English Grammar Workbook

FOR

DUMMIES®

2ND EDITION

by Geraldine Woods

WILEY

Wiley Publishing, Inc.

English Grammar Workbook For Dummies,® 2nd Edition

Published by
Wiley Publishing, Inc.
111 River St.
Hoboken, NJ 07030-5774
www.wiley.com

For general information on our other products and services, please contact our Customer Care Department within the U.S. at 877-762-2974, outside the U.S. at 317-572-3993, or fax 317-572-4002.

For technical support, please visit www.wiley.com/techsupport.

Wiley also publishes its books in a variety of electronic formats. Some content that appears in print may not be available in electronic books.

Library of Congress Control Number: 2011921767

ISBN: 978-0-470-93070-0

Manufactured in the United States of America

10 9 8 7 6 5 4 3

WILEY

About the Author

Geraldine Woods teaches English and directs the independent study program at the Horace Mann School in New York City. She is the author of more than 50 books, including *English Grammar For Dummies, SAT For Dummies, Research Papers For Dummies, College Admission Essays For Dummies, AP English Literature For Dummies,* and *AP English Language and Composition For Dummies,* all published by Wiley. She lives in New York City with her husband and two parakeets. She loves the Yankees, Chinese food, and her family.

Dedication

For Elizabeth, who, as a toddler, already shows an aptitude for grammar. And for Harry, forever in my heart.

Author's Acknowledgments

I owe thanks to my colleagues at the Horace Mann School, who are always willing to discuss the finer points of grammar. I appreciate the work of Vicki Adang, Caitie Copple, Mike Greiner, and Penny Brown, fine editors whose hard work and intelligence made this workbook much better than it would have been without them. I appreciate the efforts of my agent, Lisa Queen of Queen Literary, and the kindness of Lindsay Lefevere, Wiley's acquisitions editor.

Publisher's Acknowledgments

We're proud of this book; please send us your comments at http://dummies.custhelp.com. For other comments, please contact our Customer Care Department within the U.S. at 877-762-2974, outside the U.S. at 317-572-3993, or fax 317-572-4002.

Some of the people who helped bring this book to market include the following:

Acquisitions, Editorial, and Media Development

Project Editor: Victoria M. Adang

(Previous Edition: Kristin DeMint)

Executive Editor: Lindsay Sandman Lefevere

(Previous Edition: Kathleen M. Cox)

Copy Editor: Caitlin Copple

(Previous Edition: Sarah Faulkner, E. Neil Johnson)

Assistant Editor: David Lutton

Technical Editors: Michael Greiner, Penelope M. Brown

Editorial Manager: Michelle Hacker

Editorial Assistants: Rachelle Amick, Jennette ElNaggar

Cover Photo: © iStockphoto.com/Natalia Lukiyanova

Cartoons: Rich Tennant (www.the5thwave.com)

Composition Services

Project Coordinator: Nikki Gee

Layout and Graphics: Carl Byers, Carrie A. Cesavice, Mark Pinto, Corrie Socolovoitch, Christin Swinford

Proofreaders: Lindsay Amones, Melissa Cossell, John Greenough, Betty Kish

Indexer: Steve Rath

Publishing and Editorial for Consumer Dummies

    Diane Graves Steele, Vice President and Publisher, Consumer Dummies

    Kristin Ferguson-Wagstaffe, Product Development Director, Consumer Dummies

    Ensley Eikenburg, Associate Publisher, Travel

    Kelly Regan, Editorial Director, Travel

Publishing for Technology Dummies

    Andy Cummings, Vice President and Publisher, Dummies Technology/General User

Composition Services

    Debbie Stailey, Director of Composition Services

Contents at a Glance

Table of Contents

Introduction

Good grammar pays. I'm not joking! If you don't believe me, turn on your television. Chances are the characters who have fancy jobs or big bank accounts sound different from those who don't. I'm not making a value judgment here; I'm just describing reality. Proper English, either written or spoken, tends to be associated with the upper social or economic classes. Toning up your grammar muscles doesn't guarantee your entry to an executive corner office, but poor grammar makes it harder to fight your way in. Furthermore, with the job market becoming more competitive all the time, no one can afford to pass up an advantage in the working world. *English Grammar Workbook For Dummies,* 2nd Edition, contains lots of information and exercises geared to those who pound out quarterly reports, e-mails, tweets, memos, slide presentations, and other business communications.

If you're sitting *in* and not *at* a desk — in other words, if you're a student — good grammar pays off in different ways: with better grades and an edge in college and graduate-school admissions. Teachers have always looked favorably on well-written sentences, and grammar has become increasingly important on standardized tests. This book alerts you to material favored by the torturers — sorry, the *test writers* — and provides you with some exercises that help you become familiar with common testing formats. (If you're not clutching a number 2 pencil, don't feel left out. The skills in those exercises help you, too, by improving your grasp of proper English.)

If English is not your native language, this edition of *English Grammar Workbook For Dummies* has plenty of exercises to help you move from comprehension to mastery — the best word choice for a particular sentence, the proper way to create a plural, and so forth.

About This Book

English Grammar Workbook For Dummies, 2nd Edition, doesn't concentrate on what we English teachers (yes, I confess I am one) call *descriptive grammar* — the kind where you circle all the nouns and draw little triangles around the prepositions. A closely guarded English-teacher secret is that you don't need to know any of that terminology (well, hardly any) to master grammar. Instead, this book concentrates on *functional grammar* — what goes where in real-life speech and writing.

Each chapter begins with a quick explanation of what's right and wrong in Standard English. Next, I provide an example and then hit you with a bunch of questions. After completing the exercises, you can check your answers at the end of the chapter. I also tell you why a particular choice is correct to help you make the right decision the next time.

Conventions Used in This Book

To make your practice as easy as possible, I've used some conventions throughout this book so that from chapter to chapter or section to section you're not wondering what's going on. At the end of each chapter is the "Answers" section, which provides answers and explanations for all the exercises in that chapter. Answer pages have gray trim on the outside edge. The last exercise in each chapter is comprehensive, so you can check your mastery of the material in the entire chapter. The callout numbers pointing to the corrections in the answer key for the exercise correspond with the numbered explanations in the text.

What You're Not to Read

I promise you that I've kept the grammar jargon to a minimum in this workbook, but I must admit that I have included a couple of terms from schoolbook land. If you stumble upon a definition, run away as fast as you can and try the sample question instead. If you can get the point without learning the grammatical term, don't bother reading the definition. Likewise, feel free to skip the explanation of any question that you get right.

Foolish Assumptions

In writing the *English Grammar Workbook For Dummies,* 2nd Edition, I'm assuming that you know some English but want to improve your skills. I imagine that you aspire to a better job or want higher grades and standardized test scores. I've made two more global assumptions about you, the reader:

- ✔ I assume that you have a busy life. With this important fact in mind, I've tried to keep the explanations in this book clear, simple, and short. For the complete explanations, pick up a copy of the companion book, *English Grammar For Dummies* (Wiley), also written by yours truly.

- ✔ I also assume that you hate boring, schoolbook-style explanations and exercises. To keep you awake, I've used my somewhat insane imagination to create sentences that will (I hope) make you smile or even laugh from time to time.

How This Book Is Organized

Life gets harder as you go along, doesn't it? So does this book. Parts I and II concentrate on the basics — selecting the right verbs for each sentence, forming singulars and plurals, creating complete sentences, and so on. Part III moves up a notch to the pickier stuff. In Parts III and IV, you get to try your hand at the most annoying problems presented by pronouns (those pesky little words such as *I, me, theirs, whomever,* and others), advanced verb problems, and comparisons (*different than?* Or *different from?*). Part V is totally practical, polishing up your writing style and explaining some common word traps into which you may fall. Now for more detail.

Part I: Building a Firm Foundation: Grammar Basics

In this part I take you through the basic building blocks — *verbs* (words that express action or state of being) and *subjects* (whom or what you're talking about) — with a quick side trip into pronouns (*I, he, her,* and the like). I show you how to create a complete sentence. In this part you practice choosing the correct verb tense in straightforward sentences and find out all you need to know about singular and plural forms.

Part II: Mastering Mechanics

This part's devoted to two little things — punctuation and capital letters — that can make or break your writing. If you're not sure whether to head *North* or *north* or if you want to know where a comma belongs, this part's for you.

Part III: Applying Proper Grammar in Tricky Situations

Paging *who* and *whom,* not to mention *I* and *me!* This part tackles all the fun stuff associated with pronouns, including the reason why *everyone* can't eat *their* lunch without violating grammar rules. Part III also helps you decipher the shades of difference in verb tense (*wrote? had written?*) and voice (not *alto* or *soprano,* but *active* or *passive*). This part tackles grammar for electronic media, so you can text, tweet, and bullet-point without ending up in the grammar penitentiary.

Part IV: Upping the Interest: Describing and Comparing

Part IV doesn't tackle which stock is a better investment. Instead, it puts you through your paces in selecting and placing descriptive words and creating clear and logical comparisons.

Part V: Improving Your Writing Style

In Part V, the wind sprints and stretches are over, and it's time to compete with world-class writers. The toughest grammatical situations, plus exercises that address fluid and vivid writing, face you here. I also throw in some misunderstood words (*farther* and *further,* to name just two) and let you practice proper usage, especially as it's measured on standardized tests.

Part VI: The Part of Tens

Here you find ten ways that people trying to be super-correct end up being super-wrong and ten errors that can kill your career (or grade).

I also provide an appendix devoted entirely to comprehensive practice with the grammar skills you develop as you consult *English Grammar For Dummies* and as you complete the exercises throughout this workbook.

Icons Used in This Book

Icons are the cute little drawings that attract your gaze and alert you to key points, pitfalls, and other groovy things. In *English Grammar Workbook For Dummies,* 2nd Edition, you find these four:

I live in New York City, and I often see tourists staggering around, desperate for a resident to show them the ropes. The Tip icon is the equivalent of a resident whispering in your ear. Psst! Want the inside story that will make your life easier? Here it is!

When you're about to walk through a field riddled with land mines, it's nice to have a map. The Warning icon tells you where the traps are so you can avoid them.

The Practice icon alerts you to (surprise!) an example and a set of practice exercises so you can practice what I just finished preaching.

If you're getting ready to sweat through a standardized test, pay extra attention to this icon, which identifies frequent fliers on those exams. Not a student? No worries. You can still pick up valuable information when you see this icon.

Where to Go from Here

To the refrigerator for a snack. Nope. Just kidding. Now that you know what's where, turn to the section that best meets your needs. If you're not sure what would benefit you most, take a moment to think about the aspects of writing or speaking that make you pause for a lengthy head scratch. Do you have trouble picking the appropriate verb tense? Is finding the right word a snap but placing a comma cause for concern?

After you've done a little grammatical reconnaissance, select the sections of this book that meet your needs. Use the table of contents and the index to find more detail about what is where. If you aren't sure whether a particular topic is a problem, no problem! Try a couple of sentences and check your answers. If everything comes out okay and you understand the answers, move on. If you stub your toe, go back and do a few more until the grammar rule becomes clear. Or, if you like to start with an overview, hit the exercises in the appendix first. Then zero in on the sections that address the errors you made in those exercises.

Part I

Building a Firm Foundation: Grammar Basics

The 5th Wave   By Rich Tennant

"Oh, he's brilliant all right. But have you ever noticed the grammar in his memos? 'Org need helicon antenna...Org need ion cyclotron...Org need neutron analyzer...'"

In this part . . .

1f you've ever built a house — with real bricks or with kiddy blocks — you know that the whole thing is likely to fall down unless it's sitting atop a strong foundation. This part provides the stuff you need to lay the best foundation for your writing. Chapter 1 takes you through Verbology 101, explaining how to select the best verb for present, past, and future situations. In the same chapter you find the most useful irregular verbs and everything you need to know about the ever-helpful helping verbs, including their role in creating questions. Chapter 2 sorts verbs into singular and plural piles and helps you match each verb to the correct subject. Then you're ready to pair pronouns and nouns (Chapter 3). In Chapter 4 you distinguish between complete and incomplete sentences and practice combining sentences properly (a real favorite of standardized-test writers). Ready? I promise I won't let the roof fall on your head!

Chapter 1

Finding the Right Verb at the Right Time

. . . .

In This Chapter
▶ Putting verbs in past, present, and future tenses
▶ Practicing the perfect tenses
▶ Deciphering irregular forms
▶ Letting helping verbs lend a hand
▶ Placing verbs in questions

. . . .

As short as two letters and as long as several words, verbs communicate action or state of being. Plus, even without a new Rolex, they tell time. In this chapter I hit you with basic time questions. No, not "You're late again *because* . . . ?" but "Which verb do I need to show what's completed, not yet begun, or going on right now?" The first section hits the basic tenses (past, present, and future) and the second hits the perfect tenses, which are anything *but* perfect. After that you can work on irregulars, helping verbs, and verbs that ask questions.

Using Past, Present, and Future Tense at the Right Times

Verbs tell time with a quality known as *tense.* Before you reach for a tranquilizer, here's the lowdown on the basic tenses. The three basic tenses are *past, present,* and *future,* and each has two forms — low-carb and fat-free. Sorry, I mean *plain* (its basic time designation — present, past, or future) and *progressive* (the *-ing* form of a verb). Progressive places a little more emphasis on process or on action that spans a time period, and the present progressive may reach into the future. In many sentences either plain or progressive verbs may be used interchangeably. Here's a taste of each:

✔ *Past tense* **tells what happened at a specific, previous time or describes a pattern of behavior in the past.** In the sentence "Diane tattooed a skull on her bulging bicep," *tattooed* is a past-tense verb. In "During the Motorcycle Festival, Diane was flexing her bicep," *was flexing* is a verb in past progressive tense.

✔ *Present tense* **tells you what's going on now at the present moment, or more generally speaking, what action is recurring.** In the sentence "Grace rides her Harley," *rides* is a present-tense verb. In "Grace is always polishing her Harley" and "Grace is riding to Florida," the verbs *is polishing* and *is riding* are in present progressive tense.

✔ *Future tense* **moves into fortune-teller land.** The verb in "Grace will give Diane a ride around the block" is *will give,* which is in future tense. In "Grace will be bragging about her new motorcycle for months," *will be bragging* is in future progressive tense.

Okay, time to check out a sample problem. The *infinitive* (the grandpappy of each verb family; the verb's original form preceded by *to*) follows every sentence. Stay in that family when you fill in the blank, choosing the correct tense. When you're finished with this sample, try the practice problems that follow.

0. Yesterday, overreacting to an itty-bitty taste of arsenic, Mike _accused_ his evil twin brother of murder. *(to accuse)*

A. **accused.** The clue here is *yesterday,* which tells you that you're in the past.

1. Fashion is important to David, so he always _selects_ the latest and most popular style. *(to select)*

2. Last year's tight, slim lines _challenged_ David, who, it must be admitted, does not have a tiny waist. *(to challenge)*

3. While David _buys_ new clothes, his fashion consultant is busy on the sidelines, recommending stripes and understated plaids to minimize the bulge factor. *(to buy)*

4. David hopes that the next fashion fad _flatters_ ~~will flatter~~ a more mature, oval figure like his own. *(to flatter)*

5. Right now Diane _is writing / writes_ an article for the fashion press stating that so-tight-it-may-as-well-be-painted-on leather is best. *(to write)*

6. She once _purchased_ a purple suede pantsuit, which clashed with her orange "I Love Motorcycles" tattoo. *(to purchase)*

7. While she _modelled_ the pantsuit, the salesperson urged her to "go for it." *(to model)*

8. Two days after Diane's shopping spree, Grace _muttered_ about show-offs who "spend more time on their wardrobes than on their spark plugs." *(to mutter)*

9. However, Diane knows that Grace, as soon as she raises enough cash, _will invest_ in a suede outfit of her own. *(to invest)*

10. David, as always, _chimes ~~chimed~~_ in with the last word when he gave Grace and Diane the "Fashion Train Wreck of the Year" award. *(to chime)*

11. Two minutes after receiving the award, Diane _placed_ it on a shelf next to her "Best Dressed, Considering" medal. *(to place)*

12. Every day when I see the medal, I _wonder_ what "considering" means. *(to wonder)*

13. Grace _explained_ it to me in detail yesterday. *(to explain)*

14. "We earned the medal for considering many fashion options," she _stated_. *(to state)*

15. David, who _will visit_ Diane tomorrow, says that the medal acknowledges the fact that Grace is fashion-challenged but tries hard anyway. *(to visit)*

Putting Perfect Tenses in the Spotlight

The perfect tenses tack *has, have,* or *had* onto a verb. Each perfect tense — past perfect, present perfect and future perfect — also has a progressive form, which includes an *-ing* verb. The difference between plain perfect tense and progressive perfect is subtle. The progressive perfect is a bit more immediate than the plain form and refers to something that's ongoing or takes places over a span of time. In many sentences the plain and progressive forms may be interchanged. Here's when to use the perfect tenses:

- ✔ *Past perfect* **places one event in the past before another event in the past.** The verb in "Mike had dumped his dirty laundry in his mother's basement long before she decided to change the front-door lock" is *had dumped,* which is in past perfect tense. In the sentence "Christy, Mike's mother, had been threatening a laundry strike for years, but the beginning of mud-wrestling season pushed her to the breaking point," *had been threatening* is a past perfect progressive–tense verb.

- ✔ *Present perfect* **links the past and the present by describing an action or state of being that began in the past and is still going on.** In the sentence "Despite numerous reports of sightings around the world, Kristin has stayed close to home," the verb *has stayed* is in present perfect tense. In "Kristin has been living within two miles of the Scottish border for the last decade," *has been living* is a present perfect progressive–tense verb.

- ✔ *Future perfect* **implies a deadline sometime in the future.** In the sentence "Before sundown, David will have toasted several dozen loaves of bread," *will have toasted* is in future perfect tense. The verb in "By the time you turn on the television, *Eye on Cooking* will have been covering the toasting session for two hours, with six more to go," is *will have been covering,* which is in future perfect progressive tense.

Practice, especially with these verbs, makes perfect. (Perfect tense, get it?) Try this example and then plunge ahead. The verb you're working on appears as an *infinitive* (the basic, no-tense form) at the end of the sentence. Change it into the correct tense and fill in the blank.

Q. Kristin _____ an acceptance speech, but the Spy of the Year title went to Hanna instead. *(to prepare)*

A. **had prepared.** With two events in the past, the *had* signals the prior event. The preparing of the speech took place before the awarding of the title, so *had prepared* is the form you want.

16. Mike _____ on thin ice for two hours when he heard the first crack. *(to skate)*

17. Diane _____ Mike for years about his skating habits, but he just won't listen. *(to warn)*

18. After Mike _____ an hour in the emergency room, the doctor examined him and announced that the skater was free to go. *(to wait)*

19. After today's skating trip ends, David _____ a total of 1,232 hours for his friend and _____ countless outdated magazines in the emergency room family area. *(to wait, to read)*

20. Grace _____ to speak to Mike ever since he declared that "a little thin ice" shouldn't scare anyone. *(to refuse)*

21. Mike, in a temper, pointed out that Grace's motorcycle _____ him to the hospital even more frequently than his skates. *(to send)*

22. In an effort to make peace, Kristin _____ quietly to both combatants before the conflict escalates. *(to speak)*

23. Despite years of practice, Tim _____ success only on rare occasions, but he keeps trying to resolve his brother's conflicts anyway. *(to achieve)*

24. At times Tim's conflict-resolution technique _____ of violent finger pokes in the fighters' ribs, but he is trying to become more diplomatic. *(to consist)*

25. After Mike _____ that his brother's wisest course of action was to "butt out," Tim simply ignored him. *(to declare)*

Hitting Curveballs: Irregular Forms

Designed purposely to torture you, irregular verbs stray from the usual *-ed* form in the past tense. The irregularity continues in a form called the *past participle*. You don't need to know the terms; you just need to know what words replace the usual *-ed* verb configurations (*sang* and *sung* instead of *singed*, for example).

You can't memorize every possible irregular verb. If you're unsure about a particular verb, look it up in the dictionary. The definition will include the irregular form.

Here's a set of irregular problems to pickle your brain. Fill in the blanks with the correct irregular form, working from the verb (actually, the infinitive, the basic form of the verb family) indicated in parentheses. Check out the following example.

Q. With one leg 3 inches shorter than the other, Natalie seldom _____ into first base, even when the team was desperate for a base hit. *(to slide)*

A. slid. No *-ed* for this past tense! *Slid* is the irregular past form of *to slide*.

26. If you discover a piece of pottery on the floor, look for Natalie, who has _____ many vases because of her tendency to dust far too emotionally. *(to break)*

27. Once Natalie _____ with sadness at her first glimpse of a dusty armchair. *(to shake)*

28. David, a duster himself, _____ a manual of daily furniture maintenance. *(to write)*

29. The manual, entitled *Dust or Die,* _____ to the top of the best-seller list. *(to rise)*

30. Nearly all the copies had been _____ by fanatical cleaners. *(to buy)*

31. David once dusted the fire alarm so forcefully that it went off; the firefighters weren't amused because David had _____ the fire alarm a little too often. *(to ring)*

32. The fire chief promptly _____ to speak with the mayor about David's false alarm. *(to go)*

33. The mayor has _____ an investigation into a new category of offenses, "False Dust Alarms"; almost immediately, David _____ to protest. *(to begin)*

34. "I have _____ to a new low," sighed David. "I hear that Natalie has _____ a new hobby. Maybe I can get one too." *(to sink, to find)*

35. Natalie _____ David to a fly-catching meet, and soon his interest in grime _____ the dust. *(to take, to bite)*

36. Natalie, inspired by fly catching, _____ a tapestry with a delicate fly pattern. *(to weave)*

37. David, worried about Natalie's enthusiasm for winged pests, _____ help. *(to seek)*

38. "Leave the flies," _____ David. *(to say)*

39. "Never!" Natalie declared as she _____ her coffee. *(to drink)*

40. David soon _____ up on Natalie and her new hobby. *(to give)*

41. Every day when Natalie _____, she thought about flies. *(to wake)*

42. Her friends avoided the fly cage, which _____ in her yard. *(to stand)*

43. Natalie _____ hours watching WNET, which _____ fly-catching tips. *(to spend, to give)*

44. Eventually, Natalie _____ to realize that fly catching _____ too much. *(to come, to cost)*

45. She and David _____ a new hobby. *(to choose)*

46. They _____ miniature houses out of paper that had been _____ out. *(to build, to throw)*

47. First, David _____ a floor plan for each house. *(to draw)*

48. Next, Natalie _____ "logs" from twisted paper strips. *(to make)*

49. Unfortunately, David _____ some dog food near the houses, and his dog _____ them. *(to leave, to eat)*

50. Natalie _____ betrayed and _____ with David about what Natalie called his "criminal carelessness." *(to feel, to fight)*

Getting a Handle on Common Irregulars: Be and Have

Two irregular verbs, *to be* and *to have,* appear more frequently than a movie star with a new film to promote. And like a movie star, they tend to cause trouble. Both change according to time and according to the person with whom they're paired. (Amazing that the movie-star comparison works on so many levels!) Because they're common, you need to be sure to master all their forms, as Table 1-1 shows.

Table 1-1	Verb Forms for the Irregular Verbs *To Be* and *To Have*			
Pronoun(s)	Present-Tense Verb for "To Be"	Past-Tense Verb for "To Be"	Present-Tense Verb for "To Have"	Past-Tense Verb for "To Have"
I	am	was	have	had
you/we/they	are	were	have	had
it/he/she	is	was	has	had

Note: The form of "to be" used with helping verbs is *been.*

Fill in the blanks with the correct form of *to be* or *to have,* as in this example and the following exercises:

Q. Joyce the lifeguard _____ out in the sun long enough to fry her brain, but she intends to go inside soon because the Picnic Olympics is on television tonight.

A. **has been.** *Been* is the form used with helping verbs, such as *has.*

51. If pickling _____ necessary, I'll bring my own vinegar.

52. Whoever _____ enough cucumbers on this sort of occasion?

53. Mike replied, "I _____ totally comfortable with the amount of green vegetables in my refrigerator."

54. Kristin, never outdone, _____ a different idea.

55. "Grace and I _____ firmly in the anti-vegetable camp," she commented.

56. Two hours from now, Kristin _____ three trophies for carbo-loading.

57. Diane _____ Champion of the Potato Salad Competition for three years in a row, counting this year.

58. Grace _____ second thoughts about her entry choice; she now thinks that she should have picked sides instead of main dishes.

59. The soon-to-be-announced winners in each category _____ extremely pleased with the prizes this year.

60. Give me a taste because I _____ a judge.

61. "No kidding!" exclaimed Kristin. "I thought you _____ a participant."

62. Kristin says that Grace _____ certain to win, but I _____ not sure.

63. Grace _____ a heavy hand with hot sauce.

64. You _____ to taste her dish anyway.

65. It _____ unlikely that Grace's food will actually catch fire.

Aiding and Abetting: Helping Verbs

In addition to *has, have, had,* and the *be* verbs (*am, is, are, was, were,* and so on) you can attach a few other helpers to a main verb, and in doing so, change the meaning of the sentence slightly. Consider hiring the following helpers:

✔ **Should and must add a sense of duty.** Notice the sense of obligation in these two sentences: "David *should* put the ice cream away before he eats the whole thing." "David *must* reduce his cholesterol, according to his doctor."

✔ **Can and could imply ability.** *Could* is the past tense of *can.* Choose the tense that matches the tense of the main verb or the time period expressed in the sentence, as in these examples, "If Hanna *can* help, she will." or "Courtney *could* stray from the beaten path, depending on the weather."

✔ **May and might add possibility to the sentence.** Strictly speaking, *might* is for past events, and *may* for present, but these days people interchange the two forms: "I *may* go to the picnic if I can find a bottle of ant-killer." "I told Courtney that she *might* want to bring some insect repellent."

✔ **Would usually expresses a condition or willingness.** This helper explains under what circumstances something may happen. ("I *would* have brought the mouse if I had known about the cat problem.") *Would* may also express willingness. ("He *would* bait the trap.") *Would* sometimes communicates repeated past actions. ("Every Saturday he *would* go to the pet store for more mouse food.") The present tense of *would,* the helping verb *will,* may also indicate a condition in the present or future. ("I *will* go if I *can* find a free ticket.")

Now take a crack at this example and the following exercises. Add a helper to the main verb. The information in parentheses after the fill-in-the-blank sentence explains what meaning the sentence should have.

Q. Lisa said that she _____ consider running for Parks Commissioner, but she hasn't made her mind up yet. *(possibility)*

A. **might** or **may.** The *might* or *may* shows that Lisa hasn't ruled out a run.

66. The mayor, shy as ever, said that she _____ go to the tree-planting ceremony only if the press agreed to stay outside the forest. *(condition)*

67. Kirk, a reporter for the local radio station, _____ not agree to any conditions, because the station manager insisted on eyewitness coverage. *(ability)*

68. Whenever he met with her, Kirk _____ always urge the mayor to invite the press to special events, without success. *(repeated action)*

69. The mayor _____ make an effort to be more open to the press. *(duty)*

70. In earlier times, our mayors _____ hold weekly press conferences. *(repeated action)*

71. Lisa, who writes the popular "Trees-a-Crowd" blog, explained that she _____ rely on her imagination to supply details. *(possibility)*

72. Lisa knows that Kirk _____ leap to fame based on his tree-planting report, and she doesn't want to miss an important scoop. *(ability)*

73. All good reporters _____ know that if a tree falls or is planted in the forest, the sound is heard by a wide audience only if a radio reporter is there. *(duty)*

74. Sound engineers, on the other hand, _____ skip all outdoor events if they _____ do so. *(condition, ability)*

75. On-air talent always _____ find a way to weather all hardships, including bad weather. *(ability)*

76. Some media watchers believe that reporters _____ be a bit more modest. *(duty)*

77. In response, reporters claim that the public will not appreciate humility if they _____ choose greater entertainment value. *(ability)*

78. The mayor _____ have allowed the press at the scene had she foreseen the fuss. *(condition)*

79. The mayor _____ achieve success if she becomes more media-savvy. *(possibility)*

80. Despite her shyness she's a good mayor, and no one _____ work harder. *(ability)*

Calling into Question with Verbs

In many languages, you say the equivalent of "Ate the cookie?" to find out whether your friend gobbled up a treat. In English, you need a helping verb and a subject (the person or thing you're talking about) to create a question: "Did you eat the cookie?" (The verb *to be* is the only exception.) Notice that the combo form *(did eat)* is different from the straight past tense *(ate)*. Other question-creators, italicized in these examples, change the tense: "*Will* you eat my cookie?" or "*Do* you eat cookies?" (This last one suggests an ongoing action.) In nearly all questions, the subject follows the first (or only) verb.

Try this example and following exercises. Rewrite the statement so that it becomes a question. Add words or rearrange the sentence as needed.

Q. You found a wallet on the ground.

A. **Did you find a wallet on the ground?** The helping verb *did* precedes the subject *you*. The plain past tense, *found,* changes because it is united with a helping verb.

81. You took the wallet to the police station.

_____

82. The cops always accept lost items.

_____

83. The wallet was stolen.

_____

84. The detectives seemed interested.

_____

85. They noticed seven credit cards, each with a different name.

_____

86. The photo on the license matches a mug shot.

_____

87. The police will act swiftly.

_____

88. You want the reward for recovering stolen property.

_____

89. In the future, you will keep your eyes on the ground.

_____

90. Walking is your new hobby.

_____

Calling All Overachievers: Extra Practice with Verbs

Time to sharpen all the tools in your verb kit. Read the memo in Figure 1-1, a product of my fevered brain, and correct all the verbs that have strayed from the proper path. You should find ten.

To: All Employees

From: Christy

Subject: Paper Clips

It had come to my attention that some employees will be bending paper clips nearly every day. A few copy clerks even bended an entire box. Because of my duty as your supervisor, I would remind you that paper clips have been expensive. In my ten years of superior wisdom as your boss, I always gave you a fair deal. Does I need proof before firing you? No! However, I thinked you were responsible employees. Therefore, I will begin inspecting the desks in this office this morning. By quitting time, I will have been checking every single one. If your desk contains a bent paper clip, you would find yourself out of a job.

Figure 1-1:
A sample memo with some confused verbs.

Answers to Problems on Verbs and Verb Tenses

Have all these verb questions made you tense? If so, take a deep breath and relax. Now, check your answers to see how you did.

1 **selects.** Notice the time clues? The first part of the sentence contains the present-tense verb *is*, and the second part includes the word *always.* You're in the present with a recurring action.

2 **challenged.** Another time clue: *last year's* places you in the past.

3 **is buying** or **buys.** The second verb in the sentence *(is)* takes you right into the store with David, watching the unfolding action. Present progressive tense gives a sense of immediacy, so *is buying* makes sense. The plain present tense *(buys)* works nicely also.

4 **will flatter.** The key here is *next,* which puts the sentence in the future.

5 **is writing.** The time clue *right now* indicates an ongoing action, so the present progressive form *is writing* works well here.

6 **purchased.** Diane's bad-taste splurge happened *once,* which means it took place in the past.

7 **was modeling** or **modeled.** The second part of the sentence includes the verb *urged,* which places the action in the past. I like the past progressive *(was modeling)* here because the word *while* takes you into the process of modeling, which went on over a period of time. However, the sentence makes sense even when the process isn't emphasized, so *modeled* is also an option.

8 **muttered** or **was muttering.** The clue to the past is *two days after.* The second answer gives more of a "you are there" feel, but either is correct.

9 **will invest.** The time words here, *as soon as,* tell you that the action hasn't happened yet.

10 **chimed.** If he *gave,* you're in past tense.

11 **placed.** The expression *two minutes after* tells you that you're in the past, so you know that the action of placing the award on the shelf is in past tense.

12 **wonder.** The time clue here is *every day,* which tells you that this action is still happening at the present time and should be in present tense.

13 **explained.** The *yesterday* is a dead giveaway; go for past tense.

14 **stated.** The saga of Grace and Diane's award is in past tense, and this sentence is no exception. Even without the story context, you see the first verb *(earned)* is in past tense, which works nicely with the past-tense verb *stated.*

15 **will visit.** The time clue is *tomorrow,* which places the verb in the future.

16 **had been skating** or **had skated.** You have two actions in the past — the skating and the hearing. The two hours of skating came before the hearing, so you need past perfect tense. Either the plain or the progressive form works here also.

17 **has been warning** or **has warned.** The second half of the sentence indicates the present *(won't listen),* but you also have a hint of the past *(for years).* Present perfect is the best choice because it links past and present. I like the immediacy of progressive here (I can hear Diane's ranting), but plain present perfect is okay as well.

18 **had waited** or **had been waiting.** The waiting preceded the doctor's announcement, so you should use past perfect. Progressive adds a "you are there" feel but isn't necessary.

19 **will have waited, will have read.** The deadline in the sentence *(the end of today's trip)* is your clue for future perfect tense.

20 **has refused.** Notice the present-past link? Mike declared and Grace is acting now. Hence you need present perfect tense.

21 **had sent.** The pointing and the hospital-sending are at two different times in the past, with the hospital occurring first. Go for past perfect for the earlier action.

22 **will have spoken.** The future perfect needs an end point (in this sentence, the end of the yelling) before which the action occurs.

23 **has achieved.** If he keeps trying, you have a present-tense idea that's connected to the past (despite years of practice and on rare occasions). Present perfect connects the present and past.

24 **has consisted.** This sentence has a present-tense clue *(at times).* The sentence tells you about the past *(at times)* and the present *(is trying),* so present perfect is the one you want.

25 **had declared.** The *after* at the beginning of the sentence is your clue that one action occurs before another. Because both are in the past, you need past perfect tense for the earlier action.

26 **broken.** The verb *to break* has two irregular forms, *broke* and *broken.*

27 **shook.** *To shake* has two irregular forms, *shook* and *shaken.*

28 **wrote** or **has written.** For correct writing, use *wrote* or *has written.*

29 **rose** or **has risen.** Be sure to rise to the occasion and choose *rose* or *has risen,* not *rised.*

30 **bought.** Let this verb remind you of other irregulars, including *caught, taught,* and *thought.* Here's a sentence to help you remember: I *thought* I was in trouble because I *caught* a cold when I *taught* that class of sneezing kids, but fortunately I had *bought* tissues.

31 **rung.** The bell *rings, rang,* or *has/had rung.*

32 **went.** Take a memo: I *go,* he *goes,* I *went,* and I *have* or *had gone.*

33 **begun, began.** The plain past tense form is *began,* and the form that combines with *has, have,* or *had* is *begun.*

34 **sunk, found.** *To sink* becomes *sank* in the past tense and *has* or *have sunk* in the perfect tenses. *To find* becomes *found* in both past and present/past perfect.

35 **took, bit.** These two forms are in simple past; the perfect forms use *taken* and *bitten.*

36 **wove.** The past tense of *to weave* is *wove.*

37 **sought.** This irregular form wandered far from the original. The past tense of *to seek* is *sought.*

38 **said.** This irregular verb is the past tense of *to say.*

39 **drank.** Three forms of this verb sound like a song to accompany a beer blast: *drink, drank,* and *drunk.* The middle form, which is past tense, is the one you want here. The form that combines with *has* and *have* (in case you ever need it) is *drunk.*

40 **gave.** The verb *to give* becomes *gave* in the plain past tense (and *given* in the perfect tenses).

41 **woke.** The verb *to wake* changes to *woke* (plain past tense) or *woken* (with *has, have,* or *had*).

42 **stood.** This irregular form works for the plain past and the perfect forms of *to stand.*

43 **spent, gave.** *To spend* turns into *spent* in the plain past and perfect tenses. *To give* becomes *gave* in past tense.

44 **came** or **has come, cost.** Write it down: Natalie *came* or *has come.* Just to confuse you, the past tense of *to cost* is *cost* (in both the plain past tense and perfect tenses).

45 **chose.** They *chose* and we *have chosen.* No one *choosed,* ever!

46 **built, thrown.** Don't even consider *builded.* The correct past tense form is *built.* *To throw* becomes *threw* (plain past) or *thrown* (perfect tenses).

47 **drew.** You can't *drawed.* You either *drew* or *have/had drawn.*

48 **made.** *To make* changes into *made* for all past and perfect forms.

49 **left, ate.** Don't leave this section before you memorize this irregular form of *to leave!* The plain past form of *to eat* is *ate.* Opt for *eaten* when you have a helping verb.

50 **felt, fought.** You'll feel better when you know that *felt* works for plain past tense and the perfect tenses. *To fight* also has one form, *fought,* for both jobs.

51 **is.** Here you're in the present tense.

52 **has.** You need a singular, present-tense verb to match *who* in this sentence.

53 **am.** The verb *to be* changes to *am* when it's paired with *I.*

54 **has** or **had.** This answer depends on the tense. If you're speaking about a past event, choose *had,* but if you're speaking about something in the here and now, *has* is your best bet.

55 **are.** You need a plural to match *Grace and I.*

56 **will have.** The sentence speaks about the future.

57 **has been.** The sentence requires a link between past and present, so simple past won't do. You need present perfect, the bridge between those two time periods. *Has been* does the job.

58 **had.** The sentence calls for a contrast with *now,* so opt for past tense.

59 **will be.** Once more into the future!

60 **am** or **will be.** You may choose either present or future, depending upon the context.

61 **were.** The past tense of *to be* is required for this sentence.

62 **is, am.** The *says* tells you that present tense is needed in this sentence.

63 **has.** Here you need the singular, present tense form of *to have.*

64 **have.** The verb, *have,* doesn't express ownership in this context. Instead it implies obligation.

65 **is.** The singular subject *it* pairs with the singular verb *is.*

66 **would.** The going is dependent upon the press arrangement. Thus *would* is the best choice.

67 **could.** The agreement wasn't possible, so *could* wins the prize.

68 **would.** This helping verb expresses repeated actions in the past.

69 **should.** Once you imply duty, *should* is the helper you want.

70 **would.** Ah, the good old days! Use *would* to describe repeated actions.

71 **may** or **might.** Lisa, if she's in the mood, will cover the tree-cutting without seeing it. This possibility is expressed by the helpers *may* or *might.*

72 **can.** You need to express ability in the present tense, which *can* can do.

73 **should.** Gotta get that duty in, and *should* does the job.

74 **would, could.** *Would* expresses a condition, and *could* adds ability to the sentence.

75 **can.** You're firmly in present tense (clue word = *always*) and *can* adds a sense of ability.

76 **should.** When duty calls, opt for *should.*

77 **can.** The second half of the sentence talks about ability, so *can* works well here.

78 **would.** The first part of the sentence talks about a condition that is not actually happening, and *would* fills the bill.

79 **may** or **might.** For possibility, choose one of the two helpers.

80 **could** or **can.** Either verb form works here: *could* if you're thinking about her work record (in the past) or *can* if you're measuring her by her current 80-hour weeks.

81 **Did you take the wallet to the police station?** Typical question format: the two parts of the verb, *did* and *take,* are separated by the subject, *you.*

82 **Do the cops always accept lost items?** This one's in present tense because the original statement contains the present-tense verb, *accept.*

83 **Was the wallet stolen?** Because this sentence is about state of being, not an action, you don't need a helping verb here. However, the subject *(wallet)* should follow the verb.

84 **Did the detectives seem interested?** This one's about a state of being, but the verb, *to seem,* needs the helping verb *did* to create a question.

85 **Did they notice the seven credit cards, each with a different name?** The helper *did* precedes the subject, *they,* in this question.

86 **Does the photo on the license match a mug shot?** Here you see the same pattern: helping verb *(does),* subject *(photo),* main verb *(match).*

87 **Will the police act swiftly?** The helper, *will,* changes position to create a question instead of a statement.

88 **Do you want the reward for recovering stolen property?** In this question, you add *do* to the main verb, *want,* to land in question territory.

89 **In the future will you keep your eyes on the ground?** This question contains all the same words as the original statement. The order makes all the difference!

90 **Is walking your new hobby?** The verb, *is,* comes before the subject, *walking,* to create a question.

To: All Employees

From: Christy

Subject: Paper Clips

91 It ~~had~~ has come to my attention that some employees ~~will be~~ have **92** been bending paper clips nearly every day. A few copy clerks even **93** ~~bended~~ bent an entire box. Because of my duty as your supervisor, I ~~would~~ should remind you that paper clips ~~have been~~ are expensive. In **94** **95** my ten years of superior wisdom as your boss, I always ~~gave~~ have **96** given you a fair deal. ~~Does~~ Do I need proof before firing you? No! **97** However, I ~~thinked~~ thought you were responsible employees. **98** Therefore, I will begin inspecting the desks in this office this morning. By quitting time, I will have ~~been checking~~ checked every single one. If **99** your desk contains a bent paper clip, you ~~would~~ may find yourself out of **100** a job.

91 *Had come* is wrong because it places one action in the past before another action in the past — not the meaning expressed by this sentence. Instead, sentence one needs a verb to link past and present, and *has come* fills the bill.

92 *Will be* places the action in the future, but the memo once again seeks to establish that the bending went on in the past and continues in the present, so present perfect tense *(have been bending)* does the job.

93 *Bent* is an irregular past form. *Bended* is never correct in Standard English.

94 Because you're talking about duty, *should* works nicely here. You may also select *am reminding* because the boss is in the process of reminding the employees of paper clip prices.

95 Present tense is better because the boss is concerned about current expenses.

96 The boss is bragging about fairness in the past, which continues in the present. Thus present perfect tense *(have given)* is best. ***Note:*** The *always* may be placed between the two words of the verb *(have always given)* if you wish.

97 The pronoun *I*, though singular, takes the plural form *do*, not the singular form *does*.

98 *Thought* is the irregular past tense form of the verb *to think*.

99 No need for progressive here, because the boss wants to tell the underlings when the investigation will end, not when it will be going on.

100 You're expressing a real possibility here, so *will* or *may* works well. The helper *will* is more definite. *May* leaves a little wiggle room.

Chapter 2

Got a Match? Pairing Subjects and Verbs Correctly

In This Chapter

▶ Changing nouns from singular to plural

▶ Joining subjects and verbs according to number

▶ Dealing with subjects that appear plural but aren't

*1*n Grammarworld the difference between singular (just one) and plural (anywhere from two to a crowd) is a big deal. In this respect grammar follows real life. When the obstetrician reports on the ultrasound, the difference between one and more than one is a matter of considerable interest. In this chapter I show you how to tell the difference between the singular and plural forms of nouns, pronouns, and verbs, and I get you started on pairing them up correctly in some common sentence patterns. I also help you tackle difficult subjects such as *news, data, everyone, somebody, either,* and *neither.*

When One Isn't Enough: Forming Plural Nouns

When I was in elementary school, the only spell check was the teacher's ruler. "Don't you know you're supposed to change the *y* to *i* and add *es?*" Miss Hammerhead would inquire just before the ruler landed *(Bam!)* on a pupil's head. Hammerhead (not her real name) was teaching spelling, but she also was explaining how to form the plural of some *nouns,* the grammatical term for words that name people, places, things, or ideas. And she was a lot more accurate than a computer spell checker, which tends to allow sentences such as "Eye don't know" when you're actually trying to say, "I don't know." Here are Miss Hammerhead's lessons, minus the weaponry:

- ✔ **Regular plurals pick up an *s.*** For instance, *one snob/two snobs* and *a dollar/two billion dollars.*

- ✔ **For nouns ending in *s, sh, ch,* and *x,* tack on *es* to form the plural unless the noun has an irregular plural.** For example, *kindness/kindnesses, splash/splashes, catch/catches,* and *hex/hexes.* I tell you more about irregular plurals in a minute.

- ✔ **For nouns ending in *ay, ey, oy, uy* — in other words, a vowel before *y* — simply add an *s.*** *Monkey* becomes *monkeys* and *boy* changes to *boys.*

- ✔ **For nouns ending in *y* preceded by a consonant, change the *y* to *i* and add *es.*** *Butterfly/butterflies* and *mystery/mysteries* are two such examples.

✔ **Hyphenated nouns become plural by changing the most important word.** You can have two *mothers-in-law*, but no *mother-in-laws*, because *mother* is the defining characteristic.

✔ **When making the plural of a proper name, add *s* or *es*.** Don't change any letters even if the name ends with a consonant-*y* combo (*Smithy*, perhaps). Just add *s* for the *Smiths* and the *Smithys*. If the name already ends in *s, sh, ch, or x* (*Woods*, for example), you can add *es (Woodses)*.

✔ **Irregular nouns cancel all bets: Anything goes!** Sometimes the noun doesn't change at all, so the plural and singular forms are exactly the same *(fish/fish deer/deer)*; other times the noun does change *(leaf/leaves* and *child/children)*. When you're unsure about an irregular plural, you can check the dictionary. The definition lists the plural form for each noun.

You may be tempted to create a plural with an apostrophe (a small curved mark) and an *s*. Resist the temptation! Apostrophes don't change a singular noun to a plural.

Are you up for some multiplication? At the end of each sentence is a noun in parentheses. Write the plural in the blank, as in this example:

0. When she was angry, Jennifer often sent dinner _____ flying across the room. *(plate)*

A. **plates.** Love those regular plurals! Just add *s*.

1. Jennifer works at one of the local mental-health _____. *(clinic)*

2. Jennifer refers to these establishments as "brain _____." *(house)*

3. The town eccentric, Jennifer has dyed several _____ of her hair light green. *(thatch)*

4. Jennifer sees her unusual hair color as appropriate for both _____. *(sex)*

5. Few people know that Jennifer, an accomplished historian and mathematician, has created a series of _____ on the Hundred Years' War. *(graph)*

6. Jennifer also knows a great deal about the role of _____ in colonial America. *(turkey)*

7. The _____ of all colonies, who dropped the title of "President" because they thought the longer term was more elegant, kept track of every turkey. *(secretary-general)*

8. She discovered that the average colony had four turkeys — a guy who never paid his bills, an idiot who thought "Come here often?" was a good pickup line, and two _____ who shaved their _____ every day. *(woman, eyelash)*

9. The _____ of envy at Jennifer's scholarship were quite loud. *(sigh)*

10. However, her paper did not impress her _____. *(brother-in-law)*

11. A couple of professors think that Jennifer's _____ are filled with bats. *(belfry)*

12. Perhaps they're right, because Jennifer has encountered quite a bit of wildlife in her bell towers, including _____, _____, and _____. *(deer, squirrel, goose)*

13. Jennifer will have to put aside her research and call one of the neighboring towns' _____, who handle all stray animals. *(dogcatcher-in-chief)*

14. Anyone dealing with wild animals has to be wary of _____. *(hoof)*

15. The dogcatchers throw _____ over frightened animals. *(scarf)*

16. The _____ have worked with animals for many decades. *(Sullivan)*

17. Some _____ in the Sullivan family opt for veterinary school. *(child)*

18. _____ of the local veterinary college receive many job offers. *(alumnus)*

19. Danny Sullivan was one of three _____ for the dogcatcher position. *(runner-up)*

20. Danny went to dental school so he could work with _____ instead of dogs. *(tooth)*

Meeting Their Match: Pairing Subjects and Verbs

To make a good match, as every online-dating service knows, you have to pair like with like. So too in grammar: With two important exceptions (explained in this section), singular subjects pair with singular verbs and plural subjects with plural verbs. The good news is that most of the time English verbs have only one form for both singular and plural. "I *smirk*" and "the dinosaurs *smirk*" are both correct, even though *I* is singular and *dinosaurs* is plural. You have to worry only in these few special circumstances. Here are the rules, with italicized subjects and verbs in the examples so you can locate them quickly:

✔ **Talking about someone in the present tense requires different verb forms for singular and plural.** The singular verb ends in *s,* as in "he spits" (singular) and "they spit" (plural).

✔ **Verbs that include *does/do* or *has/have* change forms for singular and plural.** Singular verbs use *does* or *has.* ("*John does paint* his toenails blue. He *has stated* that fact.") Plurals use *do* and *have.* ("*Do* the toenails *need* more polish? No, *they have* plenty already.")

✔ ***I* pairs with plural action verbs.** The pronoun *I* is always singular, but "I go" is correct, not "I goes."

✔ ***You* may be either singular or plural, but it always pairs with plural verbs.** So *you catch* a robber, whether *you* refers to one person or ten.

✔ **The verb *to be* changes form according to the noun or pronoun paired with it.** The verbs and some matching subjects include *I am, I was, you are, he/she/it/Charlie is, he/she/it/the beanbag was* (all singular) and *we/they are, you were, we/they/teens were.*

✔ **Two subjects joined by *and* make a plural and take a plural verb.** As you discovered in kindergarten, one plus one equals two, which is a plural. ("*John and Dana plan* a bank job every two years.")

✔ **Two singular subjects joined by *or* take a singular verb.** The logic here is that you're saying one *or* the other, but not both, so two singles joined by *or* don't add up to a double. ("*Dana or John is cooking* tonight.")

✔ **Ignore interrupters when matching subjects to verbs.** *Interrupters* include phrases such as "of the books" and "except for . . ." and longer expressions such as "who golfs badly" and "which takes the cake." ("*Kristin,* as well as all her penguins, *is marching* to the iceberg today.")

Some interrupters *(as well as, in addition to)* appear to create a plural, but grammatically they aren't part of the subject and, like all interrupters, have no effect on the singular/plural issue.

✔ *Here* **and** *there* **can't be subjects.** In a *here* or *there* sentence, look for the subject after the verb. ("Here *are* five *beans.* There *is* a *bean* in your nose.")

✔ **The subject usually precedes the verb but may appear elsewhere.** ("Around the corner *speed* the *robbers,* heading for the getaway car.")

Sentences with mismatched subjects and verbs often appear on standardized tests. You have to point out the error or choose a better version of the sentence the error appears in. Number-two pencil pushers, pay special attention to this section!

Test yourself with this example. In the blank, write the correct form of the verb in parentheses.

0. John's teacher _____ uninterested in his excuses for missing homework. *(remain/remains)*

A. **remains.** The subject, *teacher,* is singular, so the verb must also be singular. The letter *s* creates a singular verb.

21. Hinting delicately that blue _____ not a natural color for nails, Nadine _____ her toes in distress. *(is/are, wriggle/wriggles)*

22. John, whose hair _____ been every color of the rainbow, says that he _____ from a toe condition. *(has/have, suffer/suffers)*

23. We _____ not buying his story. *(am/is/are)*

24. You probably _____ John because you _____ everyone the benefit of the doubt. *(believe/believes, give/gives)*

25. _____ you think that John's friends always _____ the truth? *(Does/Do, tell/tells)*

26. _____ his story fallen on disbelieving ears? *(Has/Have)*

27. I never _____ when John _____ avoiding reality. *(know/knows, am/is/are)*

28. Sometimes he _____ very odd tales. *(tells/tell)*

29. Why _____ everyone believe him? *(does/do)*

30. Nadine, who was one of John's closest friends, _____ completely dismayed by John's dishonest tendencies. *(was/were)*

31. He, along with some other thieves, _____ on his taxes all the time. *(cheats/cheat)*

32. The local police officer, in addition to everyone else on the force, _____ wanted to arrest John for years. *(has/have)*

33. Recently, John _____ spent a lot of time at the bank. *(has/have)*

34. There _____ six security guards in the safety deposit area of that bank. *(is/are)*

35. Last Tuesday, John and Dana _____ seen entering the bank. *(was/were)*

36. On the security tape, John _____ a note from his pocket and _____ it to the guard. *(removes/remove, hands/hand)*

37. "In every single one of my pockets _____ a gun," read the note. *(is/are)*

38. John, as well as the criminal mastermind Dana, _____ easily caught. *(was/were)*

39. His arrest on a variety of charges _____ being processed as we speak. *(is/are)*

40. There _____ a movie director and a literary agent in the police station trying to gain access to John. *(was/were)*

41. John's offers, in addition to a serious marriage proposal, _____ a ghostwritten autobiography and a reality television show. *(includes/include)*

42. Imagine the show: Formally dressed as always, across the screen _____ John and Dana. *(strolls/stroll)*

Taming the Brats: Choosing the Right Verb for Difficult Subjects

Like a child who has missed a nap, some subjects delight in being difficult. Difficult though they may be, *most, all, either, each,* and other brats will, with a bit of attention, quickly turn into well-behaved subjects. Here are the rules, with the example-sentence subjects and verbs in italics:

✔ **Pronouns ending in -one, -thing, and -body (everyone, something, and anybody, for example) are singular.** Even though they sometimes sound plural, *everyone is* here and *nobody needs* more grammar rules.

✔ *All, some, most, none,* and *any* **can be either singular or plural.** Subjects that can be counted are plural. ("*All* of the ears *are sticking* out. *Some* of the ears *are going* to be super-glued to scalps.") A subject that is measured but not counted is singular. ("*Most* of the sugar in his diet *comes* from his doughnut habit. *None* of his food *contains* anything nutritious.")

✔ *Either* and *neither* **alone, without** *or* **and** *nor,* **are singular.** Don't be fooled by the fact that these subjects look plural. ("*Neither* of my uncles *has agreed* to take me to the movies this afternoon.")

✔ **In** *either/or* **and** *neither/nor* **sentences, match the verb to the closest subject.** You can figure out these sentences with a ruler! ("Either *Josh* or his *partners are going* to jail. Either his *partners* or *Josh is going* to jail.")

✔ *Each* **and** *every* **are always singular, no matter what they precede.** Throw in as many plural-sounding words as you like. ("*Each* of the five thousand computers *was* on sale. *Every* video game and cellphone in the office *was stolen* from the FBI.")

These subjects are just annoying enough to attract standardized-test writers. Never fear: These exercises will prepare you for questions on this topic.

Ready to relax? I don't think so. Try these problems. Underline the correct verb from each pair.

0. Neither the fire marshal nor the police officers (was/were) aware of the bowling tournament.

A. were. The subject *police officers* is closer to the verb than *marshal.* Because *police officers* is plural, the verb must also be plural.

43. All the dancers in Lola's musical (is/are) required to get butterfly tattoos.

44. Either of the principal singers (has/have) enough talent to carry the musical.

45. Every orchestra seat and balcony box (is/are) sold already.

46. Why (does/do) no one understand that Lola's musical is extremely boring?

47. Most of the songs (has/have) been written already, but the out-of-town tryouts suggest that more work is needed.

48. Everyone (has/have) invested a substantial amount in *Whatever Lola Wants,* but no one (is/are) expecting a profit, despite the strong ticket sales.

49. Neither her partners nor Lola (is/are) willing to speculate on the critical reception.

50. Any of the reviews (has/have) the ability to make or break the production.

51. (Has/Have) either the director or the musicians agreed on a contract?

52. Everyone (agrees/agree) that Lola should cut the fifth song, "Why I Tattoo."

53. Lola is much more interested in tattoos than most of the members of the audience (is/are).

54. I don't understand the tattoo fixation because neither of Lola's parents (has/have) any tattoos.

55. Perhaps every one of Lola's 20 tattoos (is/are) a form of rebellion.

56. Some of the tattoos (is/are) to be covered by makeup, because Lola's character is an innocent schoolgirl.

57. However, each of the tattoos (has/have) special meaning to Lola, who is reluctant to conceal anything.

58. She says, "All the fame in the world (is/are) not as valuable as honesty."

59. Lola talks a good line, but all her accountants (believes/believe) that she will go along with the necessary cover-up.

60. (Has/Have) someone mentioned the Tony Awards to Lola?

61. Either Lola or her producers (is/are) sure to win at least one award — if nobody else (enters/enter) the contest.

62. Every Tony and Oscar on Lola's shelf (is/are) a testament to her talent.

63. Neither of her Tony awards, however, (has/have) been polished for a long time.

64. Perhaps someone (has/have) neglected to hire a cleaning professional to spruce up Lola's house.

65. Both of Lola's brothers (is/are) in the field of furniture maintenance.

66. (Was/Were) either of her brothers called in to consult about trophy cleaning?

67. If so, perhaps either Lola's brothers or Lola herself (is/are) on the verge of a cleaner future.

68. Most of us, I should point out, (believe/believes) that Lola will never forget to shine her Oscar statuettes.

Not What They Seem: Dealing with Deceptive Subjects

The old saying that "appearances are deceiving" certainly applies to the subjects that challenge you in this section. Some of them appear plural but take a singular verb. A couple may be either singular or plural depending upon how they're used. Here are your guidelines, with the subject and verb italicized in example sentences:

✔ *Politics, news, economics,* **and** *thesis* **are all singular.** Ignore the *s* at the end. It's not the kind of *s* that creates a plural word. Therefore, "the *news is* good," not "the *news are* good."

✔ *Statistics* **may be either singular or plural.** It's singular if it refers to the subject or a course in school, as in "*Statistics accounts* for most of my homework hours." It's plural if it refers to numbers, as in "*Statistics show* that 80 percent of all human beings hate studying grammar."

✔ **Company names are singular, even if they sound plural.** "*Sears is* (not *are*) *having* a great sale on irregular verbs today."

> ✔ **Team names usually take a plural verb.** So "the *Yankees have won* again," and "the *Rangers are losing* the game." Team names that sound singular (the *New York Liberty* or the *Utah Jazz,* for example) generally pair with a singular verb.
>
> ✔ **The dictionary is the final authority.** I can't cover all nouns here, not unless you want a workbook that you can't lift without heavy machinery. Strange words such as *data* (plural), *memorandum* (singular), *scissors* (plural), and others can fool you, unless you check the dictionary.

Sharpen your pencil and select the correct verb from the pair in parenthesis. Then hit the sentences that follow.

0. Because he had eaten five ice cream bars a day for the last month, Arthur's pants (is/are) tight.

A. **are.** Logic tells you that Arthur is putting on (or trying to put on — the zipper's stuck!) one item of clothing. However, *pants* is a plural subject and takes the plural verb *are.*

69. No matter how little studying Angie does, economics (is/are) an easy A+ for her.

70. The data (shows/show) that Angie never blows an economics test.

71. I wrote a paper on Angie's study habits; the thesis (was/were) that Angie's attention to current events helps her understand economic theory.

72. When I visit Angie, the news (is/are) always on.

73. It's difficult to drag her away from the television, though it's possible if the Giants (is/are) playing.

74. The Miami Heat, on the other hand, (does/do) not draw her attention.

75. Politics (was/were) one of Angie's hobbies when she was young.

76. Now, Angie thinks that the media (has/have) too much power.

77. Angie's fellow alumni (believes/believe) that taxes are evil, and that position is popular with some voters.

78. Angie once screamed at a political rally, "My scissors (cuts/cut) your taxes."

79. The pair of scissors she waved (is/are) in a museum now.

80. The media (loves/love) to cover Angie's career.

81. My memorandum on the subject (makes/make) my ideas perfectly clear.

82. Universal Business and Trade, a giant corporation, (agrees/agree) with me.

83. The corporation's analysis (is/are) that I should pay taxes, not the corporation.

Calling All Overachievers: Extra Practice with Hitching Subjects and Verbs

Sharpen your error-spotting skills. Tucked into the letter in Figure 2-1, written by a master criminal to his accomplice (okay, written by me, and I never even jaywalk, let alone rob banks!) are ten errors in subject-verb agreement and ten incorrect plural forms, for a total of 20 mistakes. Cross out each incorrect verb and plural and replace the error with a new, improved version.

Dear Adelie,

Oh, how I long to be with you on this cold, cold day! Neither of the iron bars of my cell have kept me from dreaming about sweeping you away to our long-planned vacation in Antarctica. Through the vast blue skys, speeding swiftly as wild turkies, go my heart.

Either my jailors or my honey have taken over every thought in my brain. I never think about the fishes in the sea. Every single one of my waking moments are devoted to you and to my ten lawyer.

I and all the other prisoners, except for my cellmate, has waited impatiently for your visit. (Don't worry about the cellmate; politics are the only thing on his mind.) Two months has passed, and everyone are impatient. I know you was busy, but the taxs are paid, your new downhill racing skies are waxed (I know you love to ski!), and still you is not here!

Here is two tickets for the policemans you befriended. They can accompany you on the train. (I know you hate to travel alone.) Speaking of alone, please bring the loots from our last job. I need escape money. Also bring two gold watchs, which are very handy for bribes.

Love,

Charlie

Figure 2-1: Practice letter with subject and verb errors.

Answers to Subject and Verb Pairing Problems

I hope you're one singular sensation at pairing subjects and verbs now. Check your work in this chapter with the following answers.

1 **clinics.** For a regular plural, just add *s*.

2 **houses.** Regular plural here: Add an *s*.

3 **thatches.** For a noun ending in *ch,* add *es*.

4 **sexes.** To a noun ending in *x,* add *es* to form a plural.

5 **graphs.** Did I fool you? The *h* at the end of the noun doesn't, all by itself, call for *es*. Only words ending in *sh* or *ch* require an added *es* in the plural form. For *graph,* a plain *s* will do.

6 **turkeys.** For nouns ending in *ay, ey,* and *oy,* add *s* to form a plural.

7 **secretaries-general.** For this hyphenated word, zero in on the important word: *secretary*. (The other word is a description, telling you what type of secretary you're talking about.) Because *secretary* ends in a *y* preceded by a consonant, you need to change the *y* to *i* and add *es*.

8 **women, lashes.** The plural of *woman* is irregular. The second noun ends in *sh,* so you must tack on *es* for a plural.

9 **sighs.** Regular plurals are fun; just add *s*.

10 **brothers-in-law.** To create the plural of a hyphenated word, add *s* to the most important word, which in this case is *brother*.

11 **belfries.** The plural of a noun ending in consonant-*y* is created by dropping the *y* and adding *ies*.

12 **deer, squirrels, geese.** The first and third nouns form irregular plurals, but good old *squirrels* follows the rule in which you simply add *s* to the singular.

13 **dogcatchers-in-chief.** The important word in this hyphenated (and fictional) title is *dogcatcher*. Create the plural by tacking on an *s* to *dogcatcher*.

14 **hooves.** This is an irregular plural. The *f* disappears completely! Why? I have no idea. Irregulars do strange things.

15 **scarves.** Another irregular, also strange, is *scarf*. You can't have two *scarfs,* just *scarves*.

16 **Sullivans.** To create the plural of a name, place an *s* at the end of the name.

17 **children.** No *s* in sight, but *children* really is plural.

18 **alumni.** This plural form has its roots in ancient Greece. *Alumni* is the all-purpose, male or mixed male-and-female form. *Alumnae* works for a group of female graduates.

19 **runners-up.** Add an *s* to the key word in this hyphenated form, and you're all set.

20 **teeth.** Irregular plurals wander all over the map. This one changes the vowels.

21 **is, wriggles.** You need two singular forms here: blue *is* and Nadine *wriggles.*

22 **has, suffers.** The verbs *has* and *suffers* are singular, as they should be, because the subject-verb pairs are *hair has* and *he suffers.*

23 **are.** The plural verb *are* matches the plural subject *we.*

24 **believe, give.** The pronoun *you* always takes a plural verb such as *believe* and *give.*

25 **Do, tell.** Both verbs are plural, matching the plural subjects *you* and *friends.* In the first pair, the subject is tucked between the two parts of the verb because the sentence is a question.

26 **Has.** You need a singular verb here to pair with the singular subject, *story.*

27 **know, is.** The pronoun *I,* though singular, pairs with the plural form *know. John* is singular and matches the singular verb *is.*

28 **tells.** Because *he* is singular, the verb *tells* must also be singular.

29 **does.** The pronoun *everyone* is singular, so it matches the singular form *does.*

30 **was.** The singular verb *was* matches the singular subject *Nadine.*

31 **cheats.** The singular subject is *He,* so you need *cheats,* a singular verb. The interrupter, *along with some other thieves,* is irrelevant.

32 **has.** Pay no attention to the interrupter, *in addition to everyone else on the force.* The real subject, *officer,* is singular and takes the singular verb *has.*

33 **has.** This one's easy. *John* is a singular subject, which pairs nicely with the singular verb *has.*

34 **are.** The subject is *guards; there* is never a subject. *Guards* is plural and takes the plural verb *are.*

35 **were.** *John and Dana* — two people, linked together by *and* (not to mention a jail sentence) — equal a plural subject, so you need the plural verb *were.*

36 **removes, hands.** Because *John* is singular, the verbs *removes* and *hands* must also be singular.

37 **is.** *Every* has magical powers. Place *every* in front of anything, even *pockets,* and you have a singular subject and a singular verb, *is.*

38 **was.** Ignore the interrupters *(as well as . . . Dana)* and zero in on the real subject, *John.* Match the singular verb *was* to the singular subject.

39 **is.** The subject is *arrest,* not *charges* or *variety. Arrest* is singular, so you need the singular verb *is.*

40 **were.** Add one *movie director* to one *agent* and what do you get? A big fat check, that's what . . . and a plural subject that takes the plural verb *were.*

41 **include.** The subject is *offers,* which matches the plural verb *include.* Everything else is camouflage.

42 **stroll.** The subjects in this sentence appear at the end of the sentence. *John and Dana* = plural, so pair them with the plural verb *stroll.*

43 **are.** You can count *dancers,* so *are* is best.

44 **has.** Without a partner, *either* is always singular and rates a singular verb, such as *has.*

45 **is.** The word *every* has the power to change *seat and balcony box* to a singular concept requiring the singular verb *is.*

46 **does.** The subject is *no one,* which is singular, so it must be paired with *does,* a singular verb.

47 **have.** The pronoun *most* may be singular (if it's used with a measurable quantity) or plural (if it's used with a countable quantity). You can count *songs,* so the plural *have* is best.

48 **has, is.** The pronouns ending in *-one* are always singular, even though they seem to convey a plural idea at times. They need to be matched with singular verbs.

49 **is.** The closest subject is *Lola,* so the singular verb *is* wins the prize, the only prize likely to be associated with Lola's musical.

50 **have.** The pronoun *any* may be either singular or plural depending upon the quantity to which it refers. Reviews may be counted (and you can be sure that Lola's investors will count them extremely carefully), so *any* takes the plural verb *have* in this sentence.

51 **Has.** The sentence has two subjects, *director* and *musicians.* The verb in this sentence has two parts, *has* and *agreed.* The subject *director* is closer to the part of the verb that changes (the *has* or the *have*); *agreed* is the same for both singular and plural subjects. The changeable part of the verb is the one that governs the singular/plural issue. Because that part of the verb is near the singular subject *director,* the singular *has* is correct.

52 **agrees.** The singular verb *agrees* matches the singular subject *everyone.*

53 **are.** The pronoun *most* can be either singular or plural. In this sentence, *members* can be counted (and it won't take too long, either, once the reviews are in), so the plural verb *are* is what you want.

54 **has.** The pronoun *neither* is always singular and needs to be paired with the singular verb *has.*

55 **is.** Did I catch you here? The expression *20 tattoos* suggests plural, but the subject is actually *one,* a singular.

56 **are.** You can count tattoos, so the pronoun *some* is a plural subject and needs to match the plural verb *are.*

57 **has.** The word *each* has the power to turn any subject to singular; *has* is a singular verb.

58 **is.** You can measure, but not count, *fame,* so a singular verb matches the singular pronoun *all.*

59 **believe.** *Accountants* are countable, so *all* is plural in this sentence and needs the plural verb *believe.*

60 **Has.** The pronoun *someone,* like all the pronouns ending in *-one,* is singular, and so is the verb *has.*

61 **are, enters.** In an *either/or* sentence, go with the closer subject, in this case, *producers*. Because *producers* is plural, it is paired with *are*, a plural verb. The singular verb *enters* matches the singular pronoun *nobody*. All pronouns ending with *-body* are singular.

62 **is.** The word *every* has the ability to make the subject singular, matching the singular verb *is*.

63 **has.** The pronoun *neither* is singular, so the singular verb *has* is needed here.

64 **has.** Pronouns ending in *-one* are always singular and thus always pair with singular verbs. Here the subject is *someone,* so *has* wins.

65 **are.** The pronoun *both* is plural, as is the verb *are*.

66 **Was.** This sentence illustrates a common error. The pronoun *either* is singular and calls for the singular verb *was*.

67 **is.** A sentence with an *either/or* combo is easy; just match the verb to the closest subject. In this sentence, the singular *Lola* is closer to the verb than *brothers,* so you need a singular verb.

68 **believe.** The pronoun *most* shifts from singular to plural and back, depending upon context. If it's associated with something that you can count (such as *us*), it's plural. Opt for the plural verb *believe*.

69 **is.** *Economics* ends in *s,* but it's a singular noun, which matches the singular verb *is*.

70 **show.** *Data look*s singular because it has no *s,* but it's actually the plural of *datum* (a word no one ever uses!). Match *data* with *show,* a plural verb.

71 **was.** The subject, *thesis,* is singular, so *was* pairs well with it. In case you're wondering, the plural of *thesis* is *theses.* Strange, huh?

72 **is.** The *news* is singular and takes the singular verb *is*. This noun has no plural form!

73 **are.** The team name sounds plural, and it is. Go for *are,* the plural verb.

74 **does.** The team name sounds singular, so the singular verb *does* works here.

75 **was.** This subject, *politics,* appears plural because of the *s,* but it's actually singular, as is the verb *was*.

76 **have.** *Media* is plural and pairs with the plural verb *have*.

77 **believe.** The subject, *alumni,* is plural and pairs with the plural verb *believe*.

78 **cut.** For reasons I can't explain, *scissors* is plural and needs a plural verb *(cut)*.

79 **is.** Now the subject is *pair,* a singular word, so go for the singular verb *is*.

80 **love.** The subject is *media,* a plural, which pairs with the plural verb *love*.

81 **makes.** *Memorandum* is singular (and, if you're curious, *memoranda* is plural). Pair *memorandum* with the singular verb, *makes*.

82 **agrees.** Company names are singular, even if they appear plural. *Agrees* is a singular verb.

83 **is.** The subject, *analysis,* is singular. (The plural is *analyses,* by the way.) *Is* is a singular verb.

Dear Adelie,

Oh, how I long to be with you on this cold, cold day! Neither of the iron bars of my cell ~~have~~ **has** kept me from dreaming about sweeping you away to our long-planned vacation in Antarctica. Through the vast blue ~~skys~~ **skies**, speeding swiftly as wild ~~turkies~~ **turkeys**, ~~go~~ **goes** my heart.

Either my jailors or my honey ~~have~~ **has** taken over every thought in my brain. I never think about the ~~fishes~~ **fish** in the sea. Every single one of my waking moments ~~are~~ **is** devoted to you and to my ten ~~lawyer~~ **lawyers**.

I and all the other prisoners, except for my cellmate, ~~has~~ **have** waited impatiently for your visit. (Don't worry about the cellmate; politics ~~are~~ **is** the only thing on his mind.) Two months ~~has~~ **have** passed, and everyone ~~are~~ **is** impatient. I know you ~~was~~ **were** busy, but the ~~taxs~~ **taxes** are paid, your new downhill racing ~~skies~~ **skis** are waxed (I know you love to ski!), and still you ~~is~~ **are** not here!

Here ~~is~~ **are** two tickets for the ~~policemans~~ **policemen** you befriended. They can accompany you on the train. (I know you hate to travel alone.) Speaking of alone, please bring the ~~loots~~ **loot** from our last job. I need escape money. Also bring two gold ~~watchs~~ **watches**, which are very handy for bribes.

Love,

Charlie

84 *85* *86* *87* *88* *89* *90* *91* *92* *93* *94* *95* *96* *97* *98* *99* *100* *101* *102* *103*

---

84 The subject of this sentence is *neither,* which, when it appears alone, is always singular, requiring the singular verb *has.*

85 To form the plural of a word ending in consonant-*y,* change the *y* to *i* and add *es.*

86 To form the plural of a word ending in vowel-*y,* just add *s.*

87 The singular subject of the verb *go* is *heart,* which in this sentence is located after the verb, an unusual but legal spot. Singular subjects take singular verbs, and *goes* is singular.

88 The sentence has two subjects connected with *either/or.* The closer subject is *my honey,* which is singular and takes a singular verb.

89 *Fish* has an irregular plural — *fish.*

90 *Every* creates a singular subject, so you need the singular verb *is.*

91 If you reach ten, you're in plural-land. The plural of *lawyer* is *lawyers.*

92 The *except for my cellmate* may distract you, but the true subject is *I and all the other prisoners,* a plural, which pairs with *have.*

93 *Politics* is singular and takes the singular verb, *is.*

94 *Two months* is plural, so use the plural verb *have.*

TIP

Time may sometimes be singular ("Five minutes is a long time") when you're referring to the total amount as one block of time. In Question 101, Charlie is counting the months separately, so plural is better.

95 *Everyone,* as well as all the pronouns with the word *one* tucked inside, is singular and takes the singular verb *is.*

96 The pronoun *you* can refer to one person or to a group, but it always takes a plural verb.

97 To form the plural of a noun ending in *x,* add *es.*

98 The noun *ski* is regular, so to form the plural, just add *s.*

99 *You* always takes a plural verb, which in this case is *are.*

100 *Here* can't be a subject, so look after the verb. Voilà! *Tickets,* a plural, takes the plural verb *are.*

101 Many things separate men and women, but both form their plurals in the same way — by changing the *a* to *e.* Hence, *policemen,* not *policemans.*

102 *Loot* is whatever you get from a crime (not counting a criminal record), whether it be one diamond or a thousand Yankee tickets. *Loots* doesn't exist.

103 To form the plural of a noun ending in *ch,* add *es.*

Chapter 3

Who Is She, and What Is It? Pronoun Basics

In This Chapter

▶ Safety in numbers: Using singular and plural pronouns correctly

▶ Proclaiming ownership with possessive pronouns

▶ Ensuring that pronouns have only one meaning

▶ Clarifying it's/its and they're/there/their

Pronouns aren't for amateurs, at least when it comes to formal grammar. These tricky words take the place of nouns and frequently come in handy. Who can write a paragraph without *I, me, ours, them, us, that,* and similar words? Unfortunately, pronouns can trip you up in a hundred ways. Never fear: In this chapter I show you how to distinguish singular from plural pronouns (and when to use each) and how to use possessive pronouns. I also help you avoid vague pronouns and guide you through the maze of *its/it's, their/there/they're, whose/who's,* and *your/you're.*

Numbering Singular and Plural Pronouns

Pronouns bump nouns from your sentences and make the words flow more smoothly. When choosing pronouns, you must follow two basic rules:

✔ Replace a singular noun with a singular pronoun.

✔ Replace a plural noun with a plural pronoun.

Pronouns have another characteristic — gender. Fortunately, the rules governing pronoun gender are nowhere near as complicated as the ones about who pays for what on the first date. Masculine pronouns *(he, him, himself)* take the place of masculine nouns, and feminine *pronouns (she, her, herself)* fill in for feminine nouns. Some pronouns are noncombatants in the gender wars *(it, itself, who, they, which,* and *that,* for example) and function in a neutral way.

Other rules also govern pronoun behavior, but I'll leave those for another time and place — specifically Chapters 2 and 9.

Just for the record, here are the most common singular and plural pronouns:

- ✔ **Singular:** *I, me, you, he, she, it, my, your, his, her, its, myself, yourself, himself, herself, itself, either, neither, everyone, anyone, someone, no one, everything, anything, something, nothing, everybody, anybody, somebody, nobody,* and *each*

- ✔ **Plural:** *we, us, you, they, them, our, ours, your, yours, their, theirs, ourselves, yourselves, themselves, both,* and *few*

The *-self* pronouns — *myself, himself,* and so on — have very limited usage. They can add emphasis ("I myself will blow up the mud balloon") or circle back to the person doing the action in the sentence ("She will clean herself later"). Resist the temptation to use a *-self* pronoun without the circling-back action ("Rachel and myself hate mud balloons," for example).

Okay, get to work. Without peeking at the answers (and I am watching), decide which pronoun may replace the underlined noun. Consider the singular/plural and gender issues. Write your choice in the blank provided.

0. I hope that Charlie Burke and Dr. Eileen Burke will attend tonight's symphony, even though Charlie is tone-deaf and <u>Eileen</u> tends to sing along. _____

A. **she.** Dr. Eileen has been known to hit the doughnut tray a little too often, but Eileen is still just one person. *She* is a singular, feminine pronoun.

1. Eileen wore a purple and red plaid hat last year, and <u>the hat</u> made quite an impression on the fashion press. _____

2. "Who is your designer, Eileen?" <u>the photographers</u> screamed. _____

3. <u>Charlie's hairpiece,</u> on the other hand, attracted almost no attention.
_____

4. At one point during the evening Eileen muttered, "Charlie, you should have ordered a limousine for <u>Charlie and Eileen.</u> _____

5. Unlike his mother, Charlie likes to travel in luxury; <u>Mama</u> usually takes public transportation. _____

6. Charlie and Eileen told <u>Charlie and Eileen</u> that they would never set one foot in a subway. _____

7. Mama says that if you're in trouble, you can always ask the subway conductor and <u>the subway conductor</u> will help. _____

8. Eileen once tried the subway but fainted when the conductor said to her, "Miss, <u>Eileen</u> will need a ticket." _____

9. Until Eileen hit the floor, <u>the subway cars</u> had never before been touched by mink.
_____

10. "Give <u>Eileen</u> a ticket, please," gasped Eileen when she awoke. _____

11. After Eileen's subway experience, <u>Eileen</u> opted for the bus. _____

12. The bus driver, Henry Todd, was very gracious to his new passenger, as <u>Henry Todd</u> was to all passengers. _____

13. Because Eileen is a little slow, the driver of the bus parked <u>the bus</u> at the stop for a few extra minutes. _____

14. As Eileen mounted the bus steps, Eileen said, "Thank you, Driver, for waiting for <u>Eileen</u>." _____

15. "I am happy to wait for <u>Eileen</u>," replied the driver. "I have 12 more years until retirement." _____

Holding Your Own with Possessive Pronouns

When I was a kid I often heard the expression, "Possession is nine-tenths of the law." I never quite understood the legal meaning, but I do know that possessive pronouns (*my, mine, your, his, her, hers, its, our, ours, their, theirs,* and *whose*) are governed by just a few, easy laws:

- ✔ **Use a possessive pronoun to show ownership.**
- ✔ **Match singular pronouns with singular owners.**
- ✔ **Match plural pronouns with plural owners.**
- ✔ **Take note of masculine (for males), feminine (for female), and neutral pronouns.**
- ✔ ***Never* insert an apostrophe into a possessive pronoun.** (If a pronoun has an apostrophe, it is part of a contraction. See the next section for more information.)

Speaking informally, many people refer to a company or store with a plural pronoun, as in "I'm going to Green's Market because *they* have great discounts on *their* marshmallows." However, *Green's Market* is singular and should be referred to with the singular pronoun *it,* which pairs with a singular verb and the possessive pronoun *its.* (Conveniently, *it* works as both a subject or an object.) The correct sentence is "I'm going to Green's Market because *it* has great discounts on *its* marshmallows."

Okay, here's a mini-test. Choose the correct possessive pronoun from the choices in parentheses and plop it into the blank.

0. The little boy grabbed a grubby handkerchief and wiped _____ nose. *(his/her/its/he's)*

A. his. Because you're talking about a *boy,* you need a masculine pronoun. Did I catch you with the last choice? *He's = he is.*

16. Jessica spent the morning polishing _____ new motorcycle, for which she had paid a rock-bottom price. *(her/hers/she's/her's)*

17. She found two scratches, so she took the cycle back to the store to get _____ fender repaired. *(it/its/their)*

18. When the store employees didn't satisfy her demand for a new fender, Jessica threatened to scratch something of _____. *(their/theirs/their's)*

19. Jessica talks a lot, but she has never taken revenge by damaging a single possession of _____. *(my/mine/mines/mine's)*

20. However, Neil and Rachel claim that Jessica once threw paint on something of _____. *(his/hers/her's/their/their's/theirs)*

21. Also, I heard a rumor that Neil had to bury _____ favorite wig, the one he styled himself, after Jessica got hold of it. *(his/her/he's)*

22. When Rachel's poodle dug up the wig, she had to use paint remover to clean _____ paw. *(it/their/its)*

23. Just to be safe, Neil will never let Jessica borrow another wig of _____ unless she takes out an insurance policy. *(his/his'/he's)*

24. Tomorrow, Neil is going to Matthews Department Store to buy a spare wig. The store is selling wigs at a 50 percent discount, and _____ wigs are Neil's favorites. *(its/their)*

25. Whenever Neil yells at Jessica, she screams, "Don't criticize _____ actions!" *(my/mine)*

26. Neil usually replies, in a voice that is just as loud, "I wouldn't dream of criticizing any action of _____." *(your/your's/yours/yours')*

27. When Neil speaks to _____ hairdresser, he will request a rush job. *(his/his'/he's)*

28. "Neil will never get his hands on any hairpiece of _____," declared Rachel and Jessica. *(our/ours/our'/ours'/our's)*

29. I think that Rachel took _____ hairpiece, and I told Neil so. *(his/his'/he's)*

30. Neil explained that he itches to get his hands on a wig of _____ someday. *(my/mine)*

31. "Over _____ dead body," I replied. *(my/mine)*

32. "I can't work on _____ dead body," answered Neil in a puzzled voice. *(your/yours/you're)*

33. As she dipped _____ fingers in paint remover, Jessica added, "You can't work on a live one either." *(her/hers/her's)*

34. Jessica and Neil seriously need to work on _____ people skills. *(his/her/their)*

35. I will buy a wig for Jessica, Neil, and myself and then style _____ new hairpieces. *(our/ours/our's)*

It's All in the Details: Possessives and Contractions

This section points out some dangers in the pronoun world and shows you how to steer clear of them. Specifically, I take you through the wonderful world of *its/it's, their/there/ they're,* and *whose/who's.* Briefly, here's how to tell them apart:

- **Its/it's:** The first word shows possession. ("The bird grasped a seed in *its* beak.") The second is a contraction meaning *it is.* ("*It's* hard to snatch birdseed from a hungry robin.")

- **Their/there/they're:** The first word shows possession. ("The birds grasped seeds in *their* beaks.") The second is a location. ("Don't go *there.*") The third is a contraction meaning *they are.* ("*They're* ready to film the nature show now.")

- **Whose/who's:** The first word shows possession. ("The bird *whose* beak is longest wins.") The second is a contraction meaning *who is.* ("*Who's* the judge?")

Try the following questions. Choose the correct word from the choices in parentheses. Underline your selection.

0. Marybelle sewed (their/there/they're) lips shut because the little brats refused to keep quiet.

A. **their.** The sentence expresses possession, so you want the first choice. The second *there* is location, and the third means *they are.* If you plug *they are* into the sentence, you're not making any sense.

36. George and Josh need watches because (their/there/they're) always late.

37. George found a watch that keeps time by counting atoms, but (its/it's) too expensive.

38. Josh, playing with the atomic watch, broke (its/it's) band.

39. I notice that (your/you're) band is broken also.

40. "(Whose/Who's) watch is this?" Josh asked innocently.

41. "(Your/You're) sure that (its/it's) not Jessica's?" asked George.

42. "Put it over (their/there/they're), and pretend you never touched it," said George.

43. "I can't lie," whispered Josh. "(Their/There/They're) security cameras caught me."

44. (Its/It's) impossible for Josh to lie anyway because he is totally honest.

45. "(Your/You're) honor demands only the truth," sighed George.

46. (Whose/Who's) going to pay for the watch, you may wonder, Josh or George?

47. (Your/You're) wrong; Josh isn't willing to pay the full cost.

48. (Their/There/They're) funds are limited, so each will probably pay half the cost of a new watch band.

49. George, (whose/who's) ideas of right and wrong are somewhat fuzzy, asked Rachel whether she would contribute to (their/there/they're) "charity campaign for underprivileged watches."

50. Rachel replied, "(Your/You're) joking!"

Making Sure Your Pronouns Are Meaningful

Unless you're a politician bent on hiding the fact that you've just increased taxes on everything but bubble gum, you're probably interested in communicating clearly. One basic rule says it all: If the meaning of a pronoun is unclear, dump the pronoun and opt for a noun instead.

In practice, this rule means that you shouldn't say things like "My aunt and her mother-in-law were happy about her success in the Scrabble tournament," because you don't know who had success, the aunt, the mother-in-law, or some other lady.

Standardized tests often hit you with a double-meaning sentence. Frequently the faulty pronoun is underlined. When asked to point out the error, keep your eye out for double-meaning pronouns.

Pronoun practice now begins. Hit these exercises with brainpower, rewriting if a pronoun may have more than one meaning. When you rewrite, choose one of the possibilities, or, if you love to work, provide two new unmistakably clear sentences. If everything is hunky-dory, write "correct" in the blank.

0. Stacy and Alice photographed her tattoos.

_____

A. **Stacy and Alice photographed Alice's tattoos.** Or, **Stacy and Alice photographed Stacy's tattoos.** Which answer is better? Neither. If you're saying something like this in real life, you know whose tattoos are under the lens. The reason the sentence needs a revision is that either meaning fits the original. To be clear, rewrite without the pronoun.

51. Chad and his sister are campaigning for an Oscar nomination, but only she is expected to get one.

_____

_____

52. Chad sent a donation to Mr. Hobson in hopes of furthering his cause.

_____

_____

53. If Chad wins an Oscar, he will place the statue on his desk, next to his Emmy, Tony, Obie, and Best-of-the-Bunch awards. It is his favorite honor.

_____

_____

54. Chad's sister has already won one Oscar for her portrayal of a kind but slightly crazy artist who can't seem to stay in one place without extensive support.

_____

_____

55. Rachel, who served as a model for Chad's sister, thought her interpretation of the role was the best.

_____

_____

56. In the film, the artist creates giant sculptures out of discarded hubcaps, although museum curators seldom appreciate them.

_____

_____

57. When filming was completed, Rachel was allowed to keep the leftover chair cushions and hubcaps, which she liked.

_____

_____

58. Rachel loves what she calls "found art objects," which she places around her apartment.

_____

_____

59. Chad's sister kept one for a souvenir.

_____

_____

60. Rachel, Chad, and Chad's sister went out for a cup of coffee, but he refused to drink his because the cafe was out of fresh cream.

_____

_____

61. Rachel remarked to Chad's sister that Chad could drink her iced tea if he was thirsty.

_____

_____

62. Chad called his brother and asked him to bring the cream from his refrigerator.

_____

_____

63. "Are you crazy?" asked Rachel as she gave Chad's sister her straw.

_____

_____

64. Chad's sister took a straw and a packet of sugar, stirred her coffee, and then placed it on the table.

_____

_____

65. Chad suddenly spotted an award-winning director. He waved to him.

_____

_____

Calling All Overachievers: Extra Practice with Basic Pronouns

Sharpen your (that's *your*, not *you're*) editing skills. Look for ten mistakes involving pronouns in the letter in Figure 3-1, written by an unfortunate merchant. After you find an error, correct it. Take note of singular/plural, gender, clarity, and confusion.

May 31, 2011

Dear Mr. Baker:

Its come to my attention that the watch you looked at yesterday in our Central Avenue store is broken. The band is disconnected from the watch, which is quite valuable. Their is no record of payment beyond a very small amount. The clerk, Mr. Sievers, told me that you paid her exactly 1 percent of the watch's price. When you and you're brother left the store, Mr. Sievers was still asking for additional funds. He's blood pressure still has not returned to normal levels.

Frankly I do not care whose to blame for the broken watchband or Mr. Sievers's medical problem. I simply want it fixed. The watch and it's band are not your property. The store needs their merchandise in good condition.

Sincerely,

E. Neil Johnson

Figure 3-1: Error-filled sample letter.

Answers to Pronoun Problems

My, my, my. You should be proud of yourself for making it through the pronoun questions in this chapter. I know I'm proud of you. Compare your answers to the answers here.

1   **it.** The hat is singular, and so is *it*.

2   **they.** More than one photographer means that you need the plural pronoun *they*.

3   **It.** The hairpiece is singular and has no gender, so *it* is the best choice.

4   **us.** Two nouns are underlined, so you're in plural territory. Because Eileen is talking about herself and Charlie, *us* fits here.

5   **she.** Mama is a singular feminine noun, so *she* is your best bet.

6   **themselves.** Two people make a plural, so *themselves,* a plural pronoun, is best.

7   **he or she.** You don't know whether the subway conductor is male or female, though you do know that you're talking about one and only one person. The best answer is *he or she,* covering all the bases.

8   **you.** Because the conductor is talking to Eileen, *you* is the best choice. *You,* by the way, functions as both a singular and a plural.

9   **they.** *Cars* is a plural noun, so *they* works best.

10   **me.** Because Eileen is talking about herself, *me* is your answer.

11   **she.** The singular, feminine *Eileen* calls for a singular, feminine pronoun, in this case, *she*.

12   **he.** The singular, masculine *Henry Todd* calls for a singular, masculine pronoun, *he*.

13   **it.** The singular *bus* isn't masculine or feminine, so *it* fills the bill.

14   **me.** *Eileen* is talking about herself here, so *me* is appropriate.

15   **you.** The driver is talking to Eileen, using the pronoun *you*.

16   **her.** You need a feminine, singular, possessive pronoun. Bingo: *her*.

17   **its.** The fender is singular, so *their* is out of bounds. Because you need a possessive (the fender belongs to the cycle), *its* is the word you want.

18   **theirs.** One of the choices — *their's* — doesn't exist in proper English. The first choice, *their,* should precede the thing that is possessed (*their* books, for example). The middle choice is just right.

19   **mine.** The last two choices don't exist in Standard English. *My* does its job by preceding the possession (*my* blanket, for example). The second choice, *mine,* can stand alone.

20   **theirs.** You need a word to express plural possession, because you're talking about Neil and Rachel. Of the three plural choices (the last three), the first should precede the possession (*their* motorcycle, for example), and the second has an apostrophe, a giant no-no in possessive-pronoun world. Only the last choice works.

21 **his.** The hairpiece belongs to Neil, so *her,* a feminine pronoun, is out. The last choice is a contraction of *he is.*

22 **its.** The first choice isn't possessive, so you can rule *it* out easily. The second choice is plural, but the pronoun refers to *poodle,* a singular noun. Bingo: The last choice, a singular possessive, is correct.

TIP

Many animal lovers don't consider *it* or *its* appropriate pronouns for family pets. If you know whether an animal is male or female, feel free to use *his/her* or *he/she.*

23 **his.** No possessive pronoun ever contains an apostrophe, so the first choice is the only possibility. *He's,* by the way, means *he is.*

24 **its.** Did I catch you here? In everyday speech, people often refer to stores and businesses as "they," with the possessive form "their." However, a store or a business is properly referred to with a singular pronoun. The logic is easy to figure out. One store = singular. So Matthews Department Store is singular, and the possessive pronoun that refers to it is *its.*

25 **my.** The pronoun *mine* stands alone and doesn't precede what is owned. *My,* on the other hand, is a pronoun that can't stand being alone. A true party animal, it must precede what is being owned (in this sentence, *actions*).

26 **yours.** In contrast to Sentence 25, this sentence needs a pronoun that stands alone. *Your* must be placed in front of whatever is being possessed — not a possibility in this sentence. All the choices with apostrophes are out because possessive pronouns don't have apostrophes. The only thing left is *yours,* which is the correct choice.

27 **his.** The contraction *he's* means *he is.* That choice doesn't make sense. The second choice is wrong because possessive pronouns don't have apostrophes.

28 **ours.** Okay, first dump all the apostrophe choices, because apostrophes and possessive pronouns don't mix. You're left with two choices — *our* and *ours.* The second is best because *our* needs to precede the thing that is possessed, and *ours* can stand alone.

29 **his.** The possessive pronoun *his,* like all possessive pronouns, has no apostrophe. The last choice, *he's,* means *he is* and isn't possessive at all.

30 **mine.** The pronoun *mine* works alone (like a private detective in an old movie). In this sentence it has a slot for itself after the preposition *of.* Perfect!

31 **my.** The form that attaches to the front of a noun is *my.* In this sentence, *my* precedes and is linked to *dead body.*

32 **your.** The possessive pronoun *your* has no apostrophe. The second choice, *yours,* doesn't attach to a noun, so you have to rule it out in this sentence. The last choice, *you're,* is short for *you are.*

33 **her.** Right away you can dump the last choice, *her's,* because possessive pronouns are allergic to apostrophes. The pronoun *hers* works alone, but here the blank precedes the item possessed, *fingers. Her* is the possessive you want.

34 **their.** Because you're talking about both *Jessica* and *Neil,* go for *their,* the plural.

35 **our.** In this sentence the possessive pronoun has to include *me,* so *our* is the winner. *Ours* isn't appropriate because you need a pronoun to precede what is being possessed *(hairpieces).* As always, apostrophes and possessive pronouns don't mix.

36 **they're.** The sentence tells you that *they are* always late, and the short form of *they are* is *they're*.

37 **it's.** You want to say that *it is* too expensive. No possessive is called for.

38 **its.** The band belongs to the watch, so possession is indicated. The possessive pronoun *its* does the job.

39 **your.** The contraction *you're* is short for *you are*, clearly not right for this context.

40 **Whose.** The sentence doesn't say, "Who is watch is this?" so go for the possessive *whose*.

41 **You're, it's.** Two pronouns, neither possessive. The sentence really means "*You are* sure that *it is* not Jessica's?"

42 **there.** The meaning of the sentence calls for a location, so *there* is the one you want.

43 **Their.** The security cameras belong to them, so *their* is needed to show possession.

44 **It's.** The sentence should begin with "*It is* impossible" and *it's* = *it is*.

45 **Your.** A possessive is called for here, not a contraction (*You're* = *You are*).

46 **Who's.** The sentence should begin with *Who is*, and *who's* = *who is*.

47 **You're.** Here you want the contraction *you're* = *you are*.

48 **Their.** The funds belong to them, so *their* is needed to show possession.

49 **whose, their.** Both spots require a possessive, showing that the fuzzy ideas belong to George and that the campaign belongs to both George and his more honest brother Josh.

50 **You're.** The joking isn't a possession. The sentence calls for the contraction *you're (you are)*.

51 **Correct.** Chad is male and his sister is female, so *she* may refer only to one person, Chad's sister. No double meanings, so no corrections.

52 **Chad sent a donation to Mr. Hobson in hope of furthering Chad's cause.** Or, **Chad sent a donation to Mr. Hobson in hope of furthering Mr. Hobson's cause.** The problem with the original is the *his*. Does *his* mean Chad's or Mr. Hobson's? The way the original reads, either answer is possible.

53 **If Chad wins an Oscar, he will place the statue on his desk, next to his Emmy, Tony, Obie, and Best-of-the-Bunch awards. The Oscar is his favorite honor.** Okay, maybe the Tony is his favorite honor, or maybe the Obie. The original is so unclear that almost anything may be plugged into the blank. Whichever one you choose, fine. Just don't let *It* stand for any one of five awards, as it does in the original.

54 **Correct.** The two pronouns in this sentence, *her* and *who,* can refer only to Chad's sister. Everything is clear, and no changes are necessary.

55 **Rachel, who served as a model for Chad's sister, thought her own interpretation was the best.** Or, **Rachel, who served as a model for Chad's sister, thought the sister's interpretation was the best.** Either answer is okay, illustrating the problem with the original. You can't tell what *her* means — *Rachel's* or *Chad's sister's*.

56 **In the film, the artist creates giant sculptures out of discarded hubcaps, although museum curators seldom appreciate the hubcaps.** Or, **In the film the artist creates giant sculptures out of discarded hubcaps, although museum curators seldom appreciate the sculptures.** The problem with the original sentence is the pronoun *them.* You have two groups of objects in the sentence: the sculptures and the hubcaps. *Them* could refer to either. To eliminate the uncertainty, replace *them* with a more specific statement.

57 **Rachel was pleased to be allowed to keep the leftover chair cushions and hubcaps.** Or, **Rachel liked the leftover chair cushions, which she was allowed to keep. She also held onto the hubcaps.** Or, **Rachel liked the leftover hubcaps, which she was allowed to keep. She also kept the chair cushions.** If you've read all three suggested answers (and more variations are possible), you understand the problem with the original sentence. What does *which* mean? *Cushions? Hubcaps? Keeping leftovers?* That last possibility, by the way, can't be expressed by a pronoun, at least not according to the strictest grammar cops. Reword so that your reader knows what *which* means.

58 **Correct.** Surprised? All the pronouns are clear, in the context of this story about Rachel. The *she* refers to *Rachel,* and the *which* refers to *objects.*

59 **Chad's sister kept one hubcap for a souvenir.** Or, **Chad's sister kept one sculpture for a souvenir.** Or, **Chad's sister kept one Rachel for a souvenir.** Just kidding about the last possible answer. (There's only one Rachel.) In the original sentence, *one* is too vague. Clarify by adding a specific souvenir.

60 **Correct.** The sentence refers to two females (Rachel and Chad's sister) and one male. Because only one male is in the sentence, the masculine pronouns *he* and *his* are clear.

61 **Rachel remarked to Chad's sister, "Chad can drink my iced tea if he is thirsty."** Or, **Rachel remarked to Chad's sister, "Chad can drink your iced tea if he is thirsty."** In the original sentence, you can't tell whether *her* refers to Rachel or to Chad's sister.

62 **Chad called his brother and asked him to bring the cream from Chad's refrigerator.** If you want to make Chad a cheapo who is always mooching someone else's stuff, reword the sentence so that Chad is asking for his brother's cream, perhaps using a direct quotation, as in **Chad called his brother and said, "Bring me some cream from your refrigerator."**

63 **"Are you crazy?" asked Rachel, giving her own straw to Chad's sister.** Or, **"Are you crazy?" asked Rachel as she picked up Chad's sister's straw and gave it to her.** The original sentence doesn't make clear who owns the straw.

64 **Chad's sister took a straw and a packet of sugar, stirred her coffee, and then placed the coffee on the table.** Or, **Chad's sister took a straw and a packet of sugar, stirred her coffee, and then placed the straw on the table.** Or, **Chad's sister took a straw and a packet of sugar, stirred her coffee, and then placed the packet on the table.** See the problem? The original sentence contains a pronoun *(it)* with several possible meanings (the straw, the sugar packet, or the coffee).

65 **Chad suddenly spotted an award-winning director, who waved to Chad.** Or, **Chad soon spotted an award-winning director. Chad waved to him.** The original sentence doesn't make clear who is waving to whom.

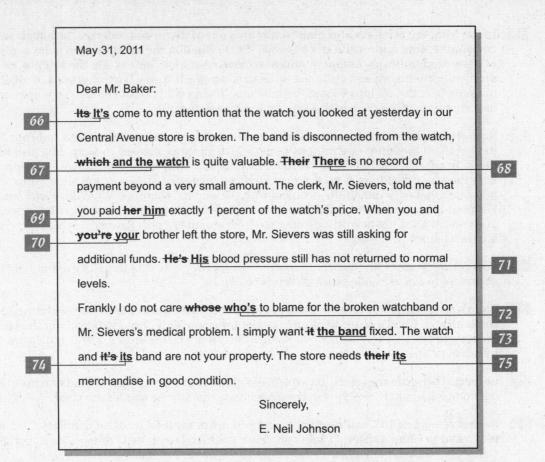

May 31, 2011

Dear Mr. Baker:

66 ~~Its~~ **It's** come to my attention that the watch you looked at yesterday in our Central Avenue store is broken. The band is disconnected from the watch, 67 ~~which~~ **and the watch** is quite valuable. ~~Their~~ **There** is no record of 68 payment beyond a very small amount. The clerk, Mr. Sievers, told me that 69 you paid ~~her~~ **him** exactly 1 percent of the watch's price. When you and 70 ~~you're~~ **your** brother left the store, Mr. Sievers was still asking for additional funds. ~~He's~~ **His** blood pressure still has not returned to normal 71 levels.

Frankly I do not care ~~whose~~ **who's** to blame for the broken watchband or 72 Mr. Sievers's medical problem. I simply want ~~it~~ **the band** fixed. The watch 73 and ~~it's~~ **its** band are not your property. The store needs ~~their~~ **its** 74 75 merchandise in good condition.

Sincerely,

E. Neil Johnson

66 In this sentence, you don't need a possessive pronoun. What you really want to say is *It has,* so *It's* is the correct word.

67 What's valuable — the watch or the band? Better to clarify by inserting the specific information.

68 *Their* is possessive, not called for in the sentence.

69 *Mr. Sievers* is male and needs a masculine pronoun *(him)*.

70 *You're* = *you are,* but the sentence needs the possessive pronoun *your.*

71 *He's* = *he is,* but the sentence calls for the possessive pronoun *his.*

72 *Who's* = *who is.* The sentence needs to read "I do not care who is to blame . . ."

73 What should be fixed, the band or the blood pressure? Clarify by changing *it* to *the band.*

74 Here the possessive *its* is needed.

75 A store is singular (one store), so *its* (singular) is what you want.

Chapter 4

Having It All: Writing Complete Sentences

In This Chapter

▶ Making sure your sentence has a subject/verb pair

▶ Avoiding fragments and run-ons

▶ Joining sentences legally for better flow

▶ Placing endmarks that set the tone

Did you hear the story about the child who said nothing for the first five years of life and then began to speak in perfect, complete sentences? Supposedly the kid grew up to be something important, like a Supreme Court justice or a CEO. I question the story's accuracy, but I don't doubt that Supreme Court justices, CEOs, or anyone else with a good job knows how to write a complete sentence.

You need to know how to do so too, and in this chapter I give you a complete (pardon the pun) guide to sentence completeness, including how to punctuate and how to combine thoughts using proper grammar. (For more on how to combine sentences stylishly, check out Chapter 17.)

The evil geniuses who write standardized tests want to know whether you can write a proper, complete sentence. Because they're seldom willing to pay teachers to read your writing, this topic often turns up on those exams in a "choose the best" multiple-choice format or in an error-recognition section. Test takers, stay alert. Business people, this chapter is also important for you, because incomplete sentences seriously mar your writing.

To write a proper, complete sentence, follow these rules:

✔ **Every sentence needs a subject/verb pair.** More than one pair is okay, but at least one is essential. Just to be clear about the grammar terms: A verb expresses *action* or *state of being;* a subject tells you *who* or *what* is acting or being.

✔ **A grammatically correct sentence contains a complete thought.** Don't leave the reader hanging with only half an idea. ("If it rains" is an incomplete thought, but "If it rains, my paper dress will dissolve" is a complete and truly bizarre thought.)

✔ **Two or more ideas in a sentence must be joined correctly.** You can't just jam everything together. If you do, you end up with a run-on or "fused" sentence, which is a grammatical felony. Certain punctuation marks and what grammarians call *conjunctions* — joining words — glue ideas together legally.

✔ **Every sentence finishes with an endmark.** Endmarks include periods, question marks, and exclamation points.

Just four little rules. Piece of cake, right? In theory, yes. But sometimes applying the rules gets a little complicated. In the following sections I take you through each rule, one at a time, so you can practice each step.

Finding Subjects and Verbs that Match

The subject/verb pair is the heart and soul of the sentence. First, zero in on the verb, the word (or words) expressing action or a state of being. Next, look for the subject, a word (or words) expressing who or what is doing that action or is in that state of being. Now check to see that the subject and verb make sense together ("Mike has been singing," "Lindsay suffered," and so forth). For practice on properly matching subjects and verbs, flip to Chapter 2.

Some words that look like verbs don't function as verbs, so you may wrongly identify them as verbs. Checking for a match between a subject and a verb eliminates these false verbs from consideration, because false-verb pairs sound incomplete. A couple of mismatches illustrate my point: "Lindsay watching" "Mike's message having been scrambled."

You try some. In the blank, write the subject (S)/verb (V) pair. If you find no true pair, write "incomplete." (By the way, Duke, who appears several times in the following sentences, is my grand-dog.)

You may find it easier to look for the verb first, and then check for the subject. Yes, I know. The verb usually appears *after* the subject. However, the verb is the heart of the sentence, so identifying the verb is a good initial step.

0. Mike, with a cholesterol count climbing higher and higher, gave up and fried some sausages. _____

A. **Mike (S)/gave (V), fried (V).** Did I catch you with *climbing?* In the preceding sentence, *climbing* isn't a verb. One clue: *cholesterol count climbing* sounds incomplete. Just for comparison, *cholesterol count is climbing* makes a subject/verb match. Hear the difference?

1. Duke, sighing repeatedly because of her inability to score more than ten points at the dog show. _____

2. Charlie fed a steak to Truffle, his favorite entrant in the Dog of the Century contest. _____

3. Duke, my favorite entrant, snarfed a bowl of liver treats and woofed for about an hour afterward. _____

4. Entered in the Toy breed category, Duke is sure to win the "Most Likely to Fall Asleep Standing Up" contest. _____

5. Having been tired out by a heavy schedule of eating, chewing, and pooping. _____

6. Duke sleeps profoundly. _____

7. Once, having eaten through the dog-food bag and increased the size of her stomach by at least 50 percent. _____

8. One of the other dogs, biting the vet gently just to make a point about needles and her preference not to have them. _____

9. The vet is not upset by Duke's reaction. _____

10. Who would be surprised by a runoff between Truffle and Duke? _____

11. Not surprised by anything, especially with liver treats. _____

12. Truffle, sniffing the new dog toy on the couch. _____

13. Toto, the winner of last century's contest in running, jumping, and sleeping.
_____

14. Duke is guided around the judges' platform and television booth by a strong handler.
_____

15. Duke loves her time in the spotlight and the attention from the national media.
_____

16. Charlie, covered in tanning cream and catching a few rays at the side of the arena.
_____

17. Truffle and Duke sniffed Charlie's tanning cream while running around the arena.
_____

18. Swiftly across the arena sped the two dogs. _____

19. Stopping next to Charlie at the arena wall, Truffle and Duke. _____

20. They lapped a few gallons of tanning cream from his skin. _____

21. Cream smells great to a dog! _____

22. Truffle's allergy to the perfume, unfortunately causing a dripping nose and a slight cough, not to mention red eyes. _____

23. Truffle's handler immediately sought help from the vet. _____

24. What's wrong? _____

25. Nothing at all, according to Toto's press release, issued after the awards ceremony.
_____

Checking for Complete Thoughts

Some subject/verb pairs form a closed circle: The thought they express is complete. You want this quality in your sentences, because otherwise your reader echoes the outlaw who, with his head in the noose, said, "Don't leave me hanging!"

Some expressions are incomplete when they're statements but complete when they're questions. To illustrate my point: "Who won the game?" makes sense, but "Who won the game" doesn't.

Try this rule on for size. If the sentence has a complete thought, write "complete." If the reader is left in suspense, write "incomplete." Remember, the number of words doesn't indicate completeness. The content does.

Q. Whenever the cow jumps over the moon. _____

A. **Incomplete.** Aren't you wondering, "What happens *whenever the cow jumps over the moon?*" The thought is not complete.

26. The cow, who used to work for NASA until she got fed up with the bureaucracy. _____

27. On long-term training flights, the milking machine malfunctioned. _____

28. Why didn't the astronauts assume responsibility for milking procedures? _____

29. For one thing, milking, which wasn't in the manual but should have been, thus avoiding the problem and increasing the comfort level of the cow assigned to the jump. _____

30. The cow protested. _____

31. She mooed. _____

32. Because she couldn't change NASA's manual. _____

33. The author of the manual, fairly well known in the field of astrophysics, having also grown up on a farm, though that experience was a long time ago. _____

34. NASA has reached out to the cow community and promised to review milking procedures. _____

35. Applying to NASA, her mother, when only a calf. _____

36. Quitting was not a bad decision, however. _____

37. Twenty years of moon jumping is enough for any cow. _____

38. Unless NASA comes up with a better way to combine moon jumping and milk producing, the administration will have to recruit other species. _____

39. Sheep, which were once rejected from moon duty. _____

40. Will NASA send a flock of sheep to the moon someday? _____

41. Not needing milking on a regular basis, though female sheep produce milk. _____

42. This species may be a better fit for life in a spacecraft. _____

43. However much the sheep practice, the training isn't as easy for them as it is for cows. _____

44. Perhaps someday, having heard "the sheep jumped over the moon," set to the same music. _____

45. The sheep may need a different song to celebrate their moon jumping adventures. _____

Improving Flow with Properly Joined Sentences

Some sentences are short. Some are long. Joining them is good. Combined sentences make a narrative more interesting. Have I convinced you yet? The choppiness of the preceding sentences makes a good case for gluing sentences together. Just be sure to do so legally, so you won't end up with a run-on sentence.

Test writers sometimes throw improperly joined sentences at you to see whether you recognize this sort of error. Read this section of the workbook carefully to ace those questions.

To join sentences correctly, you need one of the following:

✔ **A conjunction:** A *conjunction* is a grammatical rubber band that unites parts of a sentence. To connect two complete sentences more or less equally, use *and, or, but, nor,* and *for.* Be sure to put a comma before the conjunction. To highlight one thought and make the other less important, use such conjunctions as *because, since, when, where, if, although, who, which,* and *that* — among others. These conjunctions are sometimes preceded by commas and sometimes not. (For more information on comma use, check out Chapter 5.)

✔ **A semicolon:** A *semicolon* (a little dot over a comma) pops up between two complete sentences and glues them together nicely. The two complete thoughts need to be related in some way.

Some words look like conjunctions but aren't. Don't use *nevertheless, consequently, therefore, however,* or *then* to join complete thoughts. If you want to place one of these "false conjunctions" between two complete thoughts, add a semicolon and place a comma after the "false conjunction." For more information on commas, see Chapter 5. Also, don't use a dash (a long, straight, horizontal line) to link two complete sentences one after the other. A semicolon is good for that job. However, a single dash can tack words to the end of a complete sentence, so long as the addition is less than a complete sentence. Two dashes may also be used to tuck a complete sentence *inside* another complete sentence.

For the following practice questions, put on your thinking cap and decide whether you have a legally combined, correct sentence or (gasp) an illegal, glued-together mess. In the blank after the sentence, write "correct" or "incorrect." Take a stab at changing the messes to legal, complete sentences. Notice the teacher trick? I provide space to revise every sentence, including the correct ones, so you can't judge the legal sentences by the length of the blanks.

0. Kathy broke out of jail, five years for illegal sentence-joining was just too much for her.

_____

_____

A. **Incorrect.** The comma can't unite two complete thoughts. Change it to a semicolon and you're in business. **Kathy broke out of jail; five years for illegal sentence-joining was just too much for her.** An alternate correction: **Kathy broke out of jail because five years for illegal sentence-joining was just too much for her.** The *because* connects the two ideas correctly.

46. The grammarian-in-chief used to work for the Supreme Court, therefore his word was law.

_____

_____

47. His nickname, "Mr. Grammar," which had been given to him by the court clerks, was not a source of pride for him.

_____

_____

48. Nevertheless, he did not criticize those who used the term, as long as they did so politely.

_____

_____

49. He often wore a lab coat embroidered with parts of speech, for he was truly devoted to the field of grammar.

_____

_____

50. Kathy's escape wounded him deeply — he ordered the grammar cops to arrest her as soon as possible.

_____

_____

51. Kathy hid in a basket of dirty laundry, then she held her breath as the truck passed the border.

_____

_____

52. Kathy passed the border of sanity some time ago, although she is able to speak in complete sentences if she really tries.

_____

_____

53. She's attracted to sentence fragments, which appeal to something in her character.

_____

_____

54. "Finish what you start," her mother often exclaimed, "You don't know when you're going to face a grammar judge."

_____

_____

55. While she is free, Kathy intends to burn grammar textbooks for fuel — probably to heat her English classroom.

_____

_____

56. Grammar books burn exceptionally well, nevertheless, some people prefer history texts for fuel.

_____

_____

57. History books create a satisfactory snap and crackle while they are burning, the flames are also a nice shade of orange.

_____

_____

58. Because she loves history, Kathy rejected _The Complete History of the Grammatical World,_ she burned _Participles and You_ instead.

_____

_____

59. _Participles and You,_ a bestseller for more than two years, sizzled, therefore it gave off a lot of heat.

_____

_____

60. Kathy found a few sentence fragments in the ash pile, but she disposed of them quickly.

_____

_____

61. The grammar cops located Kathy's getaway car after a long search — more than a month.

_____

_____

62. The lead detective brought the evidence of Kathy's innocence to the federal prosecutor, more than twenty run-on sentences had been planted in Kathy's work by a jealous writer.

_____

_____

63. Kathy's defense attorney told her to be quiet, he invoked her right to remain grammatically silent.

_____

_____

64. The judge dropped the charges against Kathy, even though she had slugged a guard during the escape.

_____

_____

65. The grammarian-in-chief — he served for more than 60 years — will retire soon.

_____

_____

Setting the Tone with Endmarks

When you're speaking, the listener knows you've completed a sentence because the thought is complete and your tone says that the end has arrived. In writing, the tone part is taken care of by a period, question mark, or exclamation point. You must have one, and only one, of these marks at the end of a sentence, unless you're writing a comic book in which characters are allowed to say things like "You want my what??!!?" Periods are for statements, question marks are for (surprise) questions, and exclamation points scream at the reader. Endmarks become complicated when they tangle with quotation marks. (For tips on endmark/ quotation mark interactions, check out Chapter 7.)

Go to work on this section, which is filled with sentences desperately in need of an endmark. Write the appropriate endmark in the blank provided.

Q. Did Lola really ride to the anti-noise protest on her motorcycle _____

A. ? (question mark). You're clearly asking a question, so the question mark fits here.

66. No, she rode her motorcycle to the mathematicians' convention _____

67. You're not serious _____

68. Yes, Lola is a true fan of triangles _____

69. Does she bring her own triangles or expect to find what she needs at the convention _____

70. I'm not sure, but I think I heard her say that her math colleagues always bring triangles that are awesome _____

71. Do you think that she really means awful _____

72. I heard her scream that everyone loves triangles because they're the best shape in the universe_____

73. Are you going also _____

74. I'd rather have dental surgery than attend a math convention _____

75. I heard Lola exclaim that equilaterals turn her on _____

76. Are you sure that Lola loves equilaterals _____

77. I always thought that she was fond of triangles _____

78. Who in the world wants an "I love math" T-shirt _____

79. I can't believe that Lola actually bought one _____

80. Will she give me her old "I love grammar" hat _____

Proper Sentence or Not?
That Is the Question

If you've plowed your way through this entire chapter, you've practiced each sentence skill separately. But to write well, you have to do everything at once — create subject/verb pairs, finish a thought, combine thoughts properly, and place the appropriate endmark.

Take a test drive with the questions in this section. Decide whether the sentence is correct or incorrect and plop a label in the blank. If the sentence is incorrect, repair the damage. Notice that I've cleverly included a fix-it blank even for sentences that are already correct. In the military, that stratagem is called camouflage. In teaching, it's called a dirty trick.

0. Though the spaghetti sticks to the ceiling above the pan on rainy days when even one more problem will send me over the edge.

_____

_____

A. **Incorrect.** The statement has no complete thought. Possible correction: Omit *Though* and begin the sentence with *The*.

81. Bill's holiday concert, occurring early in October, honors the centuries-old tradition of his people.

_____

_____

82. The holiday, which is called Hound Dog Day in honor of a wonderful dog breed.

_____

_____

83. Tradition calls for blue suede shoes.

_____

_____

84. Having brushed the shoes carefully with a suede brush, which can be bought in any shoe store.

_____

_____

85. The citizens lead their dogs to the town square, Heartbreak Hotel is located there.

_____

_____

86. "Look for the ghost of Elvis," the hotel clerk tells every guest, "Elvis has often been seen haunting these halls."

_____

_____

87. Elvis, ghost or not, apparently does not attend the Hound Dog Day festivities because no one has seen an aging singer in a white jumpsuit there.

_____

_____

88. Why should a ghost attend Bill's festival

_____

_____

89. How can you even ask?

_____

_____

90. The blue suede shoes are a nostalgic touch, consequently, the tourists always wear them.

_____

_____

91. Personally, I prefer blue patent leather pumps, but my opinion isn't important.

_____

_____

92. Patent leather is amazing

_____

_____

93. Stay off of my shoes!

_____

_____

94. While we were talking about shoes, Bill was creating a playlist for the Hound Dog Concert.

_____

_____

95. You should plan to arrive early — everyone in town will be there.

_____

_____

Calling All Overachievers: Extra Practice with Complete Sentences

I can't let you go without pitching one more curveball at you. Read the letter in Figure 4-1, introducing a new employee to customers who apparently have good reason to be upset. Only five sentences are complete and correct; the other five have problems. Can you find the five that don't make the grade?

> To Our Valued Customers:
>
> Announcing that Abner Grey is our new Director of Customer Satisfaction, effective immediately. Abner brings a wealth of experience to our company. He served as Assistant VP of marketing for Antarctic Icebergs, Inc., until last year, when the cold finally became too much for him. His first task, to introduce himself to every customer, finding out what has been done in the past and how our relationship may be improved. Expect a phone call or a personal visit from him soon! Recognizing that our previous director was not always attentive to your needs (occupied as she was with the lawsuit, prison, and so forth), we have told Abner to work at least 90 hours per week. No more embezzlement either! Abner is completely honest, he considers "Integrity" his middle name. Call him whenever you have a problem. You will not be disappointed, furthermore, Abner will actually anticipate your needs. Rest assured that this Director of Customer Satisfaction will never see the inside of a jail cell.
>
> Sincerely,
>
> Vicki Copple

Figure 4-1:
Sample letter with incomplete and run-on sentences.

Answers to Complete Sentence Problems

Following are the answers to the practice questions in this chapter.

1 **Incomplete.** Did you zero in on *sighing?* That's part of a verb (a present participle, if you absolutely have to know), but all by itself it isn't enough to fill the verb category. Likewise, if you try to pair *sighing* with a subject, the only candidate is *Duke. Duke is sighing* would be a match, but *Duke sighing* isn't. No subject/verb pair, no sentence.

2 **Charlie (S)/fed (V).** Start with a verb search. Any action or being verbs? Yes, *fed.* Now ask who or what *fed. Charlie fed.* You have a good subject/verb match.

3 **Duke (S)/snarfed (V), woofed (V).** Your verb search (always the best first step) yields two, *snarfed* and *woofed.* Who *snarfed* and *woofed? Duke.* There you go — an acceptable subject/ verb pair.

4 **Duke (S)/is (V).** Were you tricked by *entered? Entered* may be a verb in some sentences, but in this one it isn't, because it has no subject. But *is* does have a subject, *Duke.*

5 **Incomplete.** Something's missing here: a *subject* and a *verb!* What you have, in grammarspeak, is a participle, a part of a verb, but not enough to satisfy the subject/verb rule.

6 **Duke (S)/sleeps (V).** Start with a verb search, and you immediately come up with *sleeps,* which, by the way, is an action verb, even though sleeping seems like the opposite of action. Who *sleeps? Duke,* bless her snoring little self.

7 **Incomplete.** You have two action participles — *having eaten and increased* — but no subject. Penalty box!

8 **Incomplete.** The sentence has action *(biting),* but when you ask who's *biting,* you get no answer, because *one biting* is a mismatch.

9 **vet (S)/is (V).** No action in this one, but *is* expresses being, so you're covered on the verb front. Who or what *is?* The *vet is.*

10 **Who (S)/would be (V).** Are you surprised to see *who* as a subject? In a question, *who* often fills that role.

11 **Incomplete.** A quick glance tells you that you have a verb form *(surprised),* but no subject.

12 **Incomplete.** A verb form *(sniffing)* is easy to find here, but when you ask who is doing the sniffing, you come up blank. *Truffle sniffing* doesn't match.

13 **Incomplete.** In this one you have a subject, *Toto,* but no matching verb. True, the statement talks about *running, jumping,* and *sleeping,* but those aren't matches for *Toto.* (If you care, they're actually nouns functioning as objects of the preposition *in.*)

14 **Duke (S)/is guided (V).** Start with a verb search. Any action or being verbs? Yes, *is guided.* Now ask who or what *is guided.* There you go: *Duke is guided.* You have a good subject/verb match.

15 **Duke (S)/loves (V).** A verb hunt gives you *loves,* and asking that universal question (who loves?) yields *Duke loves* — a subject/verb pair and a legal sentence.

16 **Incomplete.** Charlie makes a fine subject, but in this one he's not matched with a verb. The two verb forms in the statement, *covered* and *catching,* describe Charlie. (They're participles, if you like these grammar terms.) Neither makes a good match. *Charlie covered* sounds like a match, but the meaning here is incorrect because Charlie isn't performing the action of covering. *Charlie catching* sounds like a mismatch because it is.

17 **Truffle (S), Duke (S)/sniffed (V).** First, find the verb. If you sniff around this sentence looking for an action word, you come up with *sniffed.* Now ask, *Who sniffed? Truffle* and *Duke sniffed.* A good compound (double) subject and a matching verb make a complete sentence.

18 **dogs (S)/sped (V).** This one may have surprised you because the subjects follow the verb — an unusual, but perfectly fine position. If you follow the normal procedure (locating the verb and asking who did the action), you find *dogs,* even though they appear last in the sentence.

19 **Incomplete.** This statement contains a verb form, *stopping,* but no subject matches it. Verdict: ten years in the grammar penitentiary for failure to complete the sentence.

20 **They (S)/lapped (V).** The action here is *lapped,* which unites nicely with *they.* Completeness rules!

21 **Cream (S)/smells (V).** After you zero in on the verb, *smells,* just ask, "Who *smells*?" Resist the temptation to list all the people you know who should bathe more often and answer *cream.*

22 **Incomplete.** You have two verb forms, *causing* and *mention,* but neither pairs up with a subject. In fact, neither functions as a verb in this sentence. (*Causing* is a description and *to mention* is an infinitive, the "head" of a verb family that can't actually act as a verb in any sentence.)

23 **handler (S)/sought (V).** The action is *sought* and is performed by the *handler.*

24 **What (S)/is (V).** Okay, I can hear your protest already. Yes, *is* doesn't appear in the sentence. So how can it be a verb? See the apostrophe in *What's?* The apostrophe creates a contraction, a shortened form. Expanded, *What's* turns into *What is,* a subject/verb pair.

25 **Incomplete.** In this one you have a verb, *issued,* but no subject.

26 **Incomplete.** The reader is waiting to hear something about the *cow.* The way the sentence reads now, you have a description of *cow — who used to work for NASA until she got fed up with the bureaucracy —* but no action word to tell the reader what the cow is doing.

27 **Complete.** The sentence tells you everything you need to know, so it's complete.

28 **Complete.** The question makes sense as is, so the sentence is complete.

29 **Incomplete.** The statement gives you an idea — *milking* — and some descriptions, but it never delivers a complete thought about milking.

30 **Complete.** Short, but you have everything you need to know about the *protesting cow.*

31 **Complete.** This sentence is even shorter than the one in the preceding question, but it still delivers its complete message.

32 **Incomplete.** The word *because* implies a cause-and-effect relationship, but the sentence doesn't supply all the needed information.

33 **Incomplete.** This one goes on and on, piling on descriptions of the author. However, it never delivers the punch line. What's *the author* doing? Or, what state of being is *the author* in? The sentence doesn't tell you, so it's incomplete.

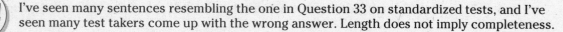

I've seen many sentences resembling the one in Question 33 on standardized tests, and I've seen many test takers come up with the wrong answer. Length does not imply completeness.

34 **Complete.** You know what NASA is doing, so this sentence is complete.

35 **Incomplete.** What did the mama cow do when she was only a calf? The sentence doesn't actually say, so it's incomplete.

36 **Complete.** This sentence makes a complete and forceful statement about quitting.

37 **Complete.** All you need to know about moon jumping (that it's enough for any cow) is in the sentence.

38 **Complete.** This sentence contains enough information to reform NASA.

39 **Incomplete.** The sentence begins to make a statement about *sheep* but then veers off into a description *(which were once rejected from moon duty)*. No other thought is attached to *sheep*, so the sentence is incomplete.

40 **Complete.** This question makes sense as is. You may wonder what NASA will do, but you won't wonder what's being asked here because the question — and the sentence — is complete.

41 **Incomplete.** The first part of the sentence is a description, and the second is a qualifier, explaining a condition *(though female sheep produce milk)*. Neither of these two parts is a complete thought, so the sentence is incomplete.

42 **Complete.** You have everything you need to know here except why anyone would want to send this species to the moon. Grammatically, this is a complete thought.

43 **Complete.** The statement comparing sheep performance to cow performance is finished, and the cows win. You're not left hanging, wondering what the sentence is trying to say. Verdict: complete.

44 **Incomplete.** The sentence contains several descriptions but no complete thought.

45 **Complete.** You have a complete thought about the *sheep and a different song*.

46 **Incorrect.** Here you have two complete thoughts (everything before the comma equals one complete thought; everything after the comma is another complete thought). A comma isn't strong enough to hold them together. Try a semicolon or insert *and* after the comma.

47 **Correct.** No problems here! The extra information about the nickname *(which had been given to him by the court clerks)* is a description, not a complete thought, so it can be tucked into the sentence next to the word it describes *(nickname)*. The *which* ties the idea to *nickname*.

48 **Correct.** Surprised? The *nevertheless* in this sentence is not used as a joiner, so it's legal.

49 **Correct.** Did I get you on this one? The word *for* has another, more common grammatical use in such expressions as *for the love of Pete, for you, for the last time,* and so on. However, *for* is a perfectly fine joiner of two complete thoughts when it means *because*.

50   **Incorrect.** The dash here can't join two complete thoughts correctly. Use a semicolon or link these ideas with *so,* preceded by a comma.

51   **Incorrect.** To connect these two ideas, look for a stronger connection word. *Then* can't do the job. Try *and then* or *but then.* Another good solution is to replace the comma with a semicolon *(; then).*

52   **Correct.** The words *although* and *if* join thoughts to another, more important, main idea about Kathy's sanity.

53   **Correct.** The tacked-on description *(which appeal to something in her character)* is legal because the *which* refers to the preceding word *(fragments).*

54   **Incorrect.** Just because you're quoting, don't think you can ignore run-on rules. The quotation itself contains two complete thoughts and thus needs to be expressed in two complete sentences. The easiest fix: Place a period after *exclaimed.*

55   **Correct.** No grammatical felonies here: Two ideas *(she is free* and *Kathy intends to burn grammar textbooks for fuel)* are linked by *while.* Did I confuse you with the dash? It's not attaching another complete sentence, so it's fine.

56   **Incorrect.** *Nevertheless* is a long word. It looks strong enough to join two complete thoughts, but in reality it isn't. Plop a semicolon before *nevertheless* and you're legal.

57   **Incorrect.** One complete thought *(History books create a satisfactory snap and crackle while they are burning)* is glued to another *(the flames are also a nice shade of orange)* with nothing more than a comma. Penalty box! Use a semicolon or add a comma after *burning* and follow it with the conjunction *and.*

58   **Incorrect.** As in the preceding question, one complete thought *(Because she loves history, Kathy rejected* The Complete History of the Grammatical World) and another *(she burned* Participles and You *instead)* are attached by a comma. I don't think so! Use a semicolon or place a *but* after *World.*

59   **Incorrect.** *Therefore* isn't a legal joiner. Substitute *so* or place a semicolon before *therefore.*

60   **Correct.** The word *but* is short, but it does the job of joining two complete sentences.

61   **Correct.** Only one complete sentence is written here. *More than a month* isn't a problem, because the dash isn't tacking on another whole sentence.

62   **Incorrect.** Two complete sentences are linked only by a comma. Doesn't work. Use a semicolon.

63   **Incorrect.** Another comma mistake! Commas don't work out at the gym or eat healthful meals, so they're too weak to join complete sentences.

64   **Correct.** Two words, *even though,* act as the conjunction (joining word) in this correct sentence.

65   **Correct.** This is a tricky sentence. Two dashes can be used to insert a complete sentence inside another complete sentence, so this sentence is fine. Just remember not to use a dash to connect two complete sentences one after the other.

66 . (period). Because this sentence makes a statement, a period is the appropriate endmark.

67 ! (exclamation point). These words may also form a question or a statement, but an exclamation point is certainly appropriate because the speaker may be expressing amazement that a biker chick likes math.

68 . (period). Another statement, another period.

69 ? (question mark). The *does* in this sentence signals a question, so you need a question mark.

70 . (period). The period is the endmark for this statement.

71 ? (question mark). Here the question mark signals a request for information.

72 . (period). This statement calls for a period.

73 ? (question mark). This sentence requests information, so place the question mark at the end.

74 ! (exclamation point). Okay, a period would do fine here, but an exclamation point adds extra emphasis. And shame on you for avoiding math. Some of my best friends are math teachers!

75 . (period). This statement needs a period as an endmark.

76 ? (question mark). The sentence requests information, so a question mark is the endmark you want.

77 . (period). I've chosen a period, but if you're bursting with emotion, opt for the exclamation point instead.

78 ? (question mark). I see this one as a true inquiry, but you can also interpret it as a scream of disbelief, in which case an exclamation point works well.

79 ! (exclamation point). I hear this one as a strong blast of surprise, suitable for an exclamation point.

80 ? (question mark). If you're asking for information, you need a question mark.

81 **Correct.**

82 **Incorrect.** The sentence is incorrect because it gives you a subject *(the holiday)* and a bunch of descriptions *(which is called Hound Dog Day in honor of a wonderful dog breed)* but doesn't pair any verb with *holiday*. Several corrections are possible. Here's one: **The holiday, which is called Hound Dog Day in honor of a wonderful dog breed, requires each citizen to attend dog obedience school.**

83 **Correct.**

84 **Incorrect.** This sentence has no subject. No one is doing the brushing or the buying. One possible correction: **Having brushed the shoes carefully with a suede brush, which can be bought in any shoe store, Bill proudly displayed his feet.**

85 **Incorrect.** This sentence is a run-on, because a comma can't join two complete thoughts. Change it to a semicolon or reword the sentence. Here's a possible rewording: **The citizens lead their dogs to the town square, where Heartbreak Hotel is located.**

86   **Incorrect.** Another run-on sentence. The two quoted sections are jammed into one sentence, but each is a complete thought. Change the comma after *guest* to a period.

87   **Correct.**

88   **Incorrect.** The sentence is incorrect because it has no endmark. Add a question mark.

89   **Correct.**

90   **Incorrect**. This sentence is a run-on. *Consequently* looks like a fine, strong word, but it can't join two complete thoughts, which you have in this sentence. Add a semicolon after *touch* and dump the comma.

91   **Correct.**

92   **Incorrect.** The sentence needs an endmark. I'd go with an exclamation point, but a period is also correct.

93   **Correct.** Surprised? This sentence gives a command. The subject is *you*, even though *you* doesn't appear in the sentence. It's implied.

94   **Correct.**

95   **Incorrect.** The dash can't connect two complete sentences. Use a semicolon.

The following answers refer to Figure 4-1.

96   Sentence 1 is incorrect because it lacks a subject/verb pair. To make the sentence correct, drop *Announcing that* or add *I am* to the beginning of the sentence.

97   Sentence 4 is incorrect because although it has two long descriptions, it doesn't complete the thought begun by *His first task*.

98   Sentence 7 is incorrect because it has neither a subject nor a verb. You could correct this by adding *We'll have* to the beginning of the sentence.

99   Sentence 8 is incorrect because it links two complete thoughts with a comma. Only a semicolon or a conjunction (a joining word such as *and*) can do that job.

100   Sentence 10 is incorrect because *furthermore* is not a conjunction. Place a semicolon in front of *furthermore*, and you're fine.

Part II
Mastering Mechanics

In this part . . .

*I*n my hometown, it's possible to find stores whose signs proclaim "merchant's sell Bagels." You have to give me a minute to shudder at the small but important mistakes (and I don't mean *mistake's*) in bagel signage. First of all, the apostrophe (the little hook at the end of the word *merchant*) is wrong, as are, by my informal count, 99.99 percent of the apostrophes I see in all sorts of official spots. Plus, despite the fact that *bagels* are extremely delicious, they don't deserve a capital letter. Sigh. Such are the daily trials of a grammarian in New York City.

Wherever you live, in this part you can practice some aspects of what grammarians call *mechanics* — punctuation and capitalization. When you're done, you'll be the master of the dreaded comma (Chapter 5), apostrophe (Chapter 6), and quotation mark (Chapter 7). Tucked into Chapter 8 are the basics of capitalization. If all these details fry your brain, feel free to refresh yourself with a bagel or two.

Chapter 5

Pausing to Consider the Comma

In This Chapter

▶ Separating items in a list with punctuation

▶ Using commas to indicate direct address

▶ Combining sentences

▶ Correctly interrupting and introducing sentences

▶ Setting descriptors off with commas

Small though they are, commas nearly always have a significant effect on the meaning of a sentence. They can indicate relationships between items or people, they keep words and numbers from running together, and they point out what's not necessary to the meaning of a sentence. In this chapter you can practice inserting and deleting commas until your writing is clear and correct.

Keeping Lists in Order with Commas and Semicolons

When you're writing a free-standing list, line breaks signal when one item in a list ends and another begins. Commas do the same thing in sentences. Perhaps Professor MacGregor wants you to do the following:

✔ Go on the Internet.

✔ Locate the origin of the handheld meat patty.

✔ Write a paper on hamburger history.

Inserted into a sentence, the line breaks in the preceding list turn into commas:

Professor MacGregor wants you to go on the Internet, locate the origin of the handheld meat patty, and write a paper on hamburger history.

Notice that the first item isn't preceded by a comma and that the last two items are separated by *and,* which has a comma in front of it. (The last comma is a style issue, not a grammatical necessity. Most people do insert a comma before the *and* or whatever word joins the last two items of the list.)

If the list is very long (and *long* is a judgment call), it may be preceded by a colon (one dot atop another). The words before the colon should be a complete thought. Here's an example:

> Ms. Sharkface required the following for every homework assignment: 12-point font, green ink, a plastic cover, at least two illustrations, a minimum of three quotations, and a list of sources.

If any item in a list has a comma *within* it, semicolons are used to separate the list items. Imagine that you're inserting this list into a sentence:

- Peter McKinney, the mayor
- Agnes Hutton
- Jeannie Battle, magic expert

In a sentence using only commas, the reader wouldn't know that Peter McKinney is the mayor and may instead think that Peter and the mayor are two separate people. Here's the properly punctuated sentence:

> Because he has only one extra ticket to the magic show, Daniel will invite Peter McKinney, the mayor; Agnes Hutton; or Jeannie Battle, magic expert.

Get to work! Insert the list from each question into a sentence (I supply the beginning) and punctuate it properly. *Note:* I use numbers to separate items on the list. Don't use numbers in your answer sentence.

Q. List of things to buy at the pharmacy: (1) industrial-strength toenail clippers (2) green shoe polish (3) earwax remover

Getting ready for his big date, Rob went to the pharmacy to purchase _____

_____

A. **Getting ready for his big date, Rob went to the pharmacy to purchase industrial-strength toenail clippers, green shoe polish, and earwax remover.** You have three items and two commas; no comma is needed before the first item on the list.

1. Supermarket shopping list: (1) pitted dates (2) chocolate-covered mushrooms (3) anchovies (4) pickles

Rob planned to serve a tasteful selection of _____

_____

2. Guests: (1) Helen Ogee, supermodel (2) Natasha Smith, swimsuit model (3) Blair Berry, auto salesperson (4) Hannah Bridge, punctuation expert (5) Jane Fine, veterinarian

Rob's guest list is heavily tilted toward women he would like to date: _____

_____

3. Activities: (1) bobbing for cabbages (2) pinning the tail on the landlord (3) playing double solitaire

After everyone arrives, Rob plans an evening of _____

_____

4. Goals: (1) get three phone numbers (2) arrange at least one future date (3) avoid police interference

Rob will consider his party a success if he can _____

_____

5. Results: (1) the police arrived at 10:00, 11:00, and 11:30 p.m. (2) no one gave out any phone numbers (3) everyone thought the host's name was Bob

Rob didn't meet his goals because _____

_____

Directly Addressing the Listener or Reader

If the name or title of the person to whom you're talking or writing is inserted into the sentence, you're in a direct-address situation. Direct-address expressions are set off from everything else by commas. In these examples, *Wilfred* is being addressed:

Wilfred, you can have the squash court at 10 a.m.

When you hit a zucchini, Wilfred, avoid using too much force.

The most common direct-address mistake is to send one comma to do a two-comma job. In the second preceding example, two commas must set off *Wilfred*.

Can you insert commas to highlight the direct-address name in these sentences?

0. Listen Champ I think you need to get a new pair of boxing gloves.

A. **Listen, Champ, I think you need to get a new pair of boxing gloves.** In this example, you're talking to *Champ*, a title that's substituting for the actual name. Direct-address expressions don't have to be proper names, though they frequently are.

6. Ladies and Gentlemen I present the Fifth Annual Elbox Championships.

7. I know Mort that you are an undefeated Elbox competitor. Would you tell our audience about the sport?

8. Elboxing is about 5,000 years old Chester. It originated in ancient Egypt.

9. Really? Man I can't believe you knew that!

10. Yes Chester the sport grew out of the natural movement of the elbow when someone tried to interfere with a diner's portion by "elbowing."

11. Excuse me a moment. The reigning champion has decided to pay us a visit. Miss William could you tell us how you feel about the upcoming match?

12. Certainly Sir. I am confident that my new training routine will pay off.

Placing Commas in Combined Sentences

Certain words — *and, but, or, nor,* and *for* — are like officials who perform weddings. They link two equals. (Always a good idea in a marriage, don't you think?) These powerful words are *conjunctions.* Forget the grammar term! Just remember to place a comma before the conjunction when you're combining two complete sentences. Here are some examples:

The wedding cake was pink, and the bride's nose was purple.

A wedding in the middle of an ice rink is festive, but the air is chilly.

The bride's nose began to run, for she had forgotten her heated veil.

You get the idea. Each conjunction is preceded by a complete sentence and a comma. The conjunction is followed by another complete sentence. (See Chapter 4 for more information on complete sentences.)

When one of these conjunctions links anything other than a complete sentence (say, two verbs), you don't need a comma.

Time to scatter commas around these sentences, starting with this example. If no comma is needed, write "no comma" in the margin.

Q. The groom skated to the center of the rink and waited for his shivering bride.

A. **No comma.** The words in front of the conjunction (*The groom skated to the center of the rink*) are a complete sentence, but the words after the conjunction (*waited for his shivering bride*) aren't. Because the conjunction *and* links two verbs (*skated* and *waited*) and their descriptions, no comma is called for. In case you're wondering, *groom* is the subject of *skated* and *waited*.

13. The best man rode in a Zamboni for he was afraid of slipping on the ice.

14. The flowers scattered around the rink and the colorful spotlights impressed the guests.

15. One of the bridesmaids whispered that her own wedding would be on a beach or in a sunny climate with absolutely no ice.

16. The guests sipped hot chocolate but they were still cold.

17. The ice-dancing during the reception made them sweat and then the temperature seemed fine.

18. Do you know who is in charge of the gifts or who is paying the orchestra?

19. I'd like to swipe a present for my blender is broken.

20. I don't need an icemaker but I'll take one anyway.

21. The happy couple drove away in a sled and never came back.

Inserting Extras with Commas: Introductions and Interruptions

Grammatically, *introductory expressions* are a mixed bag of verbals, prepositional phrases, adverbial clauses, and lots of other things. You don't have to know their names; you just have to know that an introductory expression makes a comment on the rest of the sentence or adds a bit of extra information. An introductory statement is usually separated from the rest of the sentence by a comma. Check out the italicized portion of each of these sentences for examples of introductory expressions:

> *Snaking through the tunnel,* Brad thought about potential book deals.
>
> *No,* Brad didn't blow up the enemy base.
>
> *While he was crossing the lighted area,* he called his agent instead.

Interrupters (also a grammatical mixed bag) show up inside — not in front of — a sentence. The same principle that applies to introductory expressions applies to interrupters: They comment on or otherwise *interrupt* the main idea of the sentence and thus are set off by commas. Check out these italicized interrupters:

> Cindy, *slashing the spy,* thought that Hollywood should film her adventures.
>
> There was no guarantee, *of course,* that Cindy would make it out alive.

You don't need commas for short introductory expressions or interrupters that don't contain verbs and are tied strongly to the main idea of the sentence. For example, "In the morning Brad drank 12 cups of coffee" needs no comma to separate *In the morning* from the rest of the sentence.

Up for some practice? Insert commas where needed and resist the temptation to insert them where they're not wanted in these sentences.

Q. Tired after a long day delivering pizza Elsie was in no mood for fireworks.

A. **Tired after a long day delivering pizza, Elsie was in no mood for fireworks.** The comma sets off the introductory expression, *Tired after a long day delivering pizza.* Notice how that information applies to *Elsie?* She's the subject of the sentence.

Introductory verb forms must describe the subject of the sentence. Test writers really want you to know that rule, judging from the questions they create.

22. In desperate need of a pizza fix Brad turned to his cellphone.

23. Cindy on the other hand ached for sushi.

24. Yes pizza was an excellent idea.

25. The toppings unfortunately proved to be a problem.

26. Restlessly Brad pondered pepperoni as the spies searched for him.

27. Cindy wondered how Brad given his low-fat diet could consider pepperoni.

28. Frozen with indecision Brad decided to call the supermarket to request the cheapest brand.

29. Cindy on a tight budget wanted to redeem her coupons.

30. To demand fast delivery was Brad's priority.

31. Lighting a match and holding it near his trembling hand Brad realized that time was almost up.

32. Worrying about toppings had used up too many minutes.

33. Well the survivors would have a good story to tell.

34. With determination Cindy speed-dialed the market and offered "a really big tip" for fast service.

35. As the robbers chomped on pepperoni and argued about payment Brad slipped away.

36. Let's just say that Cindy was left to clean up the mess.

Setting Descriptions Apart

Life would be much simpler for the comma-inserter if nobody ever described anything. However, descriptions are a part of life, so you need to know these punctuation rules:

✔ **If the description *follows* the word being described, it is not set off by commas if it's essential, identifying material. If the description falls into the "nice to know but I didn't really need it" (extra) category, surround it with commas.** For example, in the sentence "The dictionary *on the table* is dusty," the description in italics is necessary because it tells *which* dictionary is dusty. In "Charlie's dictionary, *which is on the table,* is dusty," the description in italics is set off by commas, because you already know *Charlie's dictionary* is the one being discussed. The part about the table is extra information.

Standardized tests often require you to decide whether descriptions such as the ones in the preceding bullet point need to be set off by commas.

✔ **For descriptions that precede the word described, place commas only when you have a list of two or more descriptions of the same type and importance.** You can tell when two or more descriptions are equally important; they can be written in different order without changing the meaning of the sentence. For example, "the *tan, dusty* dictionary" and "the *dusty, tan* dictionary" have the same meaning, so you need a comma between the descriptions. However, "*two dusty* dictionaries" is different. One description is a number, and one is a condition. Because the descriptions differ, you don't insert commas.

✔ **When descriptions containing verb forms introduce a sentence, they always are set off by commas.** An example: Sighing into his handkerchief, Charlie looked for a dust cloth. The description, *sighing into his handkerchief,* has a verb form (sighing) and thus is set off by a comma from the rest of the sentence.

Got the idea? Now try your comma skills on the following sentences. If the italicized words need to be set off, add the commas. If no commas are called for, write "correct" in the margin.

0. The *ruffled striped* blouse is at the closest dry cleaner Fleur and Sons.

A. **The *ruffled, striped* blouse is at the closest dry cleaner, Fleur and Sons.** The first two descriptions precede the word being described *(blouse)* and may be interchanged, so a comma is needed between them. The second description (which, the strictest grammarians would tell you is really an equivalent term or *appositive*) follows what's being described *(the closest dry cleaner)*. Because you can have only one *closest dry cleaner,* the name is extra, not essential identifying information, and it's set off by commas.

37. *Oscar's favorite* food *which he cooks every Saturday night* is hot dogs.

38. The place *where he feels most comfortable during the cooking process* is his *huge brick* barbecue.

39. Oscar stores *his wheat* buns in a *large plastic* tub *that used to belong to his grandpa.*

40. One of the horses *that live in Oscar's barn* often sniffs around *Oscar's lucky* horseshoe *which he found while playing tag.*

41. Oscar rode *his three favorite* horses in a race *honoring the Barbecue King and Queen.*

42. Oscar *who is an animal lover* will never sell one of his horses *because he needs money.*

43. *Being sentimental* Oscar dedicated a song to the filly *that was born on his birthday.*

44. The jockeys *who were trying to prepare for the big race* became annoyed by Oscar's song *which he played constantly;* the jockeys *who had already raced* didn't mind Oscar's music.

45. The *deep horrible* secret is that Oscar can't stay in tune *when he sings.*

46. His guitar *a Gibson* is also missing *two important* strings.

Calling All Overachievers: Extra Practice with Commas

Figure 5-1 shows an employee self-evaluation with some serious problems, a few of which concern commas. (The rest deal with the truly bad idea of being honest with your boss.) Forget about the content errors and concentrate on commas. See whether you can find five commas that appear where they shouldn't and ten spots that should have commas but don't. Circle the commas you're deleting, and insert commas where they're needed.

Annual Self-Evaluation

Well Ms. Ehrlich that time of year has arrived again. I, must think about

my strengths and weaknesses as an employee, of Toe-Ring International.

First and most important let me say that I love working for Toe-Ring.

When I applied for the job I never dreamed how much fun I would have

taking two, long lunches a day. Sneaking out the back door, is not my idea

of fun. Because no one ever watches what I am doing at Toe-Ring I can

leave by the front door without worrying. Also Ms. Ehrlich, I confess that I

do almost no work at all. Upon transferring to the plant in Idaho I

immediately claimed a privilege given only to the most experienced most

skilled, employees and started to take two, extra weeks of vacation. I

have only one more thing to say. May I have a raise?

Figure 5-1:
Comma
problems
in an
employee
self-
evaluation.

Answers to Comma Problems

Check your answers to this chapter's problems against the following solutions.

1 **Rob planned to serve a tasteful selection of pitted dates, chocolate-covered mushrooms, anchovies, and pickles.** Each item on Rob's list, including the last one before the *and*, is separated from the next by a comma. No comma comes before the first item, *pitted dates*.

2 **Rob's guest list is heavily tilted toward women he would like to date: Helen Ogee, supermodel; Natasha Smith, swimsuit model; Blair Berry, auto salesperson; Hannah Bridge, punctuation expert; and Jane Fine, veterinarian.** Did you remember the semicolons? The commas within each item of Rob's dream-date list make it impossible to distinguish between one dream date and another with a simple comma. Semicolons do the trick. Also, I hope you noticed that this rather long list begins with a colon.

3 **After everyone arrives, Rob plans an evening of bobbing for cabbages, pinning the tail on the landlord, and playing double solitaire.** Fun guy, huh? I can't imagine why he has so much trouble getting dates. I hope you didn't have any trouble separating these thrilling activities with commas.

4 **Rob will consider his party a success if he can get three phone numbers, arrange at least one future date, and avoid police interference.** All you have to do is plop a comma between each item and add *and* before the last item.

5 **Rob didn't meet his goals because the police arrived at 10:00, 11:00, and 11:30 p.m.; no one gave out any phone numbers; and everyone thought his name was Bob.** I hope you remembered to use a semicolon to distinguish one item from another. Why? The first item on the list has commas in it, so a plain comma isn't enough to separate the list items.

6 **Ladies and Gentlemen, I present the Fifth Annual Elbox Championships.** Even though *Ladies and Gentlemen* doesn't name the members of the audience, they're still being addressed, so a comma sets off the expression from the rest of the sentence.

7 **I know, Mort, that you are an undefeated Elbox competitor. Would you tell our audience about the sport?** Here you see the benefit of the direct-address comma. Without it, the reader thinks *I know Mort* is the beginning of the sentence and then lapses into confusion. *Mort* is cut away with two commas, and the reader understands that *I know that you are . . .* is the real meaning.

8 **Elboxing is about 5,000 years old, Chester. It originated in ancient Egypt.** You're talking to *Chester,* so his name needs to be set off with a comma.

9 **Really? Man, I can't believe you knew that!** Before you start yelling at me, I know that *Man* is sometimes simply an exclamation of feeling, not a true address. But *man* can be a form of address, and in this sentence, it is. Hence the comma slices it away from the rest of the sentence.

10 **Yes, Chester, the sport grew out of the natural movement of the elbow when someone tried to interfere with a diner's portion by "elbowing."** *Chester* is being addressed directly, so you need to surround the name with commas.

11 **Excuse me a moment. The reigning champion has decided to pay us a visit. Miss William, could you tell us how you feel about the upcoming match?** Here the person being addressed is *Miss William.*

12 **Certainly, Sir. I am confident that my new training routine will pay off.** The very polite *Miss William* talks to *Sir* in this sentence, so that term is set off by a comma.

13 **The best man rode in a Zamboni, for he was afraid of slipping on the ice.** The conjunction *(for)* joins two complete sentences, so a comma precedes it.

14 **No comma.** Read the words preceding the conjunction *(and)*. They don't make sense by themselves, so you don't have a complete sentence and don't need a comma before the conjunction.

15 **No comma.** Read the words after the conjunction *(or)*. You have two descriptions but not a complete sentence. Therefore, you don't need a comma before *or*.

16 **The guests sipped hot chocolate, but they were still cold.** Here you have two complete thoughts, one before and one after the conjunction *(but)*. You need a comma in front of the conjunction.

17 **The ice-dancing during the reception made them sweat, and then the temperature seemed fine.** Two complete thoughts sit in front of and behind *and*, so a comma is needed.

18 **No comma.** This one is a little tricky. The conjunction *or* joins *who is in charge of the gifts* and *who is paying the orchestra*. These two questions sound like complete sentences. However, the real question here is *Do you know*. The *who* statements in this sentence are just that: statements. No complete sentence = no comma.

19 **I'd like to swipe a present, for my blender is broken.** Both ideas — before and after the conjunction *for* — are complete, so a comma must precede *for*.

20 **I don't need an icemaker, but I'll take one anyway.** The two statements surrounding *but* are complete sentences, so you have to insert a comma.

21 **No comma.** The words after the conjunction *(and)* don't tell you who *never came back*. Without that information, the statement isn't a complete sentence. No comma needed here!

22 **In desperate need of a pizza fix, Brad turned to his cellphone.** The introductory expression here merits a comma because it's fairly long. Length doesn't always determine whether you need a comma, but in general, the longer the introduction, the more likely you'll need a comma.

23 **Cindy, on the other hand, ached for sushi.** The expression inside the commas makes a comment on the rest of the sentence, contrasting it with the actions of Brad. As an interrupter, it must be separated by two commas from the rest of the sentence.

24 **Yes, pizza was an excellent idea.** *Yes* and *no,* when they show up at the beginning of a sentence, take commas if they comment on the main idea.

25 **The toppings, unfortunately, proved to be a problem.** The *unfortunately* is short and closely tied to the meaning of the sentence. However, setting the word off with two commas emphasizes the emotional, judgmental tone. I've gone with the commas, as you see, but I can accept a case for omitting them.

26 **No comma.** The introductory word *restlessly* is short and clear. No comma is necessary.

27 **Cindy wondered how Brad, given his low-fat diet, could consider pepperoni.** The expression *given his low-fat diet* interrupts the flow of the sentence and calls for two commas.

28 **Frozen with indecision, Brad decided to call the supermarket to request the cheapest brand.** Introductory expressions with verb forms always take commas.

29 **Cindy, on a tight budget, wanted to redeem her coupons.** The phrase *on a tight budget* interrupts the flow of the sentence and comments on the main idea. Hence the two commas.

30 **No comma.** Did I catch you here? This sentence doesn't have an introductory expression. *To demand fast delivery* is the subject of the sentence, not an extra comment.

31 **Lighting a match and holding it near his trembling hand, Brad realized that time was almost up.** Introductory expressions containing verbs always take commas. This introductory expression has two verbs, *lighting* and *holding*.

32 **No comma.** The verb form *(Worrying about toppings)* is the subject of the sentence, not an introduction to another idea, so no comma is needed.

33 **Well, the survivors would have a good story to tell.** Words such as *well, indeed, clearly,* and so forth take commas when they occur at the beginning of the sentence and aren't part of the main idea.

34 **With determination, Cindy speed-dialed the market and offered "a really big tip" for fast service.** I admit that this one's a judgment call. If you didn't place a comma after *determination,* I won't prosecute you for comma fraud. Neither will I scream if you inserted one, as I did.

35 **As the robbers chomped on pepperoni and argued about payment, Brad slipped away.** This introductory statement has a subject and a verb and thus is followed by a comma.

36 **No comma.** The sentence reads seamlessly because of the word *that,* which ties the beginning of the sentence to the end of the sentence so strongly that "Let's just say" doesn't qualify as an introductory statement.

37 ***Oscar's favorite* food, *which he cooks every Saturday night,* is hot dogs.** Two words tell you more about *food,* but one is a possessive *(Oscar's)* and the other is a description *(favorite).* Because the two descriptions aren't equivalent, they aren't separated by commas. Moving on: After you find out that the food is *Oscar's favorite,* you have enough identification. The information about Oscar's datefree Saturday nights is extra and thus set off by commas. By the way, descriptions beginning with *which* are usually extra.

38 **Correct.** The term *place* is quite general, so the description is an essential identifier. The two descriptions preceding *barbecue* aren't of the same type. One gives size and the other composition. You can't easily reverse them (a *brick huge barbecue* sounds funny), so don't insert a comma.

39 **Correct.** The paired descriptions *(his* and *wheat, large* and *plastic)* aren't of the same type. *His* is a possessive, and you should never set off a possessive with a comma. *Large* indicates size, and *plastic* refers to composition. The last description nails down which *tub* you're talking about, so it isn't set off by commas. In general, descriptions beginning with *that* don't take commas.

40 **One of the horses *that live in Oscar's barn* often sniffs around *Oscar's lucky* horseshoe, *which he found while playing tag.*** Which horses are you talking about? Without the *barn* information, you don't know. Identifying information doesn't take commas. The two words preceding *horseshoe* aren't equivalent. *Oscar's* is a possessive (never set off by commas), and *lucky* is a quality that we all want in our horseshoes. The last description is extra, because we already know enough to identify which horseshoe is getting sniffed. Because it's extra, a comma must separate the description from the rest of the sentence.

41 **Correct.** The three descriptions preceding *horses* aren't of the same type: One *(his)* is possessive, and another *(three)* is a number. Commas never set off possessives and numbers. The second descriptive element, *honoring the Barbeque King and Queen,* explains which race you're talking about. Without that information, the topic could be any race. As an identifier, that phrase isn't set off by a comma.

42 **Oscar, *who is an animal lover,* will never sell one of his horses *because he needs money.*** Because you know Oscar's name, the information about loving animals is extra and thus set off by commas. The *because* statement is tricky. Without a comma, *because he needs money* is essential to the meaning of the sentence. In this version, Oscar may sell a horse because he hates the animal or wants to please the prospective buyer, but never for financial reasons. With a comma before *because,* the italicized material is extra. The sentence then means that Oscar will never sell a horse, period. The reason — *he needs the money* — may mean that the horses are worth more in Oscar's stable than they would be anywhere else. The first interpretation makes more sense, so don't insert a comma.

43 ***Being sentimental,* Oscar dedicated a song to the filly *that was born on his birthday.*** The introductory expression (which is also a description) contains a verb, so it must be followed by a comma. The second description is essential because you don't know which filly without the italicized identification. Thus, you need no comma.

44 **The jockeys *who were trying to prepare for the big race* became annoyed by Oscar's song, *which he played constantly;* the jockeys *who had already raced* didn't mind Oscar's music.** In this sentence the jockeys are divided into two groups, those who are preparing and those who are done for the day. Because the *who* statements identify each group, no commas are needed. *Oscar's song,* on the other hand, is clear. Even without *which he played constantly,* you know which song the jockeys hate. The italicized material gives you a little more info, but nothing essential, so it must be set off by commas.

45 **The *deep, horrible* secret is that Oscar can't stay in tune *when he sings.*** The first two descriptions may be reversed without loss of meaning, so a comma is appropriate. The last description also gives you essential information. Without that description, you don't know whether Oscar can stay in tune when he plays the tuba, for example, but not *when he sings.* Essential = no commas.

46 **His guitar, *a Gibson,* is missing *two important* strings.** The *his* tells you which guitar is being discussed, so the fact that it's *a Gibson* is extra and should be set off by commas.

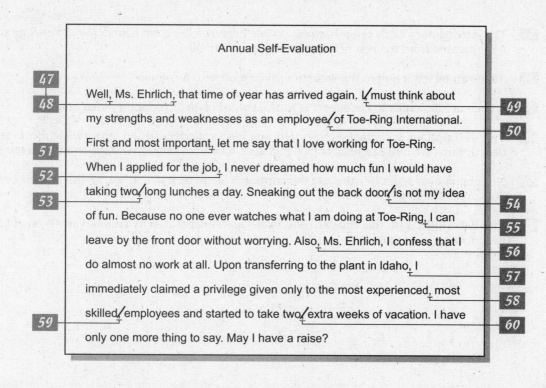

Annual Self-Evaluation

47
48 Well, Ms. Ehrlich, that time of year has arrived again. I must think about **49**
my strengths and weaknesses as an employee of Toe-Ring International. **50**
51 First and most important, let me say that I love working for Toe-Ring.
52 When I applied for the job, I never dreamed how much fun I would have
53 taking two long lunches a day. Sneaking out the back door is not my idea
of fun. Because no one ever watches what I am doing at Toe-Ring, I can **54**
55
leave by the front door without worrying. Also, Ms. Ehrlich, I confess that I **56**
do almost no work at all. Upon transferring to the plant in Idaho, I **57**
immediately claimed a privilege given only to the most experienced, most **58**
skilled employees and started to take two extra weeks of vacation. I have
59 only one more thing to say. May I have a raise? **60**

47 Commas surround *Ms. Ehrlich* because she's being directly addressed in this sentence. Also, *well* is an introductory word, so even without *Ms. Ehrlich,* you'd still need a comma after *well.*

48 See the preceding answer.

49 The pronoun *I* is part of the main idea of the sentence, not an introductory expression. No comma should separate it from the rest of the sentence.

50 The phrase *of Toe-Ring International* is an essential identifier of the type of employee being discussed. No comma should separate it from the word it describes *(employee).*

51 A comma follows the introductory expression, *First and most important.*

52 The introductory expression *when I applied for the job* should be separated from the rest of the sentence by a comma.

53 Two descriptions are attached to *lunches* — *two* and *long.* These descriptions aren't of the same type. *Two* is a number, and *long* is a measure of time. Also, numbers are never separated from other descriptions by a comma. The verdict: Delete the comma after *two.*

54 In this sentence the expression *sneaking out the back door* isn't an introductory element. It's the subject of the sentence, and it shouldn't be separated from its verb *(is)* by a comma.

55   The introductory expression *Because no one ever watches what I am doing at Toe-Ring* should be separated from the rest of the sentence by a comma.

56   *Also* is an introduction to the sentence. Slice it off with a comma.

57   A comma follows *Idaho* because it is the last word of an introductory element.

58   Two descriptions are attached to *employees: most experienced* and *most skilled.* Because these descriptions are more or less interchangeable, a comma separates them from each other.

59   No comma ever separates the last description from what it describes, so the comma before *employees* has to go.

60   Two descriptions (in this case *two* and *extra*) aren't separated by commas when one of the descriptions is a number.

Chapter 6

A Hook That Can Catch You: Apostrophes

In This Chapter

▶ Forming contractions by replacing letters and numbers with apostrophes

▶ Showing ownership with apostrophes

An apostrophe is a little hook (') that snags many writers at some point. With some practice, you can confidently place apostrophes into the proper spots in your writing.

The most common apostrophe mistake is to place one where it's not appropriate. Don't use an apostrophe in either of these circumstances:

✔ **To create a plural:** You have *one arrow* and *two arrows*, not *two arrow's*. The no-apostrophe-for-plural rule holds true for names. I am one person named *Woods*, and members of my family are the *Woodses*, not the *Woods'*.

✔ **With a possessive pronoun:** Don't use an apostrophe in a possessive pronoun (*my, your, his, hers, its, ours, theirs, whose*, and so on).

Hook into the exercises in this chapter so that no apostrophe snags you ever again.

Tightening Up Text: Contractions

Apostrophes shorten words by replacing one or more letters. The shortened word, or *contraction* (not to be confused with the thing pregnant women scream through), adds an informal, conversational tone to your writing.

The most frequently used contractions, paired with their long forms, include those in Table 6-1.

Table 6-1		Frequently Used Contractions			
Long Form	*Contraction*	*Long Form*	*Contraction*	*Long Form*	*Contraction*
Are not	Aren't	I will	I'll	We are	We're
Cannot	Can't	I would	I'd	We have	We've
Could have	Could've	It is	It's	We will	We'll
Could not	Couldn't	She has	She's	Were not	Weren't
Do not	Don't	She is	She's	Will not	Won't
He has	He's	She will	She'll	Would have	Would've

(continued)

Table 6-1 (continued)

Long Form	Contraction	Long Form	Contraction	Long Form	Contraction
He is	He's	Should have	Should've	Would not	Wouldn't
He will	He'll	Should not	Shouldn't	You are	You're
He would	He'd	They are	They're	You have	You've
I am	I'm	They have	They've	You will	You'll
I had	I'd	They will	They'll	You would	You'd

College entrance tests won't ask you to insert an apostrophe into a word, but they may want to know whether you can spot a misplaced mark or an improperly expanded contraction. An apostrophe shortens a word, and a common mistake is to re-expand a contraction into something it was never meant to be. The contraction *should've,* for example, is short for *should have,* not *should of.* The expressions *should of, could of,* and *would of* don't exist in Standard English. If you see one of these turkeys on the SAT or the ACT, you know you've found a mistake.

You also can slice numbers out of your writing with apostrophes, especially in informal circumstances. This punctuation mark enables you to graduate in 2017, marry in '23, and check the maternity coverage in your health insurance policy by early '25.

Feel like flexing your apostrophe muscles? Look at the underlined words in these sentences and change them into contractions. Place your answers in the blanks.

0. Adam said that <u>he would</u> go to the store to buy nuts. _____

A. **he'd.** This apostrophe is a real bargain. With it, you save four letters.

1. "Peanuts <u>are not</u> the best choice for an appetizer, because of allergies," commented Pam. _____

2. "<u>I am</u> sure that <u>you will</u> choose a better appetizer," she added. _____
_____

3. The store <u>will not</u> take responsibility for your purchase. _____

4. <u>Do not</u> underestimate the power of a good appetizer. _____

5. <u>You are</u> cheap if you <u>do not</u> provide at least one bowl of nuts. _____
_____

6. "Adam <u>would have</u> bought caviar, but I <u>would not</u> pass the walnut counter without buying something," commented Pam. _____ _____

7. "You <u>cannot</u> neglect the dessert course either," countered Adam. _____

8. Adam usually recommends a fancy dessert such as a maple walnut ice cream sundae, but <u>he is</u> watching his weight. _____

9. "If they created a better diet ice cream," he often says, "<u>I would</u> eat a ton of it."
_____

10. "Yes, and then <u>you would</u> weigh a ton yourself," snaps Pam. _____

11. <u>She is</u> a bit testy when faced with diet food. _____

12. Of course, Adam <u>could have</u> been a little more diplomatic when he mentioned Pam's "newly tight" slacks. _____

13. Adam is planning to serve a special dessert wine, Chateau Adam <u>1999</u>, to his guests. _____

14. He always serves that beverage at reunions of the class of <u>2006</u>. _____

15. <u>We are</u> planning to attend, but <u>we will</u> bring our own refreshments! _____ _____

Showing Who Owns What: Possessives

An apostrophe allows you to turn the awkward-sounding phrase "the pen of my aunt" into "my aunt's pen." To show possession with apostrophes, keep these rules in mind:

- **Singular owner:** Attach an apostrophe and the letter *s* (in that order) to a singular person, place, or thing to express possession ("*Henry's* tooth," the *platypus's* flipper").

- **Plural owner:** Attach an apostrophe to a regular plural (one that ends in *s*) to express possession ("the *boys'* restroom," "the *octopuses'* arms").

- **Irregular plural owner:** Add an apostrophe and the letter *s* (in that order) to an irregular plural (one that doesn't end in *s*) to express possession ("the *men's* department").

- **Joint ownership:** If two or more people own something jointly, add an apostrophe and an *s* (in that order) to the last name ("*Abe and Mary's* sofa").

- **Separate ownership:** If two or more people own things separately, everyone gets an apostrophe and an *s* ("*James's and Ashley's* pajamas").

- **Hyphenated owner:** If the word you're working with is hyphenated, just attach the apostrophe and *s* to the end ("*mother-in-law's* office"). For plurals ending in *s,* attach the apostrophe only ("*three secretary-treasurers'* accounts").

- **Time and money:** Okay, Father Time and Mr. Dollar Bill don't own anything. Nevertheless, time and money may be possessive in expressions such as *next week's test, two hours' homework, a day's pay,* and so forth. Follow the rules for singular and plural owners, as explained at the beginning of this bulleted list.

Easy stuff, right? See whether you can apply your knowledge. Turn the underlined word (or words) into the possessive form. Write your answers in the blanks provided.

Q. The style of this <u>year</u> muscle car is <u>Jill</u> favorite.

A. **year's, Jill's.** Two singular owners. *Jill* is the traditional owner — a person — but the time expression also takes an apostrophe.

16. <u>Carol</u> classic car is entered in <u>tonight</u> show. _____ _____

17. She invested <u>three months</u> work in restoring the finish. _____

18. Carol will get by with a little help from her friends; <u>Jess and Marty</u> tires, which they purchased a few years ago by combining their allowances, will be installed on her car. _____

19. The <u>boys</u> allowance, by the way, is far too generous, despite their <u>sister-in-law</u> objections. _____ _____

20. <u>Jill</u> weekly paycheck is actually smaller than the <u>brothers</u> daily income. _____ _____

21. Annoying as they are, the brothers donate <u>a day</u> pay from time to time to underfunded causes such as the <u>Children</u> Committee to Protect the Environment. _____ _____

22. Carol couldn't care less about the environment; the <u>car</u> gas mileage is ridiculously low. _____

23. She cares about the car, however. She borrowed <u>Jess and Marty</u> toothbrushes to clean the dashboard. _____

24. Now she needs her <u>helpers</u> maximum support as the final judging nears. _____

25. She knows that the <u>judge</u> decision will be final, but just in case she has volunteered <u>two thousand dollars</u> worth of free gasoline to his favorite charity. _____ _____

26. <u>Carol</u> success is unlikely because the <u>court</u> judgments can't be influenced by anything but the law. _____ _____

27. Last week, for example, the judge ruled in favor of a developer, despite the <u>mother-in-law</u> plea for a different verdict. _____

28. <u>Ten hours</u> begging did no good at all. _____

29. Tomorrow the judge will rule on the <u>car show</u> effect on the native <u>animals</u> habitat. _____ _____

30. The <u>geese</u> ecosystem is particularly sensitive to automotive exhaust. _____

Calling All Overachievers: Extra Practice with Apostrophes

Marty's to-do list, shown in Figure 6-1, needs some serious editing. Check the apostrophe situation. You need to find nine spots to insert and ten spots to delete an apostrophe.

Thing's to Do This Week

A. Call Johns doctor and arrange for a release of annual medical report.

B. Check on last springs blood pressure number's to see whether they need to be changed.

C. Ask John about his rodent problem's.

D. Find out why network's cant broadcast Tuesdays speech live, as John needs prime-time publicity.

E. Ask whether his' fondness for long speeches' is a problem.

F. Send big present to network president and remind him that you are both Yale 06.

G. Order bouquet's for secretary and National Secretaries Week card.

H. Rewrite speech on cat litter' to reflect sister-in-laws ideas'.

I. Tell opposing managers assistant that "you guys wouldnt stand a chance" in the old day's.

Figure 6-1:
Mock to-do
list, full of
apostrophe
mistakes.

Answers to Apostrophe Problems

Did you get caught on any of the apostrophe questions in this chapter? Check your answers to see how you did.

1 **aren't.** The contraction drops the letter *o* and substitutes an apostrophe.

2 **I'm, you'll.** In the first contraction, the apostrophe replaces the letter *a*. In the second, it replaces two letters, *w* and *i*.

3 **won't.** This contraction is irregular because you can't make an apostrophe-letter swap. Illogical though it may seem, *won't* is the contraction of *will not*.

4 **Don't.** Drop the space between the two words, eliminate the *o*, and insert an apostrophe to create *don't*.

5 **You're, don't.** The first contraction sounds exactly like the possessive pronoun *your*. Don't confuse the two.

6 **would've, wouldn't.** Take care with the first contraction; many people mistakenly re-expand the contraction *would've* to *would of* (instead of the correct expansion, *would have*). The second contraction, *wouldn't*, substitutes an apostrophe for the letter *o*.

7 **can't.** Did you know that *cannot* is written as one word? The contraction also is one word, with an apostrophe knocking out an *n* and an *o*.

8 **he's.** The same contraction works for *he is* (as in this sentence) and *he has*.

9 **I'd.** You're dropping the letters *woul*.

10 **you'd.** The same contraction works for *you would* (as in this sentence) and *you had*.

11 **She's.** The apostrophe replaces the letter *i*.

12 **could've.** Be careful in re-expanding this contraction. A common mistake is to write *could of*, an expression that's a total no-no.

13 **'99.** A date may be shortened, especially if you're out with Adam. Just be sure that the context of the sentence doesn't lead the reader to imagine a different century (2099, perhaps). This one is fairly clear, given that we're nowhere near 2099 or 1899.

14 **'06.** Not much chance of the reader misunderstanding which numbers are missing here (unless he or she is really old)!

15 **We're, we'll.** The apostrophes replace the letter *a* and *wi*.

16 **Carol's, tonight's.** Carol owns the car, so you just need to attach an apostrophe and an *s* to a singular form to create a singular possessive. The second answer illustrates a time/money possessive expression.

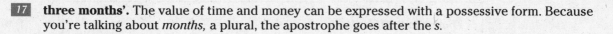

17 **three months'.** The value of time and money can be expressed with a possessive form. Because you're talking about *months,* a plural, the apostrophe goes after the *s.*

18 **Jess and Marty's.** The sentence tells you that the boys own the tires together, so only one apostrophe is needed. It's placed after the last owner's name. The possessive pronoun *her,* like all possessive pronouns, has no apostrophe.

19 **boys', sister-in-law's.** The plural possessive just tacks an apostrophe onto the *s* in regular, end-in-*s* plurals. Hyphenated forms are easy too; just attach the apostrophe and an *s* to the end.

20 **Jill's, brothers'.** The first form is singular, so you add an apostrophe and an *s.* The second form is a regular plural, so you just add the apostrophe.

21 **a day's, Children's.** The first form falls into the time/money category, and because *day* is singular, you add an apostrophe and an *s.* The second is an irregular plural (not ending in *s*), so you tack on an apostrophe and an *s.*

22 **car's.** A singular possessive form calls for an apostrophe and an *s.*

23 **Jess's and Marty's.** Okay, the brothers are close, but they draw the line at shared tooth-brushes. Each owns a separate brush, so each name needs an apostrophe.

TIP

If a word ends in *s* (*Jess,* for example), adding an apostrophe and another *s* creates a spit factor: People tend to spray saliva all over when saying the word. To avoid this unsanitary problem, some writers add just the apostrophe (*Jess'*), even though technically they've neglected the extra *s.* Grammarians generally allow this practice, perhaps because they too dislike being spit on. In all but the strictest situations, either form is acceptable.

24 **helpers'.** To create a plural possessive of a word ending in *s,* just attach an apostrophe.

25 **judge's, two thousand dollars'.** The first answer is a simple, singular possessive, so an apostrophe and an *s* do the trick. The second is a time/money possessive, and *two thousand dollars* is plural, so just an apostrophe is needed.

26 **Carol's, court's.** These two words are singular, so only an apostrophe and the letter *s* are needed to make each possessive.

27 **mother-in-law's.** The apostrophe and the letter *s* follow the last word of the hyphenated term.

28 **Ten hours'.** The apostrophe creates an expression meaning *ten hours of begging.* Because *hours* is plural, only an apostrophe is added.

29 **car show's, animals'.** The first is a singular possessive, and the second is plural.

30 **geese's.** The word *geese* is irregular. In an irregular plural, an apostrophe and the letter *s* are added.

Thing/s to Do This Week — 31

32 — A. Call John's doctor and arrange for a release of annual medical report.

33 — B. Check on last spring's blood pressure number/s to see whether they — 34

need to be changed.

C. Ask John about his rodent problem/s. — 35

36 — D. Find out why network/s can't broadcast Tuesday's speech live, as John — 38

37 — needs prime-time publicity.

39 — E. Ask whether his/ fondness for long speeches/ is a problem. — 40

F. Send big present to network president and remind him that you are

both Yale '06.

41 — G. Order bouquet/s for secretary and National Secretaries' Week card. — 43

42 —

44 — H. Rewrite speech on cat litter/ to reflect sister-in-law's ideas/. — 45
— 46

47 — I. Tell opposing manager's assistant that "you guys wouldn't stand a — 48

49 — chance" in the old day/s.

---

31 Plural words that aren't possessive need no apostrophes, so remove the apostrophe from *Things*.

32 The doctor belongs to John (in a manner of speaking), so the apostrophe is needed to show possession.

33 This time expression *(spring's)* needs an apostrophe before the *s*.

34 The plural *numbers* isn't possessive, so it shouldn't have an apostrophe.

35 A simple plural (not possessive, not a numeral, and so on) takes no apostrophe, so *problems* shouldn't have an apostrophe.

36 The *networks* aren't possessing anything here, so no apostrophe is needed in this plural.

37 In this contraction *(can't)*, the apostrophe replaces the letters *n* and *o*.

38 Time expressions sometimes use apostrophes, as in *Tuesday's*.

39 Possessive pronouns don't have apostrophes, so *his* is the word you want.

40 A plural *(speeches)* takes no apostrophe.

41 Missing numerals (in this case, *20*) are replaced by an apostrophe.

42 A simple plural *(bouquets)* doesn't take an apostrophe.

43 This plural possessive form — the *secretaries* own the week, symbolically — adds an apostrophe after the *s*.

44 In this sentence, *litter* isn't possessive and doesn't need an apostrophe.

45 A hyphenated singular form takes an apostrophe and an *s* to become possessive, so *sister-in-law's* is the correct answer.

46 The plural noun *ideas* isn't possessive, so it shouldn't carry an apostrophe.

47 A singular possessive is created by adding an apostrophe and an *s*.

48 In this contraction, the missing letter *o* is replaced by an apostrophe.

49 *Days* is just plural, not possessive, so it doesn't take an apostrophe.

Chapter 7

"Let Me Speak!" Quotation Marks

In This Chapter

▶ Differentiating between quoted and paraphrased material

▶ Punctuating sentences containing quoted material

▶ Punctuating titles of literary and media works

Quotation marks can be puzzling because they're subject to many rules, most of which come from custom rather than logic. But if you're willing to put in a little effort, you can crack the code and employ this punctuation mark correctly.

Quotation marks surround words drawn from another person's speech or writing, and, in fiction, they indicate when a character is speaking. However, they don't belong in a sentence that summarizes instead of repeating the actual words someone wrote or said. Quotation marks also enclose the titles of certain types of literary or other artworks. Sometimes quotation marks indicate slang or tell the reader that the writer doesn't agree with the words inside the quotation marks. In this chapter you put quotation marks to work in all these situations. Lucky you!

Quoting and Paraphrasing: What's the Difference?

I have something to tell you: I love Jane Austen's novels and read all six once a year. If you want to convey that fact about me, you have two choices:

"I love Jane Austen's novels and read all six once a year," wrote Woods.

Woods explained that she enjoys Jane Austen's writing and works her way through Austen's six novels annually.

The first example is a *direct quotation.* My exact words are inside the quotation marks. The second example is a *paraphrase.* The sense of what I wrote is there, but the words are slightly different. You don't have to know these terms. You do have to know that quotations, but not paraphrases, belong inside quotation marks.

Even when you're paraphrasing, you still have to cite sources for information and ideas that aren't the product of your own brain. Citation format has more rules than the U.S. tax code. For everything you ever wanted to know about citations, check out *Webster's New World Punctuation: Simplified and Applied* (Wiley) or an online source.

Now you get to try your hand at distinguishing between quotations and paraphrases. Below is a short paragraph from an imaginary news article. Following the story are sentences about something in the paragraph. Based on the paragraph and what you can infer from it, write "Quotation" if any part of the sentence is quoted. Or, write "Paraphrase" if no quotation appears. To make your task harder, I haven't inserted quotation marks anywhere in the questions. In real writing, the quotation marks would be present.

A stunningly positive annual report for Jump-Thru Hoops International, Inc., is due tomorrow. According to inside sources who wish to remain anonymous, the company will announce that profits have nearly doubled in the last year. The increase is credited to the company's newest product, the Talking Hoop. Buyers moving the hoop around their hips hear a drill sergeant screaming commands as they exercise. Company officials have high hopes for their next product, Ring-Tone Hoops.

0. The Talking Hoop has been so successful that the company has made twice as much money this year as it did last year. _____

A. **Paraphrase.** The information is from the paragraph, but the wording is different.

1. Jump-Thru Hoops International plans to market a hoop with ring tones. _____

2. The company is doing well, and profits have nearly doubled in the last year. _____

3. Go faster, Private! is what you hear when you're playing with this hoop. _____

4. The annual report should give shareholders cause for celebration. _____

5. Our best-selling product is the Talking Hoop, said Max Hippo, the president. _____

6. The Talking Hoop is used for exercise. _____

Giving Voice to Direct Quotations

The basic rule governing quotation marks is simple: Place quotation marks around words drawn directly from someone else's speech or writing, or, if you're writing the Great American Novel, place quotation marks around dialogue. The tricky part is the interaction between quotation marks and other punctuation, such as commas, periods, and the like. You also have to take into account the fact that the rules vary somewhat in different situations. The comma goes one place in a psychology paper, for example, and another place in an English essay. Sigh. Below are the most commonly accepted rules, useful in nearly all situations:

✔ **If the quotation has a speaker tag (*he murmured, she screamed,* and so forth), the speaker tag needs to be separated from the quotation by a comma.**

- If the speaker tag is *before* the quotation, the comma comes *before* the opening quotation mark: *Sharon sighed, "I hate hay fever season."*

- If the speaker tag is *after* the quotation, the comma goes *inside* the closing quotation mark: *"What a large snout you have," whispered Joe lovingly.*

- If the speaker tag appears *in the middle* of a quotation, a comma is placed before the first closing quotation mark and immediately after the tag: *"Here's the handkerchief," said Joe, "that I borrowed last week."*

✔ **If the quotation ends the sentence, the period goes *inside* the closing quotation mark.** *Joe added, "I would like to kiss your giant ear."*

✔ **If the *quotation* is a question or an exclamation, the question mark or the exclamation point goes *inside* the closing quotation mark.** *"Why did you slap me?" asked Joe. "I was complimenting you!"*

Question marks and exclamation points serve as sentence-ending punctuation, so you don't need to add a period after the quotation marks.

✔ **If the quotation is *neither* question nor exclamation, but the *sentence* in which the quotation appears is, the question mark or exclamation point goes *outside* the closing quotation mark.** *I can't believe that Joe said he's "a world-class lover"! Do you think Sharon will ever get over his "sweet nothings"?*

If the quotation is tucked into the sentence without a speaker tag, as in the previous two sample sentences, no comma separates the quotation from the rest of the sentence. Nor does the quotation begin with a capital letter. Quotations with speaker tags, on the other hand, always begin with a capital letter, regardless of where the speaker tag falls. In an interrupted quotation (speaker tag in the middle), the first word of the first half of the quotation is capitalized, but the first word of the second half is not, unless it's a proper name.

Enough with the explanations. Put the pedal to the metal in each of the following sentences. Your job is to identify the direct quotation and fill in the proper punctuation, in the proper order, in the proper places. To help you, I add extra information in parentheses at the end of some sentences and underline the quoted words. To make your life harder, I omit endmarks (periods, question marks, and exclamation points).

0. The annual company softball game is tomorrow declared Becky

A. **"The annual company softball game is tomorrow," declared Becky.** Don't count yourself right unless you placed the comma *inside* the closing quotation mark.

7. I plan to pitch added Becky, who once tried out for the Olympics

8. Andy interrupted As usual, I will play third base

9. No one knew how to answer Andy, who in the past has been called overly sensitive

10. Gus said No one wants Andy at third base

11. <u>Who wants to win</u> asked the boss in a commanding, take-no-prisoners tone

12. Did she mean it when she said that we were <u>not hard-boiled enough to play decently</u>

13. Sarah screamed <u>You can't bench Andy</u> (The statement Sarah is making is an exclamation.)

14. The opposing team, everyone knows, is <u>first in the league and last in our company's heart</u> (The whole statement about the opposing team is an exclamation.)

15. <u>The odds favor our opponents</u> sighed Becky <u>but I will not give up</u>

16. The league states that <u>all decisions regarding player placement are subject to the umpire's approval</u>

17. The umpire has been known to label us <u>out-of-shape players who think they belong in the Olympics</u> (The label is a direct quotation.)

18. <u>Do you think there will be a rain delay</u> inquired Harry, the team's trainer

19. He asked <u>Has anyone checked Sue's shoes to make sure that she hasn't sharpened her spikes again</u>

20. Surely the umpire doesn't think that Sue would violate the rule that fair play is <u>essential</u> (Imagine that the writer of this sentence is exclaiming.)

21. <u>Sue has been known to cork her bat</u> commented Harry

22. <u>The corking</u> muttered Sue <u>has never been proved</u>

Punctuating Titles

Punctuating titles is easy, especially if you're a sports fan. Imagine a basketball player, one who tops seven feet. Next to him place a jockey; most jockeys hover around five feet. Got the picture? Good. When you're deciding how to punctuate a title, figure out whether you're dealing with Yao Ming (NBA player) or Mike Smith (Derby rider), using these rules:

✔ **Titles of full-length works are italicized or underlined.** The basketball player represents full-length works — novels, magazines, television series, plays, epic poems, films, and the like. The titles of those works can be italicized (on a computer) or underlined (for handwritten works).

✔ **Titles of shorter works are placed in quotation marks.** The jockey, on the other hand, represents smaller works or parts of a whole — a poem, a short story, a single episode of a television show, a song, an article — you get the idea. The titles of these little guys aren't italicized or underlined; they're placed in quotation marks.

These rules apply to titles that are tucked into sentences. Centered titles, all alone at the top of a page, don't get any special treatment: no italics, no underlining, and no quotation marks.

When a title in quotation marks is part of a sentence, it sometimes tangles with other punctuation marks. The rules in American English (British English is different) call for any commas or periods *after* the title to be placed *inside* the quotation marks. So if the title is the last thing in the sentence, the period of the sentence comes before the closing quotation mark. Question marks and exclamation points, on the other hand, don't go inside the quotation marks unless they're actually part of the title.

If a title that ends with a question mark is the last thing in a sentence, the question mark ends the sentence. Don't place both a period and a question mark at the end of the same sentence.

All set for a practice lap around the track? Check out the titles in this series of sentences. Place quotation marks around the title if necessary, adding endmarks where needed; otherwise, underline the title. Here and there you find parentheses at the end of a sentence, in which I add some information to help you.

Q. Have you read Sarah's latest poem, Sonnet for the Tax Assessor (The sentence is a question, but the title isn't.)

A. **Have you read Sarah's latest poem, "Sonnet for the Tax Assessor"?** The title of a poem takes quotation marks. Question marks never go inside the quotation marks unless the title itself is a question.

23. Sarah's poem will be published in a collection entitled Tax Day Blues

24. Mary's fifth best-seller, Publish Your Poetry Now, inspired Sarah.

25. Some of us wish that Sarah had read the recent newspaper article, Forget About Writing Poetry

26. Julie, an accomplished violinist, has turned Sarah's poem into a song, although she changed the name to Sonata Taxiana

27. She's including it on her next CD, Songs of April

28. I may listen to it if I can bring myself to turn off my favorite television show, Big Brother and Sister

29. During a recent episode titled Sister Knows Everything, the main character broke into her brother's blog.

30. In the blog was a draft of a play, Who Will Be My First Love?

Calling All Overachievers: Extra Practice with Quotation Marks

Tommy Brainfree's classic composition is reproduced in Figure 7-1. Identify ten spots where a set of quotation marks needs to be inserted. Place the quotation marks correctly in relation to other punctuation in the sentence. Also, underline titles where appropriate.

What I Did during Summer Vacation

by Tommy Brainfree

This summer I went to Camp Waterbug, which was the setting for a famous poem by William Long titled Winnebago My Winnebago. At Camp Waterbug I learned to paddle a canoe without tipping it over more than twice a trip. My counselor even wrote an article about me in the camp newsletter, Waterbug Bites. The article was called How to Tip a Canoe. The counselor said, Brainfree is well named. I was not upset because I believed him (eventually) when he explained that the comment was an editing error.

Are you sure? I asked him when I first read it.

You know, he responded quickly, that I have a lot of respect for you. I nodded in agreement, but that night I placed a bunch of frogs under his sheets, just in case he thought about writing How to Fool a Camper. One of the frogs had a little label on his leg that read JUST KIDDING TOO.

At the last campfire gathering I sang a song from the musical Fiddler on the Roof. The song was called If I Were a Rich Man. I changed the first line to If I were a counselor. I won't quote the rest of the song because I'm still serving the detention my counselor gave me, even though I'm back home now.

Figure 7-1:
Sample school report sans quotation marks.

Answers to Quotation Problems

It's time to see if you've mastered the use of quotation marks. I'm proud of you for tackling the tough exercises in this chapter. You can quote me on that!

1 **Paraphrase.** Nothing in the sentence reflects the wording in the paragraph.

2 **Quotation.** The phrase "have nearly doubled in the past year" comes directly from the text and should be enclosed in quotation marks.

3 **Quotation.** Although the paragraph doesn't tell you what the drill sergeant says, you can infer that "Go faster, Private!" is a quotation, which should be surrounded by quotation marks.

4 **Paraphrase.** Comb through the paragraph, and you see that these words don't appear.

5 **Quotation.** The first part of the sentence, as far as the word *said,* tells you Max Hippo's exact words.

6 **Paraphrase.** The words in this sentence aren't lifted directly from the paragraph, so they're paraphrased.

7 **"I plan to pitch," added Becky, who once tried out for the Olympics.** The directly quoted words, *I plan to pitch,* are enclosed in quotation marks. The comma that sets off the speaker tag *added Becky* goes inside the closing quotation mark. A period ends the sentence.

8 **Andy interrupted, "As usual, I will play third base."** The speaker tag comes first in this sentence, so the comma is placed before the opening quotation mark. The period that ends the sentence goes inside the closing quotation mark.

9 **No one knew how to answer Andy, who in the past has been called "overly sensitive."** The quotation is short, but it still deserves quotation marks. The period at the end of the sentence is placed inside the closing quotation mark. Notice that this quotation doesn't have a speaker tag, so it isn't preceded by a comma and it doesn't start with a capital letter.

10 **Gus said, "No one wants Andy at third base."** The speaker tag is followed by a comma, and a period ends the sentence.

11 **"Who wants to win?" asked the boss in a commanding, take-no-prisoners tone.** Because the quoted words are a question, the question mark goes inside the closing quotation mark.

12 **Did she mean it when she said that we were "not hard-boiled enough to play decently"?** The quoted words aren't a question, but the entire sentence is. The question mark belongs outside the closing quotation mark.

If both the sentence and the quotation are questions, the question mark belongs inside the closing quotation mark.

13 **Sarah screamed, "You can't bench Andy!"** A comma separates the speaker tag *(Sarah screamed)* from the quotation and precedes the opening quotation mark. Because the quoted words are an exclamation, the exclamation point belongs inside the closing quotation mark.

14 **The opposing team, everyone knows, is "first in the league and last in our company's heart"!** The hint in parentheses gives rationale for the answer. Because the whole statement is an exclamation, the exclamation point belongs outside the closing quotation mark.

15 **"The odds favor our opponents," sighed Becky, "but I will not give up."** Here's an interrupted quotation, with the speaker tag in the middle. This sort of interruption is perfectly proper. The quoted material makes up one sentence, so the second half begins with a lowercase letter.

16 **The league states that "all decisions regarding player placement are subject to the umpire's approval."** This little quotation is tucked into the sentence without a speaker tag, so it takes no comma or capital letter. The period at the end of the sentence goes inside the closing quotation mark.

17 **The umpire has been known to label us "out-of-shape players who think they belong in the Olympics."** Ah yes, the joy of amateur sport! This quotation is plopped into the sentence without a speaker tag, so the first word takes no capital and isn't preceded by a comma. It ends with a period, which is slipped inside the closing quotation mark.

18 **"Do you think there will be a rain delay?" inquired Harry, the team's trainer.** Harry's words are a question, so the question mark goes inside the closing quotation mark.

19 **He asked, "Has anyone checked Sue's shoes to make sure that she hasn't sharpened her spikes again?"** This speaker tag *He asked* begins the sentence. It's set off by a comma, which precedes the opening quotation mark. The quoted words form a question, so the question mark belongs inside the quotation marks.

20 **Surely the umpire doesn't think that Sue would violate the rule that fair play is "essential"!** Okay, the parentheses tell you that the writer is exclaiming. The whole sentence is an exclamation, and the quoted word is fairly mild, so the exclamation point belongs to the sentence, not to the quotation. Place it outside the closing quotation mark. Because no speaker tag is present, the quotation begins with a lowercase letter and isn't set off by a comma.

21 **"Sue has been known to cork her bat," commented Harry.** A straightforward statement with a speaker tag *commented Harry* calls for a comma inside the closing quotation mark. The quotation is a complete sentence. In quoted material, the period that normally ends the sentence is replaced by a comma, because the sentence continues on — in this case, with *commented Harry*. Periods don't belong in the middle of a sentence unless they're part of an abbreviation.

22 **"The corking," muttered Sue, "has never been proved."** A speaker tag breaks into this quotation and is set off by commas. The one after *corking* goes inside, because when you're ending a quotation or part of a quotation, the comma or period always goes inside. Ditto at the end of the sentence; the period needs to be inserted inside the closing quotation mark.

23 **<u>Tax Day Blues</u>.** If it's a collection, it's a full-length work. Full-length works are not placed in quotation marks but are underlined if you are writing by hand or italicized if you are using a computer.

24 **<u>Publish Your Poetry Now</u>.** The book title is underlined.

25 **"Forget About Writing Poetry."** The title of an article is enclosed by quotation marks. The period following a quotation or a title in quotation marks goes inside the closing quotation mark.

26   **"Sonata Taxiana."** The period always goes inside a closing quotation mark, at least in America. In the United Kingdom, the period is generally outside, playing cricket. Just kidding about the cricket. You're using quotation marks here because a "Sonata Taxiana" isn't a full-length work.

27   <u>**Songs of April**</u>. A CD is a full-length work, so the title is underlined or, better yet, italicized.

28   <u>**Big Brother and Sister**</u>. The title of the whole series is underlined. (You can italicize it if you're typing.) The title of an individual episode goes in quotation marks.

29   **"Sister Knows Everything,"** The episode title belongs in quotation marks. The series title gets italicized (or underlined, if you're writing with a pen). The comma around this introductory expression sits inside the quotation marks.

30   <u>**Who Will Be My First Love?**</u> A question mark is part of the title, which is underlined because a play is a full-length work.

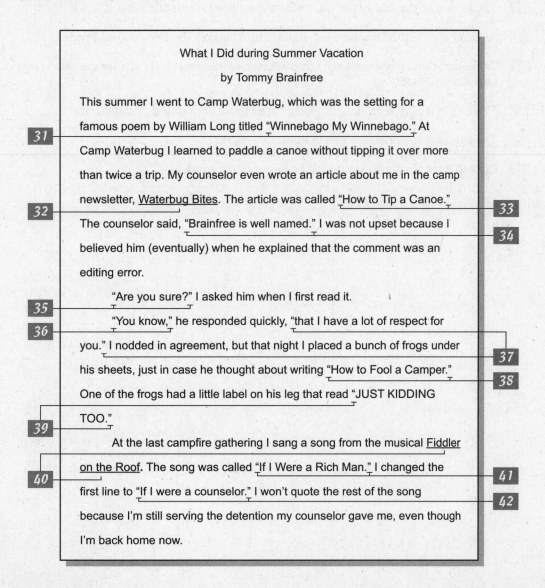

What I Did during Summer Vacation

by Tommy Brainfree

This summer I went to Camp Waterbug, which was the setting for a famous poem by William Long titled "Winnebago My Winnebago." At [31] Camp Waterbug I learned to paddle a canoe without tipping it over more than twice a trip. My counselor even wrote an article about me in the camp newsletter, <u>Waterbug Bites</u>. The article was called "How to Tip a Canoe." [33] [32] The counselor said, "Brainfree is well named." I was not upset because I [34] believed him (eventually) when he explained that the comment was an editing error.

"Are you sure?" I asked him when I first read it. [35]

"You know," he responded quickly, "that I have a lot of respect for [36] you." I nodded in agreement, but that night I placed a bunch of frogs under [37] his sheets, just in case he thought about writing "How to Fool a Camper." [38] One of the frogs had a little label on his leg that read "JUST KIDDING [39] TOO."

At the last campfire gathering I sang a song from the musical <u>Fiddler on the Roof</u>. The song was called "If I Were a Rich Man." I changed the [41] [40] first line to "If I were a counselor." I won't quote the rest of the song [42] because I'm still serving the detention my counselor gave me, even though I'm back home now.

31 Poem titles belong in quotation marks. The title of a collection of poems, on the other hand, needs to be underlined.

32 The newsletter title should be underlined.

33 An article title belongs in quotation marks. The period at the end of the sentence belongs inside the closing quotation mark.

34 Directly quoted speech belongs in quotation marks, with the period inside the closing mark.

35 The quoted words are a question, so the question mark goes inside the quotation marks.

36 The interrupted quotation with an inserted speaker tag needs two sets of marks. The comma at the end of the first part of the quotation goes inside the closing mark.

37 The period at the end of the quoted sentence goes inside the closing mark.

38 Another article title, another set of quotation marks. The period goes inside.

39 This quotation reproduces the exact written words and thus calls for quotation marks. The period goes inside.

40 The title of a play, a full-length work, needs to be underlined or italicized.

41 The title of a song needs to be in quotation marks.

42 Quoted lines from a song need to be in quotation marks.

Chapter 8

Hitting the Big Time: Capital Letters

* *

In This Chapter

▶ Choosing capitals for job titles and names

▶ Deciding which school and business terms need capitalization

▶ Finding out when to capitalize letters in titles of works

▶ Working with new media: Capitalizing in texts, e-mail, and slide presentations

▶ Determining which abbreviations get capitals

* *

Most people know the basics of capitalization: Capital letters are needed for proper names, the personal pronoun *I*, and the first letter of a sentence. Trouble may arrive with the finer points of capital letters — in quotations (which I cover in Chapter 7), titles (of people and of publications), abbreviations, presentation slides and e-mail, and school or business terms. Never fear. In this chapter you get to practice all those topics.

The major style setters in the land of grammar (yes, grammar has style, and no, grammarians aren't immune to trends) sometimes disagree about what should be capitalized and what shouldn't. In this workbook I follow the most common capitalization styles. If you're writing for a specific publication or teacher, you may want to check which 20-pound book of rules (also known as a style manual) you should follow. The most common are those manuals published by the Modern Language Association, (*MLA,* for academic writing in the humanities), the American Psychological Association (*APA,* for science and social science writing), and the University of Chicago (*Chicago or CMS,* for general interest and academic publishing).

Paying Respect to People's Names and Titles

Your name is always in caps, but titles are a different story. The general rules are as follows:

✔ **A title preceding and attached to a name is capitalized** *(Mr. Smith, Professor Wiley).* Small, unimportant words in titles (*a, the, of,* and the like) are never capitalized (Head of School Barker).

✔ **Titles written after or without a name are generally not capitalized** *(George Wiley, professor of psychology).*

✔ **Titles of national or international importance may be capitalized even when used alone** *(President, Vice President, Secretary-General).* Some style manuals opt for lowercase regardless of rank.

✔ **Family relationships are capitalized when they are used in place of a name** ("That building was designed by Mom," but "My mother is an architect").

Now that you get the idea, test yourself. In the following sentences add capital letters where needed. Cross out incorrect capitals and substitute the lowercase form. Keep your eyes open; not every sentence has an error!

0. The reverend archie smith, Chief Executive of the local council, has invited senator Bickford to next month's fundraiser.

A. **Reverend, Archie, Smith, chief, executive, Senator.** Personal names are always capitalized, so *Archie Smith* needs capitals. *Reverend* and *Senator* precede the names (*Archie Smith* and *Bickford*) and act as part of the person's name, not just as a description of their jobs. Thus they should be capitalized. The title *chief executive* follows the name and isn't capitalized.

1. Yesterday mayor Victoria Johnson ordered all public servants in her town to conserve sticky tape.

2. Herman harris, chief city engineer, has promised to hold the line on tape spending.

3. However, the Municipal Dogcatcher, Agnes e. Bark, insists on taping reward signs to every tree.

4. My Sister says that the signs placed by dogcatcher Bark seldom fall far from the tree.

5. Did you ask mom whether ms. Bark's paper detaches?

6. Few Dogcatchers care as much as agnes about rounding up lost dogs.

7. The recent dog-show champion, BooBoo, bit uncle Lou last week.

8. My Brother thinks that he wouldn't have been hurt had Agnes found BooBoo first.

9. The Mayor's Cousin, who owns a thumbtack company, has an interest in substituting tacks for tape.

10. Until the issue is resolved, Agnes, herself the chief executive of Sticking, Inc., will continue to tape.

11. Sticking, Inc., has appointed a new Vice President to oversee a merger with Thumbtack, Inc.

12. Vice president Finger of Thumbtack, Inc., is tired of jokes about his name.

13. When he was appointed Chief Financial Officer, George Finger asked grandma Finger for advice.

14. George's aunt, Alicia Bucks, had little sympathy for Finger, who is her favorite Nephew.

15. With a name like Bucks, she explained, everyone thinks you should work as a Bank President.

16. Finger next asked reverend Holy how he dealt with his unusual name.

17. However, Holy, who has been a Bishop for twelve years, shrugged off the question.

18. "My Brother is The Manager of the New Jersey Devils hockey team," Bishop Holy remarked.

19. Reginald Holy joined the Devils twenty years ago as a Player Development Director.

20. Holy hopes to be appointed President of the National Hockey League someday.

Working with Business and School Terms

Whether you bring home a paycheck or a report card, you should take care to capitalize properly. Surprisingly, the worlds of business and education have a lot in common:

✔ **The place where it all happens:** Capitalize the name of the company or school (*Superlative Widgets International* or *University of Rock and Roll*). General words that may refer to a number of businesses or academic institutions (*university, conglomerate,* and so forth) are written in lowercase.

✔ **Working units:** Business activities (*management* or *advertising*) and general academic tasks, years, and subjects (*research, sophomore, history*) aren't capitalized. The name of a specific department (*Research and Development Division, Department of Cultural Anthropology*) may be capitalized. Project names (*the Zero Task Force*) and course names (*History of Belly-Button Rings*) are capitalized.

Course titles and the names of businesses or institutions are capitalized according to the "headline style" rules of titles, which I describe in "Capitalizing Titles of Literary and Media Works" later in this chapter. Briefly, capitalize the first word, all nouns and verbs, and any important words in the title. Short, relational words such as *of, for, by,* and *from* aren't capitalized, nor are articles such as *a, an,* and *the.*

✔ **Products:** General terms for items produced or sold (*widgets, guarantees, consultation fee*) aren't capitalized. Neither are academic degrees or awards (*master's* or *fellowship*). If a specific brand is named, however, roll out the big letters (*Columbus Award for Round-Trip Travel* or *Universal Widget Lever*).

Some companies change the usual capitalization customs (*eBay* and *iPad,* for example). As a grammarian, I'm not happy, but people (and companies) have the right to ruin — sorry — *select* their own names.

Now that you have the basics, try these questions. If a word needs a capital letter, cross out the offending letter and insert the capital. If a word has an unnecessary capital letter, cross out the offender and insert a lowercase letter. You may also find a correct sentence. If you do, leave it alone!

Q. The eldest daughter of Matt Brady, founder of belly buttons international, is a senior at the university of southeast hogwash, where she is majoring in navel repair.

A. **Belly Buttons International, University of Southeast Hogwash.** The name of the company is capitalized, as is the name of the school. The year of study (*senior*) isn't capitalized, nor is the major.

21. After extensive research, the united nose ring company has determined that freshmen prefer silver rings, except Psychology majors.

22. The spokesperson for the Company commented that "gold rocks the world" of future Psychologists.

23. "I wore a gold ring to the curriculum committee during the Spring Semester," explained Fred Stileless, who is the student representative to that committee and to the board of trustees.

24. "My gold ring was a turn off for juniors," explained Fred, who hasn't had a date since he was a senior at Smith And Youngtown United high school.

25. The Spokesperson surveyed competing Products, including a silver-gold combination manufactured by in style or else, inc., a division of klepto industrials, where every worker has a College Degree.

26. Klepto's Top-Seller Task Force sells rings to Students in fifty Countries on six Continents.

27. The Task Force claims that silver attracts attention and costs less, though the department of product development can't figure out the difference in the "attractive power" of various metals.

28. Stileless, who originally majored in chemistry, said that "introduction to fashion, a course I took in freshman year, opened my eyes to beauty and made me question my commitment to Science."

29. Stileless expects to receive a bachelor's degree with a concentration in jewelry marketing.

30. Import-export Companies plan to switch their focus from gold to silver.

Capitalizing Titles of Literary and Media Works

If you write an ode to homework or a scientific study on the biological effects of too many final exams, how do you capitalize the title? The answer depends on the style you're following:

✔ **Literary, creative, and general-interest works are capitalized in "headline style."** Headline style specifies capital letters for the first and last word of the title and subtitle, in addition to all nouns, verbs, and descriptive words, and any other words that require emphasis. Articles *(a, an, the)* and prepositions *(among, by, for,* and the like) are usually in lowercase. *For Dummies* chapter titles employ headline style.

✔ **The titles of scientific works employ "sentence style,"** which calls for capital letters only for the first word of the title and subtitle and for proper nouns. Everything else is lowercased. (The title of a scientific paper in sentence style: "Cloning fruit flies: Hazards of fly bites.")

Ready to get to work? The following titles are written without any capital letters at all. Cross out the offending letters and insert capitals above them where needed. The style you should follow (headline or sentence) is specified in parentheses at the end of each title. By the way, titles of short works are enclosed in quotation marks. Titles of full-length works are italicized. (See Chapter 7 for more information on the punctuation of titles.)

Q. "the wonders of homework completed: an ode" *(headline)*

A. **"The Wonders of Homework Completed: An Ode"** The first word of the title and subtitle *(The, An)* are always capitalized. So are the nouns *(Wonders, Homework)* and descriptive words *(Completed)*. The preposition *(of)* is left in lowercase.

31. moby duck: a tale of obsessive bird watching *(headline)*

32. "an analysis of the duckensis mobyous: the consequences of habitat shrinkage on population" *(sentence)*

33. "call me izzy smell: my life as a duck hunter" *(headline)*

34. the duck and i: essays on the relationship between human beings and feathered species *(sentence)*

35. duck and cover: a cookbook *(headline)*

36. "the duck stops here: political wisdom from the environmental movement" *(sentence)*

37. duck up: how the duck triumphed over the hunter *(headline)*

38. "moby platypus doesn't live here anymore" *(headline)*

39. "population estimates of the platypus: an inexact science" *(sentence)*

40. for the love of a duck: a sentimental memoir *(headline)*

Managing Capital Letters in Abbreviations

The world of abbreviations is prime real estate for turf wars. Some publications and institutions proudly announce that "*we* don't capitalize a.m." whereas others declare exactly the opposite, choosing "AM" instead. (Both are correct, but don't mix the forms. Notice that the capitalized version does not use periods.) You're wise to ask in advance for a list of the publication's or Authority Figure's preferences. These are the general, one-size-fits-most guidelines for abbreviations:

- ✔ **Acronyms** — forms created by the first letter of each word (*NATO, UNICEF,* and so forth) — take capitals but not periods.

- ✔ **Initials and titles** are capitalized and take periods (*George W. Bush* and *Msgr. Sullivan,* for example). The three most common titles — Mr., Mrs., and Ms.— are always capitalized and usually written with periods, though trendy writers skip the period.

- ✔ **Latin abbreviations** such as *e.g.* (for example) and *ibid.* (in the same place) aren't usually capitalized but do end with a period.

- ✔ **State abbreviations** are the two-letter, no-period, capitalized forms created by the post office (*IN* and *AL*).

- ✔ **Abbreviations in texts or tweets to friends** may be informal, written without capitals or periods. If you've *gtg* (got to go), you probably don't have time for capitals. However, avoid these abbreviations when writing to someone you're trying to impress — a boss, client, or teacher.

> ✔ **When an abbreviation comes at the end of a sentence,** the period for the abbreviation does double duty as an endmark.

Okay, try your hand at abbreviating. Check out the full word, which I place in lowercase letters, even when capital letters are called for. See whether you can insert the proper abbreviation or acronym for the following words, taking care to capitalize where necessary and filling in the blanks with your answers.

Q. figure _____

A. **fig.**

41. illustration _____

42. before common era _____

43. mister Burns _____

44. united states president _____

45. national hockey league _____

46. reverend Smith _____

47. new york _____

48. Adams boulevard _____

49. irregular _____

50. incorporated _____

Calling All Overachievers: Extra Practice with Capital Letters

Use the information in this chapter to help you find ten capitalization mistakes in Figure 8-1, which is an excerpt from possibly the worst book report ever written.

Moby, the Life Of a Duck: A Book Report

If you are ever given a book about Ducks, take my advice and burn it. When i had to read *Moby Duck*, the Teacher promised me that it was good. She said that "Excitement was on every page." I don't think so! A duckling with special powers is raised by his Grandpa. Moby actually goes to school and earns a Doctorate in bird Science! After a really boring account of Moby's Freshman year, the book turns to his career as a Flight Instructor. I was very happy to see him fly away at the end of the book.

Figure 8-1:
Sample book report from a less-than-thrilled reader.

Answers to Capitalization Problems

Now that you've burned a hole through your thinking cap while answering questions about capitalization, check out the answers to see how you did.

1. **Mayor.** Titles that come before a name and proper names take capitals; common nouns, such as *servants* and *tape,* don't.

2. **Harris.** Names take capitals, but titles written after the name usually don't.

3. **municipal dogcatcher, E.** The title in this sentence isn't attached to the name; in fact, it's separated from the name by a comma. It should be in lowercase. Initials take capitals and periods.

4. **sister, Dogcatcher.** Family relationships aren't capitalized unless the relationship is used as a name. The title *Dogcatcher* is attached to the name, and thus it's capitalized.

5. **Mom, Ms.** The word *Mom* substitutes for the name here, so it's capitalized. The title *Ms.* is always capitalized, but the period is optional.

6. **dogcatchers, Agnes.** The common noun *dogcatchers* doesn't need a capital letter, but the proper name *Agnes* does.

7. **Uncle.** The title *uncle* is capitalized if it precedes or substitutes for the name. Did I confuse you with *BooBoo?* People can spell their own names (and the names of their pets) how they want.

8. **brother.** Family titles aren't capitalized unless they substitute for the name.

9. **mayor's, cousin.** These titles aren't attached to or used as names, so they take lowercase.

10. **Correct.** Names are in caps, but the title isn't, except when it precedes the name.

11. **vice president.** A title that isn't attached to a name shouldn't be capitalized.

12. **President.** In this sentence the title precedes the name and thus should be capitalized.

13. **chief financial officer, Grandma.** The first title *(chief financial officer)* isn't attached to a name. Go for lowercase. The second title *(Grandma)* is part of a name and must be capitalized.

14. **nephew.** Don't capitalize relationships, like *aunt,* unless they precede and are part of a name.

15. **bank president.** This title isn't connected to a name; therefore, it should be lowercased.

16. **Reverend.** The title precedes the name and becomes part of the name, in a sense. A capital letter is appropriate.

17. **bishop.** In this sentence *bishop* doesn't precede a name; lowercase is the way to go.

18. **brother, the, manager.** Lowercase is best for *brother, the,* and *manager* because *brother* isn't being used as a name, *the* isn't part of the title, and in any case, the title isn't connected to a name.

19. **player development director.** Another title that's all by itself. Opt for lowercase.

20 **president.** To be president is a big deal, but not a big letter.

21 **United Nose Ring Company, psychology.** Although college freshmen think they're really important (and, of course, they are), they rate only lowercase. The name of the company is specific and should be in uppercase. Don't capitalize subject areas.

22 **company, psychologists.** Common nouns such as *company* and *psychologists* aren't capitalized. (And if you've read Chapter 7, you may remember that because the quotation isn't tagged with a name, the quotation doesn't begin with a capital letter.)

23 **spring semester, Board of Trustees.** The name of the committee is generic and generally would not take capitals, though you have some elbow room here for style. Seasons, both natural and academic, take lowercase letters. The name of an official body, such as the *Board of Trustees,* is usually capitalized.

24 **and, High School.** Years in school and school levels aren't capitalized. The name of the school is (and the name includes *High School*), but an unimportant word such as *and* is written in lowercase.

25 **spokesperson, products, In Style or Else, Inc., Klepto Industrials, college degree.** A common noun such as *spokesperson* or *college degree* isn't capitalized. The names of companies are capitalized according to the preference of the company itself. Most companies follow headline style, which is explained in the section "Capitalizing Titles of Literary and Media Works" in this chapter.

26 **students, countries, continents.** Don't capitalize common nouns. Do capitalize the name of a working group, such as *Top-Seller Task Force.*

27 **task force, Department of Product Development.** In contrast to Question 26, here *task force* isn't a name but rather a common label, which takes lowercase. The name of a department should be capitalized, but the preposition (*of*) is lowercased.

28 **Introduction to Fashion, science.** Course titles get caps, but subject names and school years don't.

29 **Correct.** School degrees (*bachelor's, master's, doctorate*) are lowercased, though their abbreviations aren't (*B.A., M.S.,* and so on). Most school subjects aren't capitalized, except for languages (such as Spanish). Course names, such as Economics I, are capitalized.

30 **companies.** This term isn't the name of a specific company, just a common noun. Lowercase is what you want.

31 ***Moby Duck: A Tale of Obsessive Bird Watching*** In headline style, the first word of the title (*Moby*) and subtitle (*A*) are in caps. Nouns (*Duck, Tale,* and *Watching*) and descriptive words (*Obsessive, Bird*) are also uppercased. The short preposition *of* merits only lowercase.

32 **"An analysis of the *Duckensis mobyous*: The consequences of habitat shrinkage on population"** In sentence-style capitalization, the first words of the title and subtitle are in caps, but everything else is in lowercase, with the exception of proper names. In this title, following preferred scientific style, the names of the genus (a scientific category) and species are in italics with only the genus name in caps.

33 **"Call Me Izzy Smell: My Life As a Duck Hunter"** Per headline style, the article *(a)* is in lowercase. I caught you on *As,* didn't I? It's short, but it's not an article or a preposition, so it rates a capital letter.

34 *The duck and I: Essays on the relationship between human beings and feathered species* Sentence style titles take caps for the first word of the title and subtitle. The personal pronoun *I* is always capitalized.

35 *Duck and Cover: A Cookbook* Headline style calls for capitals for the first word of the title and subtitle and all other nouns. The joining word *and* is lowercased in headline style, unless it begins a title or subtitle.

36 **"The duck stops here: Political wisdom from the environmental movement"** Sentence style gives you two capitals in this title — the first word of the title and subtitle.

37 *Duck Up: How the Duck Triumphed over the Hunter* Because this title is in headline style, everything is in caps except articles *(the)* and prepositions *(over)*.

38 **"Moby Platypus Doesn't Live Here Anymore"** Headline style gives capital letters for all the words here because this title contains no articles or prepositions.

39 **"Population estimates of the platypus: An inexact science"** Sentence style calls for capital letters at the beginning of the title and subtitle. The term *platypus* isn't the name of a genus, so it's written in lowercase.

40 *For the Love of a Duck: A Sentimental Memoir* Headline style mandates lowercase for articles *(the, a)* and prepositions *(of)*. The first words of the title and subtitle, even if they're articles or prepositions, merit capital letters.

41 **illus.**

42 **BCE** (The Latin expression *Anno Domini* — abbreviated *AD* — means "in the year of our Lord" and is used with dates that aren't *BC,* or *before Christ*. To make this term more universal, historians often substitute *CE* or *Common Era* for AD and *BCE* or *Before the Common Era* for BC.)

43 **Mr. Burns**

44 **U.S. Pres.**

45 **NHL** (an acronym)

46 **Rev. Smith**

47 **NY** (postal abbreviation) or **N.Y.** (traditional form)

48 **Adams Blvd.**

49 **irreg.**

50 **Inc.**

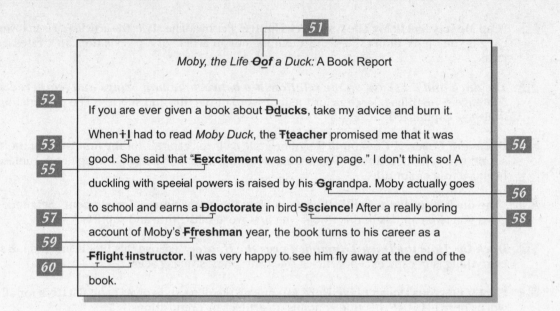

51

Moby, the Life ~~O~~of a Duck: A Book Report

52

If you are ever given a book about ~~D~~ducks, take my advice and burn it. When ~~i~~I had to read *Moby Duck*, the ~~T~~teacher promised me that it was

53

54

good. She said that "~~E~~excitement was on every page." I don't think so! A

55

duckling with ~~special~~ powers is raised by his ~~G~~grandpa. Moby actually goes

to school and earns a ~~D~~doctorate in bird ~~S~~science! After a really boring

56

57

account of Moby's ~~F~~freshman year, the book turns to his career as a

58

59

~~F~~flight ~~i~~instructor. I was very happy to see him fly away at the end of the

60

book.

51   In a headline-style title, prepositions aren't capitalized.

52   An ordinary term for animals, in this case *ducks,* is lowercased.

53   The personal pronoun *I* is always capitalized.

54   The name of the teacher isn't given, just the term *teacher,* which should be lowercased.

55   When a quotation is written without a speaker tag, the first word isn't capitalized.

56   Family relationships are capitalized only when they serve as a name.

57   Most academic degrees take lowercase.

58   Most school subjects are written in lowercase. (I must point out that English is in caps because it's so important. Okay, I'm lying. It's in caps because it's the name of a language.)

59   School years are in lowercase too.

60   Job titles, when they aren't attached to the beginning of a name, are in lowercase.

Part III

Applying Proper Grammar in Tricky Situations

The 5th Wave   By Rich Tennant

"They won't let me through security until I remove the bullets from my PowerPoint presentation."

In this part . . .

When was the last time you chatted with a grammar teacher? Never? I'm not surprised. When people find out that someone cares about proper English, they tend to staple their lips together rather than risk making an error. However, most of the issues that people obsess about are actually extremely simple. Take *who* and *whom,* for example. Deciding which one is appropriate is not rocket science; it's just pronoun case, which you can practice in Chapter 9. The same chapter explains why everyone has to bring *his* or *her,* not *their,* lunch — an issue of singular and plural pronouns. Chapter 10 tackles verb tense in difficult sentences, such as those containing several actions in the past. Chapter 11 explains how to determine a verb's mood (not irritable or ecstatic but indicative, imperative, or subjunctive) and shows you situations in which mood matters. In Chapter 12 I take you to the wonderful world of electronic communication so you can tweet, text, e-mail, blog, and create PowerPoint-style presentations without risking a stint in grammar jail.

Chapter 9

Choosing the Best Pronoun: Case, Number, and Clarity

. . . .

In This Chapter

▶ Placing subject and object pronouns in sentences

▶ Selecting *who* or *whom, he* or *him,* and *I* or *me*

▶ Keeping straight singular, plural, and possessive pronouns

▶ Pairing *who, which,* and *that* with verbs

▶ Avoiding vague pronoun references

. . . .

Have you figured out that pronouns are the most annoying part of speech in the entire universe? *Pronouns* are the words that most often take the place of *nouns* — words that name people, places, things, and ideas. Even more annoying is that sometimes pronouns replace other pronouns. In other words, when it comes to error-potential, pronouns are a minefield just waiting to blow up your speech or writing.

I cover the basics of pronoun use in Chapter 3. This chapter is for more advanced topics such as *case* (the difference, for example, between *they, their,* and *them*) and *number* (singular or plural) in complicated sentences. In this chapter I also show you how to be sure a pronoun expresses your meaning clearly. To make your life easier, I break these topics into tiny parts, so you can become an expert pronoun-chooser one small step at a time.

Pronouns are very popular with standardized-test writers, so if you plan to bubble little ovals sometime soon, work through these exercises with extra care.

Meeting the Subject at Hand and the Object of My Affection

Subjects and objects have opposite jobs in a sentence. Briefly, the *subject* is the doer of the action or whatever is in the state of being talked about in the sentence. When you say, "He and I are going to the mall," you use the subject pronouns *he* and *I. Objects* receive; instead of acting, they are acted upon. If you scold *him* and *me,* those two pronouns resentfully receive the scolding and thus act as objects. Verbs have objects, and so do some other grammatical elements, such as prepositions. (I deal with prepositions later in this chapter.) Here are the contents of the subject- and object-pronoun baskets:

> ✔ **Subject pronouns** include *I, you, he, she, it, we, they, who,* and *whoever.*
>
> ✔ **Object pronouns** are *me, you, him, her, it, us, them, whom,* and *whomever.*

Some pronouns, such as *you* and *it,* appear on both lists. They do double duty as both subject and object pronouns. Don't worry about them; they're right for all occasions. Other one-case-fits-almost-all pronouns are *either, most, other, which,* and *that.* Another type of pronoun is a reflexive, or *-self* pronoun (*myself, himself, ourselves,* and so forth). Use these pronouns only when the action in the sentence doubles back on the subject. ("They washed themselves 50 times during the deodorant shortage.") You may also insert the *-self* pronouns for emphasis. ("She herself baked the cake.") You can't use the *-self* pronouns for any other reason. A sentence such as "The cake she gave *myself* was good" is wrong. Opt for "The cake she gave *me.*"

Don't unnecessarily buddy up a pronoun and the noun it replaces. "My brother he goes swimming" is fine in many languages, but in English it's wrong because the pronoun *(he)* is meant to replace the noun *(brother).* "My brother goes swimming" or "He goes swimming" are both correct.

In the following sentences choose the correct pronoun from the parentheses, if — and only if — a pronoun is needed in the sentence. (If no pronoun is needed, select "no pronoun.") Take care not to send a subject pronoun to do an object pronoun's job, and vice versa.

0. Peyton took the precious parchment and gave (she/her) a cheap imitation instead.

A. **her.** In this sentence, Peyton is the one taking and giving. The pronoun *her* is on the receiving end because Peyton gave the imitation to *her. Her* is an object pronoun.

1. Maria, Peyton, and (I/me/myself/no pronoun) found a valuable item.

2. The parchment, which Peyton (he/him/no pronoun) discovered in the back pocket of a pair of jeans, is covered with strange symbols.

3. George Morse of Codebusters (he/him/no pronoun) is an expert at decoding ancient parchments.

4. Codebusters may contact Matt first, or the company may wait until Matt realizes that (he/him/himself/no pronoun) needs help.

5. Arthur, the president of Codebusters, knows that Maria (she/her/herself/no pronoun) is good at figuring out obscure symbols.

6. Peyton won't tell (I/me/myself/no pronoun) a thing about the parchment, but Maria (she/her/herself/no pronoun) did nod quietly when I mentioned Martians.

7. Peyton's friends — Lucy and (she/her/herself/no pronoun) — are obsessed with Martians and tend to see Little Green Men everywhere.

8. If the Martians and (she/her/herself/no pronoun) have a message for the world, (they/them/themselves/no pronoun) will make sure it gets maximum publicity.

9. Elizabeth and (I/me/myself/no pronoun) will glue (we/us/ourselves/no pronoun) to the all-news channel just in case Peyton (he/him/himself/no pronoun) decides to talk.

10. Sure enough, Peyton just contacted the authorities, Dan Moore and (he/him/himself/no pronoun), to arrange an interview.

11. Elizabeth (she/her/herself/no pronoun) favors sending NASA and (we/us/ourselves/no pronoun) the parchment.

12. I pointed out that NASA's scientists (they/them/themselves/no pronoun) know a lot about space, but nothing about ancient parchments.

13. Matt checked the Internet, but it had little to offer (he/him/himself/no pronoun) except the number for Codebusters.

14. (I/me/I myself/no pronoun) think that the parchment is a fake.

15. Matt told Maria and (I/me/myself/no pronoun) that he would call Codebusters.

16. Yesterday, Elizabeth (she/her/herself/no pronoun) showed Matt and (I/me/myself/no pronoun) some parchment scraps from Peyton's room.

To "Who" or To "Whom"? That Is the Question

Why are *who* and *whom* such a pain? Probably because they tend to occur in complicated sentences. But if you untangle the sentence and figure out (pardon the expression) *who* is doing what to *whom,* you'll be fine. Here's the deal: If you need a subject (someone doing the action or someone in the state of being described in the sentence), *who* is your guy. If you need an object (a receiver of the action), go with *whom.*

A good trick is to see if you can substitute the words *he* or *she* or *they.* If so, go with *who.* If *him, her,* or *them* is a better fit, opt for *whom.*

Take a ride on the *who/whom* train and select the proper pronoun from the parentheses in the following sentences.

Q. (Who/Whom) can decode the message? Codebusters!

A. **Who.** The verb *can decode* needs a subject, someone to do that action. *Who* is for subjects, and *whom* is for objects.

17. Does Peyton know (who/whom) should get the information after Maria has decoded it?

18. Matt will discuss the parchment with (whoever/whomever) the buyer sends.

19. (Who/Whom) is his buyer?

20. His buyer is (whoever/whomever) believes Matt's sales pitch.

21. Also, Matt will sell the parchment to (whoever/whomever) is willing to pay.

22. I don't think NASA is interested, despite Matt's claim that an expert from NASA, (who/whom) isn't saying much, was seen checking "Mars" and "Alien Life Forms" on the Internet.

23. Do you know (who/whom) the expert consulted?

24. No one seems to know (who/whom) Matt saw.

25. Peyton remains capable of conspiring with NASA, Codebusters, and (whoever/whomever) else is able to sell a fraudulent document.

26. Matt, (who/whom) I do not trust, has the most sincere face you can imagine.

27. Peyton, (who/whom) Matt once scolded for cutting class, has a reputation for sincerity.

28. I once heard Peyton explain that those (who/whom) have an honest face can get away with anything.

29. "If you are one of those people (who/whom) can fake sincerity," he said, "you can accomplish anything."

30. Peyton states this theory to (whoever/whomever) is willing to listen.

Linking Up with Pronouns in "To Be" Sentences

Most verbs express action, but mingling with this on-the-go group are forms of the verb *to be* (*am, is, are, was, were, has been, will be,* and the like). These verbs are like giant equal signs linking two equivalents, and for that reason they're sometimes called *linking verbs.* "Jeremy is the president" is the same as "Jeremy = president." If you've studied algebra, or even if you haven't, you know that these statements mean the same even when reversed ("the president is Jeremy").

This incredibly boring explanation leads to an important pronoun fact: A subject pronoun serves as the subject of a linking verb, and to preserve reversibility, subject pronouns also *follow* linking verbs, in the same spot where you normally expect an object. Therefore, the answer to *Who's there?* is "It is *she*" instead of "It is *her*" because you can reverse the first ("She is it") and not the second ("Her is it").

When you select pronouns for a linking-verb sentence, be aware that sometimes the verb changes, so to sound right, a reversible sentence may need a verb adjustment from singular to plural or vice versa. "It is they" is reversible, at least in theory, because *they* is a subject pronoun, even though "they is" doesn't pass a sound check until you change the verb to *are.*

Can you select the appropriate pronoun from the parentheses? Give it a whirl in the following example and practice exercises. Just to make life more interesting, I'm sprinkling action verbs into the mix — for more information on pronouns with action verbs, see the earlier section, "Meeting the Subject at Hand and the Object of My Affection."

0. Miley knows that the true culprit is (he/him).

A. **he.** Who is *he?* Only the gossip columnist knows for sure. The grammarian, on the other hand, is positive that a subject pronoun is the one you want after the linking verb *is.* Reverse that portion of the sentence to check yourself: *Him* is the *culprit?* I don't think so. *He* is the *culprit?* Bingo.

31. The FBI recently announced that the criminals responsible for the theft of an ancient parchment are (they/them).

32. I met with three FBI agents and promised (they/them) that the parchment would be returned to the rightful owner.

33. The "rightful owner," according to Maria, is (she/her), because Maria herself purchased the jeans in which the document was discovered.

34. "I can't read the code," added Maria, "but I know a good pair of jeans when I see one, and besides, the lawful purchaser of both the jeans and the parchment is (I/me)."

35. Matt isn't so sure; it is (he/him) who will have to go to jail if the FBI decides not to buy Maria's story that "the seller said the document was included in the price."

36. The FBI agent told (they/them) that the document is vital to national security.

You Talkin' to Me, or 1? Pronouns as Objects of Prepositions

Prepositions, not to be confused with *propositions* (such as "Are you busy tonight?") are words that express relationships. (Come to think of it, *propositions* concern relationships too.) Common prepositions include *by, for, from, in, on, of, about, after,* and *before.* Prepositions always have objects, and sometimes those objects are pronouns. Check out the italicized objects of prepositions in these examples:

Give that umbrella to *me,* or I'll break it over your *head.*

The embroidery on the *umbrella* was done by *me* alone.

In the first sample sentence, *me* and *head* are objects of the prepositions *to* and *over.* In the second, *umbrella* and *me* are objects of *on* and *by.* Luckily, you don't have to worry about *umbrella* and *head.* They're nouns, and they don't change no matter where they appear in the sentence. But the pronoun does change (sigh), depending upon its job in the sentence. And if its job is to be an object of a preposition, it must be an object pronoun. You can't give an umbrella to *I,* nor was the embroidery done by *I alone.* Not in this grammatical universe, anyway.

The *-self* pronouns (*myself, himself, ourselves, themselves,* and the like) can serve as objects of prepositions, but only if the action in the sentence doubles back, as in "I talk to myself all the time." In this example sentence, *myself* is the object of the preposition *to.*

Take a stab at the following sentences, selecting the correct pronoun from the pair in parentheses. I cleverly (she said modestly) scatter a few subjects in the exercise.

0. I won't accept any packages from (he/him) because last week he sent a quart of pickled cabbage to (I/me), and my mailbox was sticky for days.

A. **him, me.** The preposition *from* needs an object, so your first answer has to be *him.* To is also a preposition and should be followed by the object pronoun *me.*

37. Jessica sang songs to Mom and (he/him/himself) whenever the moon was full.

38. Her latest CD is titled *Of Mom, (I/Me/Myself), and the Moon.*

39. I'm going to download some songs, although a lot of issues remain between Jessica and (I/me/myself).

40. Once, she stole my dog Spike and asked for a reward when she returned Spike to (I/me/myself).

41. Spike ran after (she/her) and took a large bite out of her nose, and (I/me) applauded.

42. Aggressive though Spike may be, you can't put much past (he/him), and for that reason (he/him) is a great watchdog.

43. Spike likes to walk behind (we/us) when we approach the house; he growls at (whoever/whomever) comes too close.

44. "At (who/whom) is this dog snarling?" asked Jessica, as she snarled back at (he/him/himself).

45. "(He/Him/Himself) thinks the letter carrier wants to rob us, so Spike tries to keep an eye on (he/him)," I replied as (I/me/myself) pieced together a ripped catalogue.

46. "You have to run around (they/them)," I said to (she/her/herself), speaking of Spike and my mother.

47. Carefully separating the letters addressed to "Spike" from the letters meant for Jessica or (I/me/myself), the letter carrier told (he/him/himself) that even dogs deserved good service.

48. Spike's pen pals generally include a dog biscuit when writing to (he/him/himself), but no one ever sends presents to (I/me/myself).

49. Spike's letters sometimes contain meaty bones from (whoever/whomever) really wants to catch his attention.

50. Jessica and (I/me/myself) are as fond of meaty bones as (he/him) is, but (we/us/ourselves) seldom chew any in public.

Matching Possessive Pronouns to "-ing" Nouns

I cheated a bit with the title of this section. When I say *-ing* noun, I mean a noun made from the *-ing* form of a verb (*swimming, smiling, puttering,* and similar words). I'm not talking about nouns that just happen to contain those three letters, such as *king, wingding,* and *pudding,* among others. Nor am I talking about *-ing* verb forms used as verbs or as descriptions of other nouns. (For those of you who enjoy grammar terms, the *-ing*-noun-made-from-a-verb-form is actually a *gerund.*)

Here's the deal with pronouns and *-ing* nouns. You should put a possessive form in front of these nouns. Why? Because that form keeps the focus in the right place. Take a look at this sentence:

Carrie hates (me/my) auditioning for the new reality show, *Nut Search*.

Putting on your thinking cap, you can see that Carrie doesn't hate *me*. Instead, Carrie hates the whole reality-show project. The possessive pronoun *my* is the best choice because it shifts the reader's attention to *auditioning*, where it belongs, because *auditioning* is what Carrie hates.

The possessive form of a *noun* should also be your choice for the spot in front of an *-ing* noun. In the preceding sample sentence, the correct form is "Carrie hates Rick's auditioning."

If you're facing a standardized test, don't nod off during this exercise. The SAT and other exams include this topic!

Try your hand at the following example and practice exercises. Circle the pronouns you love and ignore the ones you hate. To keep you alert, I've inserted a few sentences that don't call for possessive pronouns. Keep your eyes open!

Q. Although I'm not a literary critic, I think that (he/him/his) writing a novel on his phone is a bad idea.

A. his. The bad idea here is the *writing*, not *he* or *him*. The possessive pronoun shifts the attention to the task, which is the point of the sentence.

51. St. John Lincoln of the *Times* needs help with (he/him/his) editing and must hire assistants; Lincoln looks forward to (they/them/their) correcting his grammar.

52. Lincoln said that he loved everything the employment agency did last week except (they/them/their) sending him too many pronoun-obsessed writers.

53. When Lori went for an interview, she saw (he/him/his) reading a review of *The Pronoun Diet;* (she/her) saying that the book was "trash" bothered Lincoln.

54. "I object to (she/her) insisting on one pronoun per paragraph," he muttered, as he eyed (she/her) ring, which sparkled intensely.

55. When I applied, Lincoln looked favorably upon (I/me/my) editing, but he hated (I/me/my) pronouncing his first name incorrectly.

Missing in Action: Choosing Pronouns for Implied Comparisons

Sometimes, what you don't say is more important than what you do say, especially when it comes to pronouns. In a sentence with an implied, not stated, comparison, you sometimes have to add the missing words before you can select the proper pronoun. Take a look at this example:

George has more cauliflower than (I/me).

Before you underline anything, add the missing word:

George has more cauliflower than (I/me) do.

Clearly *I* is the pronoun you want, because *me* can't act as the subject of the verb *do*. To sum up: In an implied comparison, throw in the missing words and figure out whether a subject or an object pronoun is called for. When you know that fact, your choice is easy.

Go for it! Select the appropriate pronoun and circle it. Remember to add the missing words (mentally) before answering.

0. Grandpa always gives Oscar more vegetables than (I/me).

A. **I or me.** No, I haven't lost my mind. The answer here depends upon the meaning you're trying to express. If you want to say that "Grandpa gives Oscar more vegetables than I give Oscar," go for *I.* If your meaning is that "Grandpa gives Oscar more vegetables than Grandpa gives to me," the answer you want is *me.*

56. Oscar is as careful as (she/her) when he's weeding, but somehow he pulls out more plants than (she/her).

57. The chipmunks consider Oscar their friend because he breaks as much garden fence as (they/them).

58. With the fence down, the chipmunks munch more vegetables than (we/us).

59. Oscar has planted fewer tomato plants than (I/me).

60. Oscar gives more zucchini to the chipmunks than (I/me), because I hate the taste of zucchini.

61. The chipmunks seem to enjoy their vegetables as much as (he/him).

62. Sometimes we take the chipmunks to the wilderness, which Oscar seems to enjoy more than (they/them); the chipmunks prefer our suburban garden.

63. Because she took a course in "Wild Food," Oscar's sister believes that the little animals have fewer chances to find food in the wilderness than (she/her).

Making Pronouns Get Along

Pronouns substitute for nouns, but in a sincere effort to ruin your life, they also match up with other pronouns. Some matches are straightforward:

When Charlie yelled at me, I smacked him and poured glue on his homework.

In the preceding example, the pronoun *his* refers to the pronoun *him*, which stands in for the noun *Charlie.* But some pronoun/pronoun pairs are devilish:

Everybody eats lunch.

Doesn't that comment sound plural? But *everybody* is a singular pronoun and pairs with the singular verb *eats*. Other singular pronouns include *someone, anyone, no one, somebody, anybody, nobody, everything, something, anything, nothing, each, either,* and *neither*.

Because you have only one body, if you see *-one* or *-body* in a pronoun, the pronoun is singular.

If you extend the logic and match another pronoun — such as a possessive — to these singular pronouns, you need a singular form. I often hear sentences such as "Everyone needs their lunch pass" — a grammatical felony because the singular *everyone* doesn't agree with the plural *their*. And in the grammar world, agreement (matching up all plurals with other plurals and singulars with other singulars) is a Very Big Deal. To get out of the grammatical penitentiary, substitute *his or her* for *their*: "Everyone needs his or her lunch pass." Of course, not every pronoun is singular. *Both, several, few,* and *many* are plurals and may match with *their* or other plural words.

When you're selecting pronouns, don't forget about gender. If you're talking about a single female, use *she, her,* or *hers*. If you're talking about a single male, opt for *he, him,* or *his*. If you don't know, *his or her* or *he or she* is a safe bet.

Test writers want to know that you can make pronouns agree with other pronouns. When you're wielding a number two pencil, remember that singular goes with singular and plural with plural.

Scan the following example sentence and practice exercises and plop a pronoun that makes sense in each blank.

0. Neither of my aunts has a wart on _____ nose.

A. **her.** The singular pronoun *neither* must pair with another singular pronoun. True, the sentence refers to *aunts,* a plural. But the word *neither* tells you that you're talking about the aunts individually, so you have to go with a singular pronoun. Because *aunts* are female, *her* is the word you want.

64. My cousins are easily located in a crowd because both have warts on _____ noses.

65. My cousin Amy opted for surgery; relieved that the procedure went well, everybody sent _____ best wishes.

66. Many of the get-well cards sported miniature warts on _____ envelopes.

67. A few even had little handwritten messages tucked into _____ illustrations.

68. Because Amy is pleased with the result of her surgery, I'm sure that someone else in her family is going to get _____ nose done also.

69. "Doesn't everyone need more warts on _____ nose?" reasoned Amy.

70. Anybody who disagreed with Amy kept quiet, knowing that _____ opinion wouldn't be accepted anyway.

71. Each of the implanted warts has _____ own unique shape.

72. Several of Amy's new warts model _____ appearance on a facial feature of a famous movie star.

73. Although someone said that _____ didn't like the new warts, the crowd reaction was generally positive.

74. Neither of the surgeons who worked on Amy's nose has opted for a similar procedure on _____ own schnoz.

75. I assume that nothing I say will change your mind about the nose-wart question; _____ will "go in one ear and out the other," as my mother used to say.

76. Aftercare is quite extensive; not one of the warts will continue to look good unless Amy gives _____ a lot of attention.

77. Both Amy and her sister Emily look forward to having _____ portraits painted, warts and all.

Multitasking Pronouns: Who, That, and Which

Most pronouns are either singular or plural, masculine or feminine or neuter, popular or unpopular, good at math or barely passing arithmetic. Okay, I went a little too far, but you get the point. The characteristics of most pronouns are fixed. But a couple of pronouns change from singular to plural (or back) and from masculine to feminine without a moment's pause. *Who, which,* and *that* take their meaning and characteristics from the sentences in which they appear. Here's what I mean:

May, who was born in April, wants to change her name. (The *who* is feminine and singular because it replaces the feminine, singular *May.*)

Her sisters, who were named after their birth months of June and August, support May's changes. (The *who* is feminine and plural because it replaces *sisters.*)

A change in the meaning of *who, which,* or *that* would be an interesting but useless fact except for one issue. Whether a subject pronoun is singular or plural affects what sort of verb (singular or plural) is paired with it. In the preceding sample sentences, the *who* is paired with *was* when the *who* represents *May* and with *were* when the *who* represents *sisters.*

Deciding singular/plural verb issues is especially tough sometimes:

She is one of the few quarterbacks who (is/are) ready for prime time.

She is the only quarterback who (is/are) negotiating with the Jets.

The key to this sort of sentence is deciding what the pronoun represents. If *who* means *she,* then of course you opt for a singular verb because *she* is a singular pronoun. But if *who* means *quarterbacks,* the verb should be plural, because *quarterbacks* is plural. Logic tells you the answers:

She is one of the few quarterbacks who *are* ready for prime time.

She is the only quarterback who *is* negotiating with the Jets.

How many are ready for prime time? A few quarterbacks are ready — you football fans can make the list — and she's one of them. The *who* in the first example clearly stands in for *quarterbacks,* a plural. In the second example just one person is negotiating — *she.* Therefore, *who* is singular and so is the verb paired with it.

The preceding examples involve *who,* but *that* and *which* behave the same way when they show up in similar sentences. Follow the same logic, and you'll choose the correct verb for these subject pronouns.

Standardized testers, bless their little hearts, like to throw these changeable pronouns around to see whether you can decode their meaning and pair them up with proper verbs.

Catch as many correct verbs as you can in the following example sentence and practice exercises. I promise that at least one of each pair in parentheses is what you want.

0. Kristin is one of the many lawyers on the fishing boat who (want/wants) to catch a shark.

A. **want.** How many lawyers want to catch a shark, according to this sentence? One or more than one? The sentence tells you that quite a lot of lawyers are in that category, so the *who* stands in for the group of lawyers. Touchdown! A plural verb is needed to match the plural *who.*

78. The shark that Kristin caught was the only one that (was/were) hungry enough to take the bait that Kristin offered.

79. The bait that (was/were) on sale at the market was extremely cheap.

80. "I know that there is at least one shark that (likes/like) peanut butter," reasoned Kristin.

81. Kristin's fellow shark fans, who (sails/sail) even in the winter, read a lot about these animals on the Internet.

82. The only one of the shark sites that (doesn't/don't) appeal to Kristin is the one sponsored by the Stop Fishing Society.

83. Could it be that Kristin is one of the shark fans who (believes/believe) the Great White is a misunderstood, gentle giant?

84. Why did Kristin choose a bait that (is/are) completely unappetizing when dunked in salt water?

85. One of the many experienced sailors who (was/were) laughing at Kristin's bait exclaimed, "Peanut butter can't catch anything!"

86. I'm going to take Kristin's shark to the only taxidermist that (is/are) willing to stuff such a catch.

87. In the mouth of the shark he is planning to mount a jar of one of the many brands of peanut butter that (is/are) shark-friendly.

88. The taxidermist has a contract with several peanut butter manufacturers, which (advertises/advertise) in unusual spots.

89. Recently, one of the manufacturers that (is/are) particularly interested in social networking launched a new brand, which (is/are) called "FaceNut."

90. FaceNut is the only one of this company's new products that (spreads/spread) as quickly as a rumor on the Internet.

91. I personally have tasted FaceNut's peanut butter, which (goes/go) nicely with grape jelly.

92. When I tried it on one of the fishcakes that (contains/contain) shark meat, however, FaceNut tasted terrible.

Limiting Pronouns to Specific References

Pronoun rules are far more rigid than even the U.S. tax code. The underlying principle, that one pronoun may replace one and only one matching noun, bends only a tiny bit by allowing *they,* for instance, to take the place of more than one name. (*Ida, Mary,* and *Joan,* for example, may be replaced by *they.*) In informal speech and writing, pronouns are sometimes sent to fill other roles. But if you're going for correct, formal English — and on standardized tests, you are! — don't ask a pronoun to violate the rules.

A common error is to ask a pronoun to stand in for an idea expressed by a whole sentence or paragraph. (Pronouns can't replace verbs or noun/verb combos.) The pronouns *that, which,* and *this* are often misused in this way. Therefore, you can't say, "Jeffrey handed in a late, error-filled report, which annoyed his boss," because *which* refers to an entire idea. In the correct sentence, "Jeffrey's report, which annoyed his boss, was late and error-filled," *which* refers to *report,* a noun.

Sometimes the best way to fix one of these sentences is to eliminate the pronoun entirely: "The fact that Jeffrey's report was late and error-filled annoyed his boss."

Another common mistake is to send in a pronoun that approaches, but doesn't match, the noun it's replacing, as in "Jeffrey's sports marketing course sounds interesting, but I don't want to be one." One what? *Sports marketing course?* I don't think so. The *one* replaces *sports marketer* (or *sports marketing executive*), but the sentence has no noun to match *one.* A better sentence is "Jeffrey's sports marketing course sounds interesting, but I don't want to enroll in it." Now *it* replaces *sports marketing* — a better match.

Fix the pronoun problem in the following example sentence and practice exercises. Some are correct as written. When you find one, write "correct" in the blank. Rewrite the clunkers so that every pronoun refers to an appropriate noun. Remember that sometimes you have to dump the pronoun entirely in order to correct the mistake. *Note:* The incorrect sentences have more than one answer; in the following example, I show you two possibilities, but in the answers section of this chapter, I provide only one possible answer.

0. Jeffrey's dream job features a corner office, three-hour lunches, and frequent "research" junkets to Tahiti, which is unlikely given that he has no skill whatsoever.

_____

_____

A. **Given that he has no skill whatsoever, Jeffrey is unlikely to get his dream job, which features a corner office, three-hour lunches, and frequent "research" junkets to Tahiti.** The preceding sentence is just one possible solution, in which the pronoun *which* takes the place of *job*. Here's another: **The fact that Jeffrey has no skill whatsoever makes his dream job, which features a corner office, three-hour lunches, and frequent "research" junkets to Tahiti, unlikely.** Any sentence that achieves the goal of one noun out, one pronoun in is fine. The original doesn't work because *which* replaces an entire sentence, "Jeffrey's dream job features a corner office, three-hour lunches, and frequent 'research' junkets to Tahiti."

93. Jeffrey jogged for an hour in an effort to work off the pounds he had gained during his last three-hour lunch, but this didn't help.

_____

_____

94. He's always admired the superhero's flat-ab look, but no matter how hard he tries, he can't be one.

_____

_____

95. The 15 sit-ups that were prescribed by his exercise coach didn't help at all.

_____

_____

96. Jeffrey's next fitness effort ended in disaster; that did not discourage him.

_____

_____

97. He simply ignored the arrest warrant and continued to run; this was only a temporary solution.

_____

_____

98. Next, Jeffrey joined a gym, where he recites Shakespeare's sonnets, which help him to stay focused.

_____

_____

99. The great poet inspired Jeffrey to study it also.

_____

_____

100. "No, I did not see the car when I directed my bicycle into the street," testified Jeffrey, "but that wasn't the cause of the accident."

_____

_____

101. "The driver was distracted by his cellphone, which rang at the exact moment I started to ride," explained Jeffrey.

_____

_____

102. The judge was not impressed by Jeffrey's testimony and fined him, and Jeffrey paid it.

_____

_____

103. When Jeffrey paid the fine, the court clerk quoted Shakespeare, which impressed Jeffrey very much.

_____

_____

104. "I see you are a sonneteer," commented Jeffrey as he smiled and gave the clerk a romantic look; she wasn't impressed by this at all.

_____

_____

Calling All Overachievers: Extra Practice with Tricky Pronoun Situations

Here's a field trip report (see Figure 9-1), written by a battle-weary teacher after a particularly bad day. Can you find 20 pronoun errors that cry out for correction? Circle the mistakes and give a thought to how you would fix them.

Three chaperones and myself left school at 10:03 a.m. with 45 freshmen, all of who were excited about our visit to Adventure Land. The day it passed without incident, which was a great relief to me. My friend Jim and me sat in the Adventure Land Bar and Grille for five hours while the youngsters visited Space Camp, Pirates' Mountain, and other attractions that is overpriced but popular. Each of the students at my table (Alex and another boy) objected to me eating such good food and said they wanted one too. The bus driver and myself explained that everyone was supposed to eat their school-issued lunch. This was a disappointment, and the two students — Alex and him — threw them at me. We got on one of the vans that was overdue for maintenance. The motor whirred loudly, and it scared whomever heard the noise. We drove to Makoski Brake and Wheel Repairs because the driver said their expertise was what we ourselves needed. Makoski is also the only one of the many repair shops on Route 9 that take credit cards, which was helpful because I had spent all my money in the Adventure Land Bar and Grille.

Figure 9-1:
A field trip report, written by a teacher who doesn't use pronouns correctly. (Shame!)

Answers to Advanced Pronoun Problems

I hope all these pronoun problems didn't trip you up too badly. See how you did by taking a look at the answers and explanations.

1 **I.** The pronoun *I* is one of the subjects of the verb *found. Me* is for objects. *Myself* is only for emphasis *(I myself)* or for actions that bounce back on the subject. ("I told myself not to stand under a tree during a thunderstorm!")

2 **No pronoun.** Because the noun *Peyton* is present in the sentence, no pronoun is needed to replace it.

3 **No pronoun.** Because *George Morse* acts as the subject, you don't need a pronoun to act as the subject.

4 **he.** The verb *needs* must have a subject, and the subject pronoun *he* fills the bill.

5 **No pronoun.** *Maria* is the subject of the verb *is,* so you don't have to double up with a pronoun after *Maria.*

6 **me, no pronoun.** In the first part of the sentence, the pronoun receives the action *(Peyton won't tell whom? Me.)* In the second, *Maria* is already nodding, so you don't need an additional pronoun.

7 **she.** The tough part about this sentence is that the pronoun choice is camouflaged by other words *(Peyton's friends* and *Lucy).* If you isolate the pronoun, however, you see that it is *she* who is *obsessed* with Martians. You need the subject pronoun. To add a technical grammatical explanation — stop reading now before you die of boredom! — the subject is *Peyton's friends,* and the expression *Lucy and she* forms an appositive to the subject. An appositive is always in the same case as the word it matches.

8 **she, they.** Two parentheses, two subjects. The verbs *have* and *will make* need subjects; *she* and *they* fill the bill.

9 **I, ourselves, no pronoun.** In the first part of the sentence, you need a subject for *will glue.* You can rule out *me* because *me* is an object pronoun. The pronoun *myself* works only for emphasis, in which case the sentence would read *Elizabeth and I myself. (Elizabeth and myself* is never correct, because the *-self* pronouns don't substitute for subject pronouns.) In the second parentheses, you're looking for an object for the verb *will glue.* The pronoun *we* drops out right away because it's for subjects only. The next choice, *us,* is tempting, but because the actor and the receiver are the same, *ourselves* is better. Finally, the noun *Peyton* is the subject of the verb *decides,* so you can immediately eliminate *he* (subject pronoun) and *him* (object pronoun). I don't see a need for emphasis, so *himself* also drops out.

10 **him.** Like Sentence 7, this one has lots of camouflage. Cover everything between *contacted* and the pronoun choice. What's left? *Peyton just contacted he/him/himself.* Can you hear the correct answer? *Peyton contacted he?* I don't think so! You need the object pronoun *him.* You can't use *himself* because the action isn't doubling back on the subject (as in "He told *himself* not to worry"). If you really want a grammatical explanation, and surely you have better things to do with your time, *authorities* is the object of the verb *contacted,* and *Dan Moore and him* forms an appositive. An appositive is always in the same case as its equivalent.

11   **No pronoun, us.** *Elizabeth* is doing the action, so you have no reason to add a pronoun after her name. Moving to the second parenthesis, you see that the pronoun is on the receiving end of the verb *will glue.* You can't plug in *we* because *we* is for subjects, and receivers are objects. *Ourselves* doesn't fit because the *-self* pronouns are only for emphasis *(we ourselves will go . . .)* or for situations in which the actor and receiver are the same *(I told myself . . .).*

12   **No pronoun.** A subject for the verb *know* ((NASA's scientists) is already present in this sentence. Don't throw in an extra pronoun!

13   **him.** The verb *offer,* even in the infinitive form *(to offer),* takes the object pronoun *him.*

14   **I** or **I myself.** The first choice is an ordinary subject pronoun; the second is emphatic. Do you want to scream this phrase or just say it? Your call.

15   **me.** *Matt told* is a subject-verb pair, so you need an object pronoun *(me)* to receive the action.

16   **No pronoun, me.** *Elizabeth* is the subject of the verb *showed,* and doubling up makes no sense. In the second parenthesis, the object pronoun *me* receives the action from the verb *told.* You can probably "hear" the correct answer if you use your thumb to cover the words *Matt and.* By isolating the pronoun, you quickly determine that *Elizabeth showed I* is a nonstarter. *Elizabeth showed me* sounds — and is — correct.

17   **who.** Focus on the part of the sentence containing the *who/whom* issue: *who/whom should get the information.* The verb *should get* needs a subject, so *who* is the proper choice.

18   **whomever.** The buyer is sending someone, so the pronoun you plug in receives the action of *sending.* Receivers are always object pronouns, so *whomever* wins the prize.

19   **Who.** The verb *is* needs a subject, and *who* is a subject pronoun — a match made in heaven.

20   **whoever.** The verb *believes* needs a subject. *Whoever* is a subject pronoun.

21   **whoever.** This one is tricky. When you hear the word *to* (a preposition), you may want to jump for the object pronoun, because *prepositions* are completed by object pronouns such as *whomever.* But in this sentence, the verb *is* needs a subject, and *whoever* fills that role. For those who dig grammar (if you quake at the word, don't read this part), the object of the preposition *to* is the whole clause, *whoever is willing to pay.*

22   **who.** Somebody *isn't saying,* so you need a subject pronoun. *Who* fills the bill.

23   **whom.** This sentence is easier to figure out if you isolate the part of the sentence containing the who/whom choice: *who/whom the expert consulted.* Now rearrange those words into the normal subject-verb order: *the expert consulted whom. Whom* is the object of the verb *consulted.*

24   **whom.** As in the previous sentence, isolating and rearranging are helpful: *who/whom Matt saw, Matt saw whom.* The pronoun *whom* serves as the object of the verb *saw.*

25   **whoever.** The verb *is* needs a subject, so *whoever* has to do the job.

26   **whom.** Concentrate on the part of the sentence between the commas. Rearrange the words into the normal subject-verb order: *I do not trust who/whom.* Now do you see that it has to be *whom?* The pronoun *I* is the subject, and *whom* is acted upon, not an actor.

27 **whom.** The action from the verb *scolded* goes to an object, and the object pronoun *whom* fills that role.

28 **who.** The verb *have* just has to have a subject (verbs are picky that way), so here you need *who*.

29 **who.** The verb *can fake* pairs with the subject pronoun *who* in this sentence.

30 **whoever.** Did I fool you here? The preposition *to* needs an object, so at first glance *whomever* looks like a winner. However, the verb *is willing* requires a subject, and that subject is *whoever*. So what about the preposition? No sweat: The object of the preposition is the whole statement (a clause, in grammatical terms) *whoever is willing to listen.*

31 **they.** Okay, I know it doesn't sound right, but you can reverse "the criminals are they" to get "they are the criminals." To put it another way, *they* is a subject pronoun and belongs after the linking verb *are.*

32 **them.** *To promise* isn't a linking verb; it expresses action. After an action verb you need an object pronoun, and *them* fits that description.

33 **she.** The *rightful owner* is *she,* and *she* is the *rightful owner.* See how neatly that reverses?

34 **I.** The subject pronoun *I* belongs after the linking verb *is.*

35 **he.** *It* is *he* and *he* is *it* . . . in more ways than one! If the FBI goes after Matt, he is certainly *it,* as far as felony charges go. Speaking grammatically, I must point out that *he* is a subject pronoun and should appear after the linking verb *is.*

36 **them.** Telling is an action, so you need an object pronoun here, and *them* is an object pronoun.

37 **him.** The preposition *to* needs an object. In this sentence it has two — *Mom and him.* The pronoun *him* works as an object.

38 **Me.** The preposition *of* has three objects, including *me.*

39 **me.** The preposition *between* calls for two objects. In this sentence, *Jessica* is one and *me* is the other. Don't fall into the *between-and-I* trap; *between* calls for objects, not subjects. Also, stay away from *myself.* The *-self* pronouns are appropriate only when you're doubling back ("I told *myself*") or emphasizing ("I *myself* will cook the meal").

40 **me.** The preposition *to* requires the object pronoun *me.*

41 **her, I.** The preposition *after* needs an object, and *her* takes that role. In the second parenthesis, you're looking for a subject for the verb *applauded,* and *I* does the job.

42 **him, he.** Did you know that *past* may sometimes be a preposition? The object pronoun *him* works well here. In the second part of the sentence, go for *he* because the verb *is* requires a subject, and *he* is a subject pronoun.

43 **us, whoever.** This is a hard one; if you got it right, you deserve an ice cream sundae. The pronoun *us* is best as an object of the preposition *behind.* But the preposition *at* is *not* completed by the pronoun *whomever.* Instead, *whoever* functions as the subject of the verb *comes.* The whole thing — *whoever comes too close* — is the object of the preposition *at.*

44 **whom, him.** Change the first part of this question to a statement and you'll get this one right away: *This dog is snarling at whom.* The preposition *at* is completed by the object *whom.* The second preposition, also *at,* needs an object, which is the object pronoun *him.*

45 **He, him, I.** The verb *thinks* takes the subject pronoun *he.* The preposition *on* needs an object, and *him* gets the job. Finally, *I* is the subject pronoun paired with the verb *ripped.*

46 **them, her.** *Around* is a preposition in this sentence, so it takes the object *them.* The object pronoun *her* is the object of the preposition *to.*

47 **me, himself.** The preposition *to* needs an object, so choose *me.* In the second part of the sentence, the *letter carrier* is talking to *himself.* Because the action circles back to the subject, a *-self* pronoun is appropriate.

48 **him, me.** You can't write *to he* or *I,* because *he* and *I* are subject pronouns, and the preposition *to* can't bear to be without an object pronoun.

49 **whoever.** The preposition *from* needs an object, but in this tricky sentence, the entire expression *whoever really wants to catch his attention* is the object, not just the first word. The pronoun *whoever* functions as the subject of the verb *wants.*

50 **I, he, we.** First off, you need a subject pronoun (I) for the verb *are.* Next, you need another subject (he) for the verb *is.* Finally, you need the subject pronoun *we* to match with the verb *chew.*

51 **his, their.** *Lincoln* doesn't need help with a person; he needs help with a task *(editing).* Whose editing is it? *His.* Moving on, Lincoln doesn't look forward to a person but to an action *(correcting).* Whose *correcting? Their correcting.*

52 **their.** Lincoln didn't hate the people at the agency, but he didn't love *their sending* pronoun-lovers. The possessive pronoun shifts the focus to the action, where it should be.

53 **him, her.** I snuck this one in to see if you were awake. *Lori saw him.* What was he doing? *Reading,* but the *reading* is a description tacked onto the main idea, which is that she saw *him.* A possessive isn't called for in the first part of this sentence. In the second part, what bothered Lincoln? Not the person *(she)* but the action *(her* saying that the book was "trash"). Select *her* to keep the emphasis on the action.

54 **her, her.** The objection isn't to a person *(she)* but to an action *(insisting).* I tucked one regular possessive pronoun problem into the end of the sentence, to see whether you were paying attention. Here, the ring belongs to *her.*

55 **my, my.** The point in this sentence is Lincoln's reaction to the *editing* and to the *pronouncing.* The possessive pronoun *my* keeps the reader's attention on *editing* and *pronouncing,* not on *me.*

56 **she, she.** For these implied comparisons, add the missing words. *Oscar is as careful as she is* and *he pulls out more plants than she does.*

57 **they.** Add in the implied verb (do) and you hear the answer immediately: *as they do.* The pronoun *they* is the subject of the verb *do.*

58 **we.** The *chipmunks munch more than us munch?* I don't think so! They *munch more than we munch.*

59 **I.** Tack the missing words to the end of the sentence, and you hear *than I have planted*. You need a subject (I) for the implied verb *have planted*.

60 **me.** The missing words are in the middle of the sentence. *Oscar gives more zucchini to the chipmunks than he gives to me.* The object pronoun *me* is required here.

61 **he.** How much do they enjoy veggies? *As much as he does.* The subject pronoun *he* is the one you want here.

62 **they.** *Than* begins a comparison, and *they do* finishes it. The verb *do* is implied here.

63 **she.** Once again, *than* signals a comparison. The implied verb is *does*, and *she* is its subject.

64 **their.** The plural pronoun *both* matches with the plural possessive pronoun *their*.

65 **his or her.** Technically you can answer "his best wishes" and be grammatically correct, but I always opt for the more inclusive term "his or her." Don't pair the plural *their* with the singular *everyone*.

66 **their.** The plural pronoun *many* is a good mate for the plural possessive *their*.

67 **their.** The pronoun *few* is plural, and so is *their*. What a pair!

68 **his or her.** The singular possessive *his or her* links up nicely with the singular *someone*.

69 **his or her.** Once again you're matching a possessive with the singular pronoun *everyone*.

70 **his or her.** The singular pronoun *anybody* must be paired with a singular possessive pronoun (or two, for gender fairness), so go for *his or her*.

71 **its.** Yes, the sentence refers to warts, but the *each* indicates that you're talking about one wart at a time. The singular *each* matches the singular possessive pronoun *its*.

Never confuse the possessive pronoun *its* with the shortened form of *it is* (it's). The possessive has no apostrophe.

72 **their.** The pronoun *several* moves you into plural territory, where *their* rules.

73 **he or she.** The pronoun *someone* is singular (notice the *one* inside the word?) and must pair with the singular *he or she.*

74 **his or her.** If you know that the surgeons are both men (or both women), use one of the singular pronouns (either *his* or *her*). Absent gender knowledge, go for the inclusive *his or her* (writing both singular pronouns). No matter what, don't opt for the plural *their* because *neither* is singular.

75 **it.** The singular *nothing* pairs with the singular pronoun *it* in this sentence.

76 **it.** The singular *not one* needs the singular *it*.

77 **their.** The plural pronoun *both* tells you that the girls are springing for two portraits. It also tells you that you need the plural pronoun *their*.

78 **was.** The clue here is *the only one*. Not all, or even some, sharks would take Kristin's unusual bait. *Only one was hungry enough*. The pronoun *that* is singular.

79 **was.** The pronoun *that* replaces *bait*, a singular word that must match with the singular verb *was*.

80 **likes.** Now Kristin is talking about *one shark*, and the pronoun *that* is singular.

81 **sail.** The pronoun *who* refers to *fans*, so the *who* is plural and takes a plural verb, *sail*.

82 **doesn't.** The *only* tells you that the pronoun *that* is singular and is therefore desperate for a singular verb, *doesn't*. Okay, not desperate, but you get the idea.

83 **believe.** She's not the only one; she's one out of a crowd. The people in the crowd *believe*.

84 **is.** The pronoun *that* represents *bait*, so *that* is singular and takes the singular verb *is*.

85 **were.** How many people are doubled over in mirth? Not just one. (Knowing Kristin, I'd guess thousands.) The *who* is plural, as is its verb, *were*.

86 **is.** Just one taxidermist, so singular is the way to go.

87 **are.** Strange as it may sound, more than one brand of peanut butter is shark-friendly. (No sharks were harmed in the grinding or bottling operation.) Bingo, you need a plural.

88 **advertise.** The pronoun *which* represents *manufacturers*, a plural noun that pairs with the plural verb *advertise*.

89 **are, is.** For the first parenthesis, ask yourself how many manufacturers are interested. One? More than one? Because the answer is more than one, you need a plural verb. The second choice hinges upon the meaning of *which*. Here the pronoun refers to *brand*, a singular noun, so *which* is singular, as is the verb paired with *which*.

90 **spreads.** Because *FaceNut is the only one*, you need the singular verb *spreads* to match the singular pronoun *that*.

91 **goes.** In this sentence the pronoun *which* refers to *peanut butter*, a singular noun, so *which* is singular and takes the singular verb *goes*.

92 **contain.** How many *fishcakes* contain shark meat? More than one, so the pronoun *that* is plural and pairs with the plural verb *contain*.

93 **Jeffrey jogged for an hour in an effort to work off the pounds he had gained during his last three-hour lunch, without success.** The easiest way to fix the pronoun problem (in the original sentence, *this* incorrectly refers to a complete sentence, not to a single noun) is to eliminate *this*. You can dump *this* with any number of rewrites, including the one given here.

94 **He's always admired the superhero with flat abs, but no matter how hard he tries, he can't be one.** Now the pronoun *one* refers to *superhero*. In the original, the noun *superhero* doesn't appear, just the possessive *superhero's*, which doesn't match the nonpossessive pronoun *one*.

95 **Correct.** The pronoun *that* replaces one word: *sit-ups*.

96 **The fact that Jeffrey's next fitness effort ended in disaster did not discourage him.** Eliminate the pronoun and you eliminate the problem, which is the pronoun *that*. *That* may not refer, as it does in the original sentence, to a whole sentence *(Jeffrey's next fitness effort ended in disaster)*.

97 **As a temporary solution, he simply ignored the arrest warrant and continued to run.** The pronoun *this* needs a one-word reference, but in the original, *this* replaces everything that appears before the semicolon. As usual, an easy fix is to rewrite without a pronoun.

98 **Correct.** Surprised? The pronoun *which* refers to *sonnets*. One word out and one in: You're okay.

99 **The great poet inspired Jeffrey to study poetry also.** In the original, no one can figure out what *it* means. The solution is to insert a noun *(poetry)* and dump the pronoun.

100 **"No, I did not see the car when I directed my bicycle into the street," testified Jeffrey, "but my distraction wasn't the cause of the accident."** One possible fix is to cut *that* and insert a specific. I've chosen *distraction,* but you may select *blindness, lack of awareness,* or something similar.

101 **Correct.** The pronoun *which* refers to *cellphone,* a legal use.

102 **The judge was not impressed by Jeffrey's testimony and fined him, and Jeffrey paid the $500.** Okay, pick any amount you want, so long as you dump the *it.* Why is *it* illegal? The original sentence has no *fine,* just the verb *fined.* A pronoun replaces a noun, not a verb.

103 **When Jeffrey paid the fine, he was impressed by the court clerk, who quoted Shakespeare.** The problem here is the pronoun *which*. In the original sentence, the *which* refers to the fact that the court clerk spouted sonnets while Jeffrey counted out his money. In my suggested rewrite, I drop the pronoun *which* altogether.

104 **"I see you are a sonneteer," commented Jeffrey as he smiled and gave the clerk a romantic look; she was not impressed by Jeffrey's efforts at all.** The original sentence contains a vague pronoun *(this).* You can eliminate this vagueness in a couple of different ways; just write a noun instead of *this* and you're all set.

105 — Three chaperones and ~~myself~~ I left school at 10:03 a.m. with 45 freshmen, all

106 — of ~~who~~ whom were excited about our visit to Adventure Land. The day ~~it~~ — 107

108 — passed without incident, which was a great relief to me. My friend Jim and

109 — ~~me~~ I sat in the Adventure Land Bar and Grille for five hours while the

youngsters visited Space Camp, Pirates' Mountain, and other attractions that

110 — ~~is~~ are overpriced but popular. Each of the students at my table (Alex and

111 — another boy) objected to ~~me~~ my eating such good food and said they wanted

112 — ~~one~~ some too. The bus driver and ~~myself~~ I explained that everyone was — 113

114 — supposed to eat ~~their~~ his or her school-issued lunch. This was a — 115

116 — disappointment, and the two students — Alex and ~~him~~ he — threw them at — 117

me. We got on one of the vans that ~~was~~ were overdue for maintenance. The — 118

motor whirred loudly, and it scared ~~whomever~~ whoever heard the noise. We — 120

119 — drove to Makoski Brake and Wheel Repairs because the driver said ~~their~~ its — 121

expertise was what we ~~ourselves~~ needed. Makoski is also the only one of the

122 — many repair shops on Route 9 that ~~take~~ takes credit cards, which was helpful — 124

123 — because I had spent all my money in the Adventure Land Bar and Grille.

105 The *-self* pronouns are for actions that double back on the subject or for emphasis — not the case here — so replace *myself* with *I*.

106 The preposition *of* needs an object, not a subject (like *who*). *Whom* is an object pronoun.

107 The noun *day* does all the work here, and the sentence doesn't need an extra pronoun. Delete *it*.

108 The pronoun *which* can't refer to an entire sentence, as it does in the original. Here's a better sentence: "I was relieved that the day passed without incident."

109 The pronoun *I* is for subjects, and *me* for objects.

110 The pronoun *that* refers to all the overpriced rides, so the pronoun is plural and takes the plural verb *are*.

111 The kids aren't objecting to *me* but rather to the teacher's *eating*. The possessive pronoun *my* places the emphasis where it belongs.

112 The pronoun *one* must refer to a specific item of food — a sandwich, a meal, or something similar. *Some*, on the other hand, can refer to *such good food*. Think of the sentence this way: The teacher is eating *some good food* but not *one good food*.

113 The pronoun *I* is a subject. *Myself* can receive action or double up with another pronoun for emphasis. In this sentence *myself* isn't filling either role, so it's incorrect.

114 The pronoun *everyone* is singular, and in the original it's paired with *their*, a plural. Pair *everyone* with a singular pronoun, *his or her*.

115 What was a disappointment? The whole idea — that students are supposed to eat mystery meat. But no pronoun can stand in for a subject/verb combo, so the sentence doesn't work. A better sentence would begin "They were disappointed."

116 *Alex and he* are appositives (equivalents) of *the two students*, which is the subject of the sentence. An appositive must be in the same case as the word(s) it refers to.

117 The pronoun *them* can only mean the kids' lunches, but *lunch* is in the neighborhood, not *lunches*. To correct this error, rewrite the sentence to eliminate the pronoun (which is too far away from *lunch* anyway): ". . . and threw food at me."

118 More than one van needed maintenance, so *that* is plural and so is the verb *(were)* paired with it.

119 Okay, *it* may be the motor, but the more likely meaning of this sentence is that the noise was scary, not the motor. Therefore, *it* refers to *the motor whirred loudly*. Penalty box! A pronoun shouldn't stand in for a subject/verb combo.

120 The verb *heard* needs a subject, and *whoever* is a subject pronoun.

121 The repair shop is singular, but *their*, the pronoun referring to it, is plural. Replace with the singular *its*.

122 The sentence doesn't justify emphasis, so *ourselves* is unnecessary.

123 If *only one* is in the sentence, you know that you're in singular territory. The pronoun *that* is singular and needs the singular verb *takes*.

124 Rewrite the sentence to eliminate the pronoun, because *which* must not refer to a subject/verb combination. A better version: "Because I had spent all my money, I was pleased that the garage accepted credit cards."

Chapter 10

Tensing Up: Choosing the Right Verb for Tricky Sentences

In This Chapter

▶ Choosing the proper tense to summarize speech and state unchanging facts

▶ Writing about art and literature in the proper tense

▶ Indicating timing with verbals

Did Arthur say that he *has* or *had* a cold? *Is* or *was* Mars a planet? *Did* or *does* Hamlet talk too much? And what effect do verbals — hybrid forms that are half verb, half another part of speech — have on the timing of events in a sentence? If you're sure of all these issues, drop the book and go fishing. If you're not completely certain, try your hand at the exercises on verb tense in this chapter.

Speaking of the Past and Things That Never Change

Humans love to gossip, so I bet that right now you have a story to tell. Because you're telling (actually, retelling) something that already happened, your base of operations is past tense. Note the past-tense verbs in italics:

> She *caught* Arthur with Stella, but he *told* her that he *was* only tying Stella's bow tie and not nibbling her neck. Then she *said* that Arthur *brought* her a box of candy with a note saying that no one else *had* eyes like hers.

The verb tenses are all in the past because that's where a *summary of speech* usually resides. So even if she still *has* incomparable eyes, in this paragraph the verb *had* is better. However, if you're talking about something that will never change, that is forever true, present tense is the only one that makes sense, no matter what else is going on in the sentence. Take a look at this example:

Wrong: "Marty told me that the earth was a planet."

Why it is wrong: What is the earth now, a bagel? The unchanging fact, that the earth is a planet, must be expressed in present tense, despite the fact that all other summarized speech should be in past tense.

Right: "Marty told me that the earth is a planet."

Another important exception to the stay-in-past-tense-for-speech-summary rule pops up when you're writing about a work of art or literature. See "Romeo Lives! Writing about Literature and Art in Present Tense" in this chapter for more information.

A common error is to switch from one tense to another with no valid reason. I often hear people say something like "He finally *texted me*. He *says* that the big dance *is* a waste of time!" The writer begins in past tense *(texted),* but the next two verbs *(says, is)* are in present tense. Penalty box. If you start in past tense, stay there, unless the content requires a change. The correct way to explain what went on is to say, "He finally texted me. He said the big dance was a waste of time."

Take a crack at circling the right verb from the choices in parentheses. Just to be sure you're paying attention, I sneak in a few verbs that don't summarize speech, as well as a few forever-true statements.

Q. At yesterday's tryouts for the reality show *Grammarian Idol,* Roberta (tells/told/will tell) the producer that she (likes/liked/will like) selecting pronouns while dangling 20 feet above the ground.

A. **told, liked.** The first answer is easy. If the tryouts were yesterday, the fact that Roberta lied to the producer (she actually hates pronouns) has to be in past tense. *Told* is past tense. The second part is trickier. Roberta may continue to like selecting pronouns, but past tense is the way to go, because a person's feelings can always change.

1. The director of *Grammarian Idol* explained to the candidates that he (has/had/will have) to select a maximum of 30 contestants.

2. Most of the contestants eagerly replied that they (want/wanted/would want) to make the final 30.

3. Those selected were set to compete against 14 other candidates, because the producers made two separate groups, and 15 (equals/equaled) half of 30.

4. Roberta, who (likes/like/had liked) to play hard to get, screamed at the director that he (doesn't/didn't) have the faintest idea how to select the best applicants.

5. One contestant who didn't make the cut, Michael Hooper, told me that Roberta (is/was/had been) the clear winner of the first two challenges — the noun toss and the pronoun shuffle.

6. For the first challenge, a noun, which (is/was) a word naming a person, place, thing, or idea, (is/was) thrown into a container resembling a basketball hoop.

7. During the second contest, the pronoun *I,* which (is/was) capitalized, (is/was) moved around the racetrack by contestants who (wear/wore) blindfolds.

8. Michael whispered something surprising: Roberta (fails/failed/had failed) the psychological test.

9. The test comes from Austria, which (is/was) in Europe.

10. A month ago, when the psychologist (asks/asked) Roberta her feelings about various parts of speech, Roberta said that the linking verbs (do/did) present a problem.

11. "Why (don't/didn't) you like linking verbs?" (continues/continued) the psychologist.

12. Roberta explained that any form of the verb _to be_ (annoys/annoyed) her; she also said she hated any verb she (encounters/encountered) in science class.

13. Her science teacher (is/was) not Roberta's favorite, she explained, although she (admires/admired) his vegetarian philosophy.

14. Vegetarians (don't/didn't) eat meat.

15. "I (try/tried) to avoid sentences about science," said Roberta in her interview.

16. She went on to say that adjectives (are/were/had been) her favorite part of speech.

17. The psychologist later reported that he (is/was/had been) worried about Roberta's reaction to punctuation.

18. Roberta apparently said that commas (are/were/had been) "out to get her."

19. She remarked that exclamation points (threaten/threatened/had threatened) her also.

20. An exclamation point (is/was) formed by placing a dot under a vertical line; vertical lines (run/ran) up and down, not side to side.

21. Roberta related well to the psychologist, who complained that quotation marks (hem/hemmed) him in and (make/made) him feel trapped.

22. Roberta and the psychologist disagreed, however, when Roberta said that the semicolon (is/was) the best punctuation mark.

23. The director said that he (doesn't/didn't) know what to make of Roberta's punctuation obsession.

24. He declared that she (is/was) too unstable for a show that relies heavily on question marks.

25. The assistant director, on the other hand, whispered that Roberta (is/was) faking a punctuation phobia just to attract attention.

26. "She answered only half of the questions correctly," he continued; because half of 100 (is/was) 50, Roberta (fails/failed).

27. Marty, rejected by _Grammarian Idol,_ probably won't be hired as a science teacher because he told the interviewer that each molecule of water (has/had) three oxygen atoms.

28. Science has never been Marty's best subject, as I realized when he explained that water (covers/covered) nine tenths of the planet.

29. In fact, land (makes/made) up about a quarter of the earth's surface.

30. Marty sniffed and said that he (has/had) a cold and couldn't think about the earth anyway.

Romeo Lives! Writing about Literature and Art in Present Tense

At the end of Shakespeare's *Romeo and Juliet* (spoiler alert!) the title characters die. Yet every time you open the book or go to the theater, they live again. Because the events in the book or play are always happening, present tense is generally the best choice when you're writing about literature. Not always, of course. At times you want to explain that one event in the story occurred before another. In such a situation, past tense may be the only way to talk about the earlier event. Other types of art also rely on present tense. In Picasso's famous portrait of Gertrude Stein, for example, her massive form *looks* — not *looked* — like a monument carved from a block of stone.

If you write about the act of creating art, past tense is best, as in "Picasso *painted* Gertrude Stein's portrait." (*Painted* is a past-tense verb.)

Time to tense up. In the blank, write the correct form of the verbs (actually, the infinitives, the leaders of each verb family) that appear in parentheses at the end of the sentence. To keep you off balance, I mix sentences about artworks (present tense usually preferred) with sentences about the artistic process or the artist (often in past tense). After the sample question, I base the exercise on nonexistent artworks. Have fun.

0. In Jane Austen's *Sense and Sensibility,* Marianne _____ her ankle. *(to sprain)*

A. **sprains.** To write about this event in Austen's novel, present tense is best.

31. The horizontal bands in Lola's paintings _____ random, but she _____ the width of each band using a complex formula involving horses at her local racetrack. *(to appear, to calculate)*

32. Lola, who also _____ a mystery novel, _____ a character who _____ his lunch money every day and often _____. *(to write, to create, to bet, to win)*

33. The character's name _____ William, and in every scene he _____ a hat. *(to be, to wear)*

34. William _____ the murder of a veterinarian; in one scene a parrot _____ a vital clue, but William _____ the bird perhaps because earlier the parrot _____ William. *(to investigate, to provide, to ignore, to bite)*

35. When asked about her writing, Lola _____ that William _____ loyalty, honor, and the need for a reliable birdseed provider. *(to maintain, to represent)*

36. Followers of Lola's blog _____ for years on William's fear of parrots, which they _____ "parrot-noia"; in fact, today someone _____ about that topic. *(to comment, to call, to write)*

37. The parrot _____ a poet; he _____ sonnets and sometimes _____ them loudly. *(to be, to favor, to recite)*

38. As of today Lola _____ 17 copies of her novel, which _____ place in New York City. *(to sell, to take)*

Putting Events in Order with Verbals

In Chapter 1 I explain the basic and "perfect" tenses of verbs (past, present, future, past perfect, present perfect, and future perfect). Here I drop you into a vat of boiling grammar as you choose the best tense for some complicated elements called verbals. Verbals, as the name implies, have a link with verbs, but they also have a link with other parts of speech (nouns, adjectives, and adverbs). Verbals never act as the verb in a sentence, but verbals do influence the sense of time that the sentence conveys. Keep your eye out for infinitives, participles, and gerunds — the three types of verbals.

- **Infinitives** are what you get when you add "to" to verbs. Infinitives may function as nouns or take a descriptive role. ("*To be* safe, Alice packed a few hundred rolls of breath mints." In this sentence, *to be* is an infinitive.)

- **Participles** are the *-ing* or *-ed* or *-en* form of verbs, plus a few irregulars. They're also the form of the verb that joins up with *has, have,* or *had*. Participles describe, often explaining what action someone is doing. ("*Inhaling* sharply, Elaine stepped away from the blast of peppermint that escaped from Alice's mouth." In this sentence, *inhaling* is a participle giving information about *Elaine.* The verb is *stepped.*)

- **Gerunds** are the *-ing* form of verbs, used as nouns. ("*Going* to the beach is fun." *Going* is a gerund. The verb is *is.*)

Verbals give time information. The plain form (without *has, have, having,* or *had*) shows action happening at the same time as the action expressed by the main verb in the sentence. The perfect form (with *has, have, having,* or *had*) places the action expressed by the verbal before the action of the main verb.

The tricky part about choosing either the plain or perfect form is to decide whether the events are actually simultaneous, at least in the grammatical sense. First, figure out how important the timeline is. If the events are so closely spaced so as not to matter, go for the plain form. If it matters to the reader/listener that one event followed or will follow another, go for a perfect form.

Sequence of tenses — the combination of verbs and verbals to express the order of events — is a frequent flyer on college entrance tests.

In the example and the practice exercises that follow, get out your time machine and read about a fictional tooth whitener called "GreenTeeth." The content is strange, but all you need to worry about is locating and circling the correct verbal form.

Q. (Perfecting/Having perfected) the new product, the chemists asked the boss to conduct some market research.

A. **Having perfected.** The two events occurred in the past, with the chemists' request closer to the present moment. The event expressed by the verbal (a participle, if you absolutely have to know) attributes another action to the chemists. The perfect form (created by *having*) places the act of *perfecting* prior to the action expressed by the main verb in the sentence, *asked*.

39. (Peering/Having peered) at each interview subject, the researchers checked for discoloration.

40. One interview subject shrieked upon (hearing/having heard) the interviewer's comment about "teeth as yellow as sunflowers."

41. (Refusing/Having refused) to open her mouth, she glared silently at the interviewer.

42. With the market research on GreenTeeth (completed/having been completed), the team tabulated the results.

43. The tooth whitener (going/having gone) into production, no further market research is scheduled.

44. The researchers actually wanted (to interview/to have interviewed) 50 percent more subjects after GreenTeeth's debut, but the legal department objected.

45. Additional interviews will be scheduled if the legal department succeeds in (getting/ having gotten) participants to sign a "will not sue" pledge.

46. "(Sending/Having sent) GreenTeeth to the stores means that I am sure it works," said the CEO.

47. (Deceived/Having been deceived) by this CEO several times, reporters were skeptical.

48. (Interviewing/Having interviewed) dissatisfied customers, one reporter was already planning an exposé.

49. (Weeping/Having wept), the marketing team applauded the boss's comment.

50. Next year's Product Placement Awards (being/having been) announced, the GreenTeeth team is celebrating its six nominations and looking for future dental discoveries.

Calling All Overachievers: Extra Practice with Verb Tenses

You need to know how to summarize speech, state unchangeable facts, make literary references, and create a timeline with verbals to edit this accident report, filed by a security guard. Check out the report in Figure 10-1 and circle the proper verbs or verbals in the parentheses.

GMT Industries Incident Report

Date: 8/29/10   Time: 1:10 a.m.   Place: Loading dock

(Proceeding, Having proceeded) from the locker room, I noticed smoke (coming, having come) from a doorway that leads to the loading dock. (Knowing, Having known) that no deliveries were scheduled, I immediately became suspicious. I radioed the other guard on duty, Faulkner. Faulkner, not (turning, having turned) off the television, couldn't hear me. (Screaming, Having screamed) into the radio that I needed him right away, I crept up to the door. I was so scared that I (understand, understood, had understood) how Hamlet feels when he (meets, met, had met) the ghost.

As I waited, (touching, having touched) the door to see whether it was getting hot, I sincerely wished (to find, to have found) Faulkner and (to strangle, to have strangled) him for not (replying, having replied) when I called. (Arriving, Having arrived), Faulkner apologized and explained that the show (is, was, had been) his favorite. He also said that he (has, had) a clogged ear that he (has, had) not been able to clean out, no matter how many toothpicks he (uses, used).

"(Speaking, Had spoken) of heating up," I remarked, "the door is cool." I reminded him that fire (is, was) hot, and where there's smoke (there is, there was) fire. Then Faulkner and I, (hearing, having heard) a buzz from the other side of the door, ran. I told Faulkner that the buzz (is, was) not from a bomb, but neither of us (being, having been) in the mood to take chances, we headed for the locker room. We did not put the television on again, Faulkner's show (being, having been) over for more than ten minutes. We waited for the police to arrive, (calling, having called) them some time before. We didn't hear the director yell, "Cut!" In no way did we intend (to disrupt, to have disrupted) the film crew's work or (to ruin, to have ruined) the dry ice that caused the "smoke." (Respecting, Having respected) Hollywood for many years, Faulkner and I wish Mr. Scorsese only the best with his next film.

Figure 10-1:
Sample
accident
report.

Answers to Advanced Verb Tense Problems

Now that you've seen just how tricky verbs can be, use this section to check your answers to the practice questions.

1 **had.** The tip-off is the verb *explained,* which tells you that you're summarizing speech. Go for the past tense *had.*

2 **wanted.** *Replied* is a clue that you're summarizing speech, so *wanted,* the past tense, is best. The last choice, by the way, imposes a condition (he *would* do something under certain circumstances). Because the sentence doesn't impose a condition, that choice isn't appropriate.

3 **equals.** Math doesn't change, so the verb must be in present tense.

4 **likes, didn't.** The first choice has nothing to do with summary of speech and is a simple statement about Roberta. The present tense works nicely in this spot. The second choice *is* a speech summary (well, a *scream* summary, but the same rule applies), so the past-tense verb *didn't* fills the bill.

5 **was.** The sentence tells you that *Michael Hooper told.* The past tense works here for summary of speech.

6 **is, was.** The definition of a noun won't change, so you need present tense for the first parenthesis. In the second, you're simply telling what happened on the show, so past tense rules.

7 **is, was, wore.** The rules of grammar are constant, and permanent conditions are best expressed by present tense, so *is* should be your choice in the first parenthesis. The next two verb choices require past tense because they express actions that took place in the past.

8 **failed.** You can arrive at the answer in two separate ways. If Michael *whispered,* the sentence is summarizing what he said. Another way to look at this sentence is to reason that Michael is telling you something that already happened, not something happening in the present moment. Either way, the past tense *failed* is best.

9 **is.** Austria isn't going anywhere, so this sentence expresses an unchangeable condition. Go for present tense.

10 **asked, did.** The first answer comes from the fact that the psychological test was in the past. The second is summary of speech (Roberta's words) and calls for past tense.

11 **don't, continued.** Give yourself a pat on the back if you got this one. The quotation marks indicate that the words are exactly what the psychologist said. The speech isn't summarized; it's quoted. The present tense makes sense here because the tester is asking Roberta about her state of mind at the moment. The psychologist's action, however, took place in the past, so *continued,* a past-tense verb, is what you want for the speaker tag.

12 **annoyed, encountered.** Straight summary of speech here, indicated by the verb *explained.* Therefore, past tense is best for both parentheses.

13   **was, admired.** Once again, this sentence summarizes speech and thus needs past-tense verbs.

14   **don't.** The definition of *vegetarian* is unchangeable; opt for present tense.

15   **try.** This statement isn't a summary, but rather a direct quotation from Roberta. She's speaking about her current actions, so present tense fits.

16   **were.** Roberta's comments are summarized, not quoted, so past tense is appropriate.

17   **was.** The psychologist may still be worried (I would be, if I were treating Roberta!), but the summary of what he said should be in simple past tense.

18   **were.** The parentheses contain two past-tense verbs, *were* and *had been*. The *had* form is used to place one event further in the past than another, a situation that isn't needed here, when you're simply summarizing what someone is saying and not placing events in order. Go for simple past tense.

19   **threatened.** Roberta's remark about exclamation points is summarized speech calling for past tense.

20   **is, run.** Present tense is your choice here because the description of punctuation marks doesn't change.

21   **hemmed, made.** The psychologist's comments should, like all summarized speech, be reported in simple past tense.

22   **was.** I like semicolons too, though I hesitate to say that they're the best. Whatever I say about them, however, must be summarized in simple past tense.

23   **didn't.** *The director said* is your cue to chime in with simple past tense, because you're reporting his speech.

24   **was.** *He declared* tells you that you're reporting what he said. Thus, past tense is the way to go.

25   **was.** The word *whispered* is the key here because it indicates summarized speech, which calls for simple past tense.

26   **is, failed.** Because 50 is half of 100, an unchangeable fact, you need present tense. The second part of the sentence relates what Roberta did, so past tense is best here.

27   **had.** The composition of a water molecule is a constant, but this sentence talks about what Marty said, not about an unchangeable fact. Therefore, past tense is correct here.

28   **covered.** The verb *explained* tells you that you're in summary-of-speech land, where past tense rules.

29   **makes.** The amount of land doesn't change; go with present tense.

30   **had.** Colds come and go; they aren't unchangeable conditions. The summary of speech rule doesn't change. Past tense is what you want.

31 **appear, calculated.** The first part of the sentence describes a work of art, so the present-tense verb *appear* is what you want. The second part of the sentence explains how the artwork was created, an event that took place in the past. Therefore, opt for the past-tense verb *calculated*.

32 **wrote, created, bets, wins.** The first two verbs describe the process of making art, and because the process is over, past tense works well here. The second two verbs apply to the artwork (the novel), so you need present tense.

33 **is, wears.** For these simple statements about a literary work, use present tense.

34 **investigates, provides, ignores, bit.** The first three statements are in present tense, as comments about literature and art generally are. The last verb is a little tricky; the sentence explains why William ignores the bird by citing an earlier event. Because the order of events is important, the past-tense verb *bit* is best.

35 **maintained, represents.** The verb *asked* tells you that Lola's comments also took place in the past, so the past-tense verb *maintained* is correct. The symbolic meaning, however, doesn't change and should be expressed in present tense.

36 **have commented, call, wrote.** The first choice that confronts you in this sentence is the actions of Lola's readers. Because their actions span past and present, present perfect tense is best for the first parenthesis. Moving on: The second parenthesis addresses the comments that exist on the blog. While blogs don't generally rise to the level of literature, they are written works, so present tense applies in this situation. The last part of the sentence describes what someone did in the past, so you need a past-tense verb.

37 **is, favors, recites.** These three verbs talk about events in Lola's novel, so present tense is what you need.

38 **has sold, takes.** The first part of the sentence spans past and present, and present perfect tense is (pardon the pun) perfect for that sort of situation. The novel's setting is described in present tense, because that's the tense for writing about literature.

39 **Peering.** Here the two actions take place at the same time. The researchers check out the subjects' teeth and check for trouble. The perfect form (with *having*) is for actions at different times.

40 **hearing.** Once again, two actions take place at the same time. Go for the plain form.

41 **Refusing.** The "not in this universe will I open my mouth" moment is simultaneous with an "if looks could kill" glare, so the plain form is best.

42 **having been completed.** The plain form *completed* would place two actions (the completing and the tabulating) at the same time. Yet common sense tells you that the tabulating follows the completion of the research. The perfect form (with *having*) places the completing before the tabulating.

43   **having gone.** The decision to stop market research is based on the fact that it's too late; the tooth whitener, in all its glory, is already being manufactured. Because the timeline matters here and one action is clearly earlier, the perfect form is needed.

44   **to interview.** The *have* form places the action of interviewing *before* the action expressed by the main verb in the sentence. Dump the *have* form.

45   **getting.** Three actions are mentioned in this sentence: scheduling, succeeding, and getting. The first action is placed in the future, so don't worry about it. The last two actions take place at the same time, because the minute somebody signs a legal paper, the attorneys are successful. As it expresses a simultaneous action, the plain form of the verbal (without *having*) is appropriate.

46   **Sending.** The CEO's statement places two things, sending and being sure, at the same time. Bingo: The plain form is best.

47   **Having been deceived.** The point of the sentence is that one action (deceiving the reporters) precedes another (being skeptical). You need the perfect form to make the timeline work.

48   **Interviewing.** The interviews and the planning of an exposé are simultaneous, so the plain form is best.

49   **Weeping.** The marketers are all choked up as they clap their hands and hope for a very big raise. Plain form works because the two things happen at the same time.

50   **having been.** The celebration and "time to get back to work" movement take place after the announcement, so you want the perfect tense.

GMT Industries Incident Report

Date: 8/29/10 Time: 1:10 a.m. Place: Loading dock

51 **Proceeding** from the locker room, I noticed smoke **coming** from a doorway **52**

that leads to the loading dock. **53** **Knowing** that no deliveries were scheduled, I

immediately became suspicious. I radioed the other guard on duty, Faulkner.

54 Faulkner, not **having turned** off the television, couldn't hear me. **Screaming** into **55**

the radio that I needed him right away, I crept up to the door. I was so scared that I

56 **understood** how Hamlet feels when he **meets** the ghost. **57**

58 As I waited, **touching** the door to see whether it was getting hot, I sincerely

59 wished **to find** Faulkner and **to strangle** him for not **replying** when I called. **60**

62 **Arriving**, Faulkner apologized and explained that the show **was** his favorite. He **61**

64 also said that he **had** a clogged ear that he **had** not been able to clean out, no **63**

66 matter how many toothpicks he **used**. **65**

67 "**Speaking** of heating up," I remarked, "the door is cool." I reminded him that

68 fire **is** hot, and where there's smoke **there is** fire. Then Faulkner and I, **hearing** a **70**

69 buzz from the other side of the door, ran. I told Faulkner that the buzz **was** not from **71**

72 a bomb, but neither of us **being** in the mood to take chances, we headed for the

locker room. We did not put the television on again, Faulkner's show **having been** **73**

over for more than ten minutes. We waited for the police to arrive, **having called** **74**

them some time before. We didn't hear the director yell, "Cut!" In no way did we

75 intend **to disrupt** the film crew's work or **to ruin** the dry ice that caused the **76**

77 "smoke." **Having respected** Hollywood for many years, Faulkner and I wish Mr.

Scorsese only the best with his next film.

51 The proceeding and the noticing took place at roughly the same time, so the plain form is the one you want here.

52 The noticing and the coming of the smoke were more or less simultaneous, so go for the plain form here. The perfect form would place one action earlier than another, which is contrary to the intended meaning.

53 The suspicions arose from the knowledge that no deliveries were scheduled, so the knowing and the act of suspecting are simultaneous. Use the plain verbal.

54 This sentence emphasizes the order of events. Because the television was not turned off first, Faulkner couldn't hear. The perfect form works to show an earlier action (not turning off the television).

55 The screaming and the creeping are simultaneous; go for the plain form.

56 The comment *I was so scared* is in past tense, so *understood* makes sense in the first blank.

57 The reference to literature *(Hamlet)* requires present tense.

58 The touching of the door and the waiting are simultaneous, calling for a plain (no sprinkles added) verbal.

59 The narrator *wished to find* Faulkner (everyone's looking for him, including his bookie), and the wishing and finding are more or less simultaneous. Plain form doesn't set up any special order of events.

60 The plain infinitive *to strangle* is appropriate because the narrator *wished to find and to strangle* Faulkner all at the same time. The actions are presented equally, not in time order.

61 The calling and replying are presented as simultaneous acts, so go for plain, not perfect.

62 The apologizing and the arriving are going on at the same time; a plain form is therefore best.

63 This verb expresses summarized speech, so past tense is what you want.

64 Another speech summary is expressed by this verb, so go for past tense.

65 In summarizing speech, always opt for past tense.

66 All these verbs fall into the category of summarized speech and thus take the past tense.

67 The *I* in the sentence is *speaking* now, so the plain form is needed.

68 Fire is always hot, so present tense works here.

69 This unchangeable fact (fire is never without smoke) calls for present tense.

70 These two cowards took off at exactly the same time they heard a buzz — no time lag here! The perfect form would indicate two consecutive events, but these events were simultaneous and thus need the plain form.

71 Summarized speech, indicated by *told,* calls for past tense.

72 *Being* keeps the speakers in the moment. The writer is not placing the mood before another action. Go for plain form.

73 The perfect form is appropriate because the speaker is putting events in order. First, the show ends. Second, they don't turn on the television.

74 In hopes of saving his job, the writer emphasizes the order of events, using the perfect form to place the calling of the police earlier on the timeline.

75 The intending and the disrupting are simultaneous, so plain form is best.

76 Plain form works here because the intending and the ruining occur at the same time.

77 Here the writer is emphasizing a longstanding respect for the film world. The perfect form extends the respectful feeling into the past.

Chapter 11

Are You and Your Verbs in the Right Mood?

. . . .

In This Chapter

▶ Getting a handle on verb moods for facts and commands

▶ Choosing verbs for statements, commands, and condition-contrary-to-fact sentences

. . . .

*V*erbs have mood swings. One minute they're *indicative,* the just-the-facts sort of verb. ("The dishes *are* dirty. No one *has washed* them. Little colonies of mold *grew* all over the sink.") Then they're issuing orders in *imperative* mood. ("*Wash* the dishes. *Stop* whining. *Don't think* your allowance is off limits!") Sometimes, a *subjunctive* mood pops up. ("If I *were* rich enough to hire a maid, I wouldn't ask for your dishwashing help. I'm not a millionaire, so I request that 7 p.m. *be* the official dishwashing hour.")

You don't need to know the grammatical terms; you just need to understand how to use each mood correctly. Never fear. In this chapter I take you through all three moods, with a little extra attention on the subjunctive, which is the one most likely to trip you up and to appear on standardized exams.

Indicating Facts: Indicative Mood

Just about everything I *say* about verbs in this book actually *applies* to indicative verbs, which, as the name implies, *indicate* facts. Indicative mood *is* the one you *use* automatically, stating action or being in any tense and for any person. *Do* you *want* to see some samples of indicative verbs? No problem. Every verb in this paragraph *is* in indicative mood. I *have placed* all the verbs in italics so you *can locate* them easily.

Indicative verbs change according to the time period you're talking about (the *tense*) and, at times, according to the person doing the action. I cover the basics on verb use in Chapters 1 and 2. For the pickiest (and trickiest) verb-tense issues, turn to Chapter 10.

If you're in the mood, circle the indicative verb that works best in each of the following sentences. The verb choices are in parentheses.

0. Mr. Adams (holds/held) a performance review every June.

A. **holds.** Both choices are indicative, but the present tense works better. The clue is the expression *every June.*

1. Each employee (is/was) summoned annually to Adams' office for what he calls "a little chat."

2. All the workers (know/will know) that the "chat" is all on Adams' side.

3. Adams (likes/like) to discuss baseball, the economy, and the reasons no one (will/would) receive a raise.

4. "(Is/Was) business good these days?" he always says.

5. He always (mentions/will mention) that he may have to make personal sacrifices to save the company.

6. Sacrifices! He (means/meant) that he (earns/will earn) only a million instead of two million next year!

Issuing Commands: Imperative Mood

The command, also known as the imperative mood, is fairly easy to work with because an imperative verb is the same whether you're talking to one person or 20, to a peasant or to a queen. The command form is simply the infinitive minus the *to*. In other words, the unchanged, plain form of the verb. ("*Stop* sniveling, Henry. *Pull* yourself together and *meet* your new in-laws." The command-form verbs are *stop, pull,* and *meet.*) Negative commands are slightly different. They take the infinitive-minus-*to* and add *do not.* ("*Do not mention* our engagement. *Do not let them find* out we're getting married!" *Do not mention* and *do not let* are negative commands.)

Fill in the blanks with commands for poor Henry, who is meeting his prospective in-laws. The base verb you're working with appears in parentheses at the end of each sentence.

0. _____ quietly on the couch, Henry, while I fetch Daddy. *(to sit)*

A. **Sit.** The command is formed by dropping the *to* from the infinitive.

7. Henry, _____ my lead during the conversation. *(to follow)*

8. If Mom talks about Paris, _____ your head and _____ interested. *(to nod, to look)*

9. Dad hates fake accents, so _____ French. *(to speak, negative command)*

10. _____ them to show you slides of last year's trip to Normandy. *(to ask)*

11. _____ asleep during the slide show, if you can help it! *(to fall, negative command)*

12. _____ some of Mom's potato salad, even if it's warm. *(to eat)*

13. _____ about unrefrigerated mayonnaise and the risk of food poisoning. *(to talk, negative command)*

14. When she ignores you and serves the potato salad anyway, just _____ an appointment with your doctor and _____ quiet. *(to make, to keep)*

Telling Lies or Commanding Indirectly: Subjunctive Mood

The subjunctive is a very big deal in some languages; whole terms were devoted to it in my college Spanish class. Fortunately for you, in English the subjunctive pops up only rarely, in two situations: condition-contrary-to-fact and indirect commands.

Condition-contrary-to-fact means that you're talking about something that isn't true. ("If I *were* famous, I would wear sunglasses to hide my identity." The verb *were* is subjunctive. "*Had* I *known* the secret password, I would have passed the bouncer's test and entered the club." The verb *had known* is subjunctive.)

Notice that the subjunctive changes some of the usual forms. In indicative, the pronoun *I* is paired with *was*. (See the section on indicative mood earlier in this chapter for more detail.) The switch to *were* in the first sample sentence tells you that you're in contrary-to-fact land. In the second sample sentence, the *had* doesn't do its usual indicative job, which is to place events earlier in the past than other past-tense events. (See Chapter 1 for more details on this use of *had*.) Instead, in a subjunctive sentence the *had* means that I didn't know the secret password, and I didn't socialize with sports stars and supermodels.

Condition-contrary-to-fact sentences always feature a *would* form of the verb. In Standard English, the *would* form never appears in the part of the sentence that is untrue. Don't say, "If I would have known . . ." when you didn't know. Say, "If I had known, I would have . . ."

Subjunctive verbs also express commands indirectly. ("The bouncer requested that he *remove* himself from the line as soon as possible." The verb *remove* is subjunctive. "The club owner declared that guests wearing nerdy clothes *be* denied entry." The verb *be* is subjunctive.)

Subjunctive, indirect commands are formed by dropping the *to* from the infinitive. In the first example sentence, the pronoun *he* normally (that is, in indicative mood) pairs with *removes*. In subjunctive, the infinitive *to remove* loses the *to* and becomes *remove*. In the second example, *guests* pairs with *be,* which is created by dropping *to* from the infinitive *to be*. The indicative form would be *guests are*.

Write the correct verb in the blank for each exercise in this section. The verb you're working with appears in parentheses after each sentence. Just to keep you honest, I tucked in a few sentences that don't require subjunctive. Keep your eyes open.

0. If Ellen _____ for her turn at the wheel, she wouldn't have wrapped her car around that telephone pole. *(to prepare)*

A. had prepared. The *had* creates a subjunctive here, because Ellen didn't prepare for her road test. Instead, she went to a drive-in movie, as a passenger.

15. The motor vehicle tester asked that Ellen _____ ready for her exam at 9 a.m. *(to be)*

16. The test would have gone better if Ellen _____ a morning person. *(to be)*

17. "If it _____," explained the instructor, "you will be required to take the test as soon as the roads are plowed." *(to snow)*

18. If the snow plow _____ the entire route, Ellen would have passed. *(to cover)*

19. Unfortunately, the supervisor of the snow-removal crew declared that the highways _____ cleaned first. *(to be)*

20. Terrified of ice, Ellen requested that the examiner _____ her test. *(to postpone)*

21. If he _____, Ellen would have taken the test on a sunny, warm day. *(to refuse, negative form)*

22. If Ellen _____ about the examiner, the motor vehicle department would have investigated. *(to complain)*

23. If an examiner _____ unfair, the motor vehicle department schedules another test. *(to be)*

24. The department policy is that if there _____ a valid complaint, they dismiss the examiner promptly. *(to be)*

25. If Ellen _____ the test five times already, she would have been more cheerful about her grade. *(to take, negative form)*

Calling All Overachievers: Extra Practice with Moody Verbs

If you master the three moods (cranky, irritable, ready to bite someone's head off), try your hand at this exercise. The progress report in Figure 11-1 has some serious mood problems. Check out the underlined verbs, circle the ones that are correct, and cross out and correct the ones that are in the wrong mood.

Progress Report: Coffee Break Control

From: Ms. Bell, Coffee Break Coordinator

To: Ms. Schwartz, Department Head

Re: Coffee Break Control

As you <u>know</u>, I <u>were</u> now in charge of implementing the new directive that every employee <u>submits</u> to a coffee-residue test. If a test <u>were</u> given at a time when coffee-sipping <u>were</u> not <u>authorized</u> and the results <u>were</u> positive, the policy <u>require</u> that the worker "<u>donates</u>" a pound of coffee to the break room.

<u>Do not asked</u> me to describe the union's reaction to this directive. If I <u>would tell</u> you what the shop steward <u>would have said</u>, you <u>had blushed</u>. All I <u>would say</u> is that the steward <u>were</u> not happy.

<u>Would</u> you <u>have known</u> about the reaction before issuing the directive, you <u>would have had reconsidered</u>. One more thing: the coffee stains on my shirt, if they <u>were to remain</u>, should not make you <u>thought</u> that I <u>were drinking</u> coffee outside of the official break time. These stains <u>result</u> from coffee being thrown at me.

Figure 11-1:
This progress report contains some verbs that are in the wrong mood.

Answers to Verb Mood Problems

Are you happy because you've completed all the practice questions, or are you in a snit because you want more? Either way, you, just like the verbs, are entitled to your mood. Now it's time to check your answers.

1 **is.** The sentence speaks of an ongoing situation, so present tense is best.

2 **know.** The workers have been through this "chat" many times, so the act of knowing isn't in the future but in the present.

3 **likes, will.** The present-tense form for talking about someone (*Adams,* in this sentence) is *likes.* The future-tense verb *will* explains that in the coming year, as always, employees will be shopping for bargains.

4 **Is.** The expression *these days* is a clue that you want a present-tense verb that talks about something or someone.

5 **mentions.** If an action *always* occurs, present tense is the best choice.

6 **means, will earn.** The boss is talking about the future (the clue is *next year*). The talking takes place in the present (so you want *means*), but the earning is in the future (hence, *will earn*).

7 **follow.** The command is formed by stripping the *to* from the infinitive.

8 **nod, look.** Drop the *to* and you're in charge, commanding poor Henry to act interested even if he's ready to call off the engagement rather than listen to one more story about French wine.

9 **don't speak** or **do not speak.** The negative command relies on *do* and *not,* as two words or as the contraction *don't.*

10 **Ask.** Poor Henry! He has to request boredom by dropping the *to* from the infinitive *to ask.*

11 **Do not fall.** Take *to* from the infinitive and add one *do* and *not* and you have a negative command.

12 **Eat.** Henry's in for a long evening, given the command *eat,* which is created by dropping *to* from the infinitive.

13 **Don't talk** or **Do not talk.** The negative command needs *do* or it dies. You also have to add *not,* either separately or as part of *don't.*

14 **make, keep.** Drop the *to* from each infinitive and you're in imperative mood.

15 **be.** The subjunctive is needed for this indirect command, signaled by the verb *asked.*

16 **were.** Ellen likes to sleep until midafternoon. As she's not a morning person, the subjunctive verb *were* expresses condition-contrary-to-fact. The verb *were* is better than *had been* because Ellen still *is* not a morning person, and *had been* implies that her grouchiness is in the past.

17 **snows.** Surprise! This one isn't subjunctive. The instructor is talking about a possibility, not a condition that didn't occur. The normal indicative form, *snows,* is what you want.

18 **had covered.** The plow didn't finish (the clue here is *would have passed*), so subjunctive is needed.

19   **be.** An indirect command is created by the verb *declared.* The subjunctive *be* fits nicely.

20   **postpone.** The indicative (the normal, everyday form) of *to postpone* is *postpones,* when the verb is paired with *examiner.* Here the indirect command created by *requested* calls for the subjunctive *postpone.*

21   **had not refused.** The examiner stood firm: Take the test or die. Thus the first part of this sentence is condition-contrary-to-fact and calls for the subjunctive.

22   **had complained.** Ellen said nothing, as revealed by the conditional *would have investigated* in the second part of the sentence. Subjunctive is the way to go!

23   **is.** Did I get you here? The possibility expressed in the *if* portion of the sentence calls for a normal, indicative verb *(is).* Stay away from subjunctive if the statement may be true.

24   **is.** The first part of this sentence is not condition-contrary-to-fact. It expresses a possibility and thus calls for the normal, indicative verb *(is).*

25   **had not taken.** She has taken it five times, so the statement isn't true and needs a subjunctive verb.

Progress Report: Coffee Break Control

From: Ms. Bell, Coffee Break Coordinator

To: Ms. Schwartz, Department Head

Re: Coffee Break Control

26 **27** As you **know**, I ~~were~~ **am** now in charge of implementing the new directive that

28 every employee ~~submits~~ **submit** to a coffee-residue test. If a test ~~were~~ **is** given at a **29**

30 time when coffee-sipping ~~were~~ **is** not **authorized** and the results ~~were~~ **are** positive, **31**

32 the policy ~~require~~ **requires** that the worker ~~"donates"~~ **"donate"** a pound of coffee to **33**

the break room.

Do not ~~asked~~ **ask** me to describe the union's reaction to this directive. If I ~~would tell~~

34

35 ~~were to tell~~ you what the shop steward ~~would have~~ **said**, you ~~had blushed~~ **would** **36**

37 **blush**. All I ~~would say~~ **will say** is that the steward ~~were~~ **was** not happy. **38**

~~Would~~ **Had** you ~~have~~ **known** about the reaction before issuing the directive, you **39**

40

41 **would have** ~~had~~ **reconsidered**. One more thing: the coffee stains on my shirt, if they

~~were to~~ **remain**, should not make you ~~thought~~ **think** that I ~~were drinking~~ **drank** coffee **43**

42

45 outside of the official break time. These stains **resulted** from coffee being thrown at **44**

me.

26 Correct.

27 The indicative form *(I am)* is called for here because the sentence expresses a truth, not a condition-contrary-to-fact or a command.

28 This part of the sentence expresses an indirect command, *that every employee submit.* The indicative verb that matches the singular subject *every employee* is *submits,* but the subjunctive form *(submit)* is needed here.

29 A normal indicative verb works here because possibility exists.

30 The indicative *is* works best in this sentence, which expresses a real possibility and not a condition-contrary-to-fact.

31 Because the possibility exists, the indicative is called for.

32 This statement is simply a fact, so the indicative is needed.

33 The second part of the sentence is an indirect command *(the worker donate)* and needs the subjunctive.

34 The imperative mood, the command, calls for the infinitive minus the *to.* As this is a negative command, *do not* is added. In the original, the *-ed* at the end of *ask* is wrong.

35 The writer is *not* telling, so a subjunctive verb form is needed to express a condition-contrary-to-fact.

36 The report referred to concerns what was actually *said.* Indicative rules!

37 In a sentence expressing a condition-contrary-to-fact, the "untrue" portion should be subjunctive, with the "would" statement in the other part of the sentence. This sentence reverses the proper order (and plops a correct indicative verb, *said,* in the middle). Another possible correction: "Had I told you . . . you would blush."

38 A plain indicative verb is needed for this statement.

39 The original has a subjunctive *(were)* but indicative is called for in this simple statement.

40 The sentence expresses an untruth, so you need subjunctive. The corrected sentence reads "Had you known about the reaction. . . ."

41 The original has two "would" statements. The "would" doesn't belong in the "untrue" portion of the sentence. Replace the first with a *had* statement: *Had you known.* Dump the unnecessary had from the second verb, and you're left with the correct answer: *you would have reconsidered.*

42 This sentence doesn't express a condition-contrary-to-fact. Instead, it talks about a possibility. Go with indicative, not subjunctive.

43 Stay in the indicative present here, not past.

44 Indicative past is needed here because the stains were already on the shirt. Therefore, the coffee-drinking took place in the past.

45 Go for past indicative, as the writer is talking about one event in the past.

Chapter 12

Writing for Electronic Media

In This Chapter

▶ Adapting traditional grammar rules to texts, e-mails, and blog posts

▶ Creating proper and effective presentation slides

When you and your 5,000 closest friends communicate on a social networking site, should you worry about grammar? The answer is a definite *maybe*. The new media — texts, instant messages, e-mails, blog posts, and the like — have bent some of the traditional grammar rules and even broken a few. You may be surprised to hear that I'm not tearing my hair out about these changes. In fact, I'm actually happy that more people are turning to the written word to communicate. However, some rules may be broken without creating confusion, and some may not. No matter where, when, or how you're communicating, the only rule you can never break is this one: **You must be clear.** If your reader or listener is left wondering what you mean, you've strayed too far from proper grammar.

In this chapter I explain what you can get away with — and when — and what sends you to the grammar penitentiary. I also show you the ins and outs of PowerPoint-style presentations, so you can fire off bullet points with confidence.

Knowing Your Audience: The Right Writing for the Right Situation

In some situations you may want to write informally, of course without sacrificing meaning. If you're dealing with a friend or co-worker, you can generally drop a few words and punctuation marks, especially if you're limited to 100 or so characters (letters and spaces) in your message. Your peers probably don't care about capital letters either (though in my experience every crowd has at least one stickler for the rules, and yes, I'm the stickler in *my* crowd). When you're aiming upward — writing to a boss, teacher, escape-pod leader, and the like — proper English is safest. Blog posts fall somewhere in the middle. You may want a relaxed, just-kicked-off-my-shoes tone. In that case, go for informal language. If you want readers to see you as an authority, stick with Standard English.

Most instant messages make do without a "greeting" — the *Dear Sir,* or *Hi, Pamela!* sort of comment — and a closing such as *Sincerely, Best,* and the like. E-mails usually *do* include a greeting line and a closing. Capitalize the greeting and the name, and the *first* word of the closing. If a closing (*Sincerely yours,* for example) has more than one word, capitalize the first word only.

Take a look at these excerpts from texts (notes sent via cellphone), instant messages (written, real-time "chat"), tweets (140-character messages to groups), blogs (periodic diary-like entries on the Web), and e-mails (notes sent via computer). The intended audience is identified in parentheses at the end of each. Decide whether the message is acceptable or not. If it isn't, try to figure out what changes are needed. Write "acceptable" or "unacceptable" (plus your correction) in the space provided.

Q. Luigi's 8 p.m.? Respond asap. *(Text to co-worker)*

A. Acceptable. Assuming the co-worker knows where Luigi's is located, the meaning ("Do you want to have dinner at Luigi's restaurant tonight at 8?") is clear. The abbreviation *asap* ("as soon as possible") is standard, though it's usually capitalized. Because your co-worker will probably understand the entire message, you're fine.

1. i cooked three chickens tonight and im now on p 5567 of How to Cook Everything. It was terible. Don't ever put a sardine near a chicken ever. *(blog post from cookbook reviewer)* _____

2. Met client. Deal okay if shipping included. Your thoughts? *(text to boss)*

_____

3. Tell your representative to vote no on the bill to ban toothpaste. Defy the dental lobby! *(tweet to voters from lobbyist)* _____

4. Mr. Smarva, sorry, can't hand in my homework my cat ate it I'll do better tomorrow From Leo *(e-mail to teacher)* _____

5. Judging from the horizontal strips of some metallic substance and the marks of a crude pickax, this archaeological site was a prehistoric mine. *(blog post from archaeologist)*

_____

6. dude, can't come now maybe later *(instant-message to friend)* _____

7. ctn prof here ttyl *(text to close friend)* _____

8. Hi, Grandpa. The speaker was great. Thanks for arranging her visit.
Best,
Alice
(e-mail to relative) _____

9. Blue Beak's last set was a screech, seriously, where do they find those notes. *(post on a music blog)* _____

10. tlion for 9s only *(tweet to high school students)* _____

Shortening Your Message

A character in Shakespeare's *Hamlet* proclaims that "brevity is the soul of wit." It's also the soul of most new media. Maybe because electronic media zings words back and forth quickly, readers expect to get the point fast. Whatever the reason, you need to know how to say more with fewer words when you text, send an instant message, or tweet (send a 140-character message).

In this section I explain how to cut away elements of Standard English. Before you cut, be sure to consider the identity of the person reading your message. The preceding section, "Knowing Your Audience: The Right Writing for the Right Situation," explains when you can break grammar rules. This section concentrates on how a message may be shortened.

Here are some guidelines for the chopping block:

- **Consider dropping the subject.** If I type "attended meeting," you can probably figure out that *I* attended the meeting. If someone else went, you should include the name ("Bob attended meeting") unless the reader knows whom you're discussing.

- **You can usually drop articles.** *A, an,* and *the* are seldom important.

- **Use abbreviations, but carefully.** Some abbreviations (such as *FYI* for "for your information") are commonly known, but others (*F2F* for "face to face") may mystify readers who don't frequent social-networking sites. Think about your reader as you type an abbreviation. When in doubt, write the whole word.

- **Never drop punctuation that adds meaning.** If you type, "Deal?" you're asking someone to commit. "Deal" either conveys information ("I agree to your terms") or gives a command ("deal with it"). The question mark makes a difference.

Sharpen your knife and whittle down these messages so that they're short but understandable. Assume that you are writing to a co-worker or friend and that your goals are accuracy, clarity, and brevity. I provide one possible answer for each message; your own response may differ, but check the explanation to see whether you missed anything.

Q. I don't know what you mean about Lola. _____

A. **Lola — meaning?** or **Lola?** These two words and a question mark are probably enough to convey the confusion. If you're writing to a friend who understands you well, **Lola?** may be enough.

11. You should know that Lola is in jail and needs ten thousand dollars in bail. She was arrested for driving without a license. She needs your help.

_____

_____

12. Her lawyer is hopeful that Lola will be sentenced to probation and community service.

_____

13. Lulu will visit Lola as soon as possible. Lulu will probably arrive at the jail around noon.

_____

14. The bad news for Lola is that the judge, Larry Saunders, was once flattened by a motorcycle. He's bitter and will probably throw the book at Lola because she was riding a motorcycle when she was arrested.

_____

_____

15. Lola claimed that her license had been shredded when she washed her jeans.

_____

16. Will you attend the press conference when Lola is released?

_____

Powering Up Your Presentation Slides

Do you spend your days dodging bullets? I'm not talking about target practice but rather the little round dots, stars, or checkmarks that create lists in PowerPoint-style presentation slides and in other spots (memos, for example). If you are dodging bullets, it may be because you're not sure what to capitalize and where to place punctuation marks. To help you, here are some bullet points on bullet points:

- **A title or introductory sentence should precede every list.** Notice that _this_ list is set up by a sentence (_To help you, here are some bullet points on bullet points_).

- **Titles should be centered and capitalized.** The rules for capitals are in Chapter 8. Don't place quotation marks around a centered title. Also, avoid full-sentence titles.

- **Introductory sentences, if complete, may end with a colon.** A colon (one dot on top of another) sets up this bulleted list. Don't place a colon in a partial sentence, such as "Projected earnings for 2018 are." Omit punctuation entirely after that sort of introduction.

- **If the bullet point is a complete sentence, capitalize the first word and use an end-mark (period, question mark, exclamation point).** The bullet points in this list are complete sentences, so they follow this rule.

➤ **If the bullet point isn't a complete sentence, don't capitalize the first word or use an endmark.** This sort of list often follows an introductory statement that isn't a complete sentence.

➤ **Grammatically, every bullet point should match.** If one bullet point is a complete sentence, all the bullet points should be complete sentences. Or, all the bullet points may be phrases. In grammar terms, the items should be *parallel*. I discuss parallel structure in detail in Chapter 16.

Time to target some bullet points. Below are some sample "slides" from a presentation, without capital letters or punctuation. Add capital letters and punctuation where needed. If the items on the list have matching grammatical structures, add or delete words to make the items parallel.

Q.

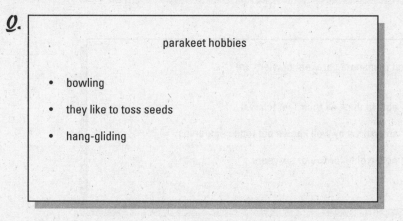

> parakeet hobbies
>
> • bowling
>
> • they like to toss seeds
>
> • hang-gliding

A. **Capitalize *Parakeet* and *Hobbies*. Change the second bullet point to "seed-tossing."** Did you notice the absence of punctuation? The title stands alone, and the items on the list aren't complete sentences. No punctuation is needed.

17.

> parakeets need the following items for bowling
>
> • three-toed bowling shoes
>
> • beak-adapted bowling balls
>
> • featherweight pins

18.

the best-selling bowling shoes for parakeets have

- they have room for overgrown claws

- most are in brightly colors

- many include a complimentary seed stick

- they have clips rather than laces

19.

most prominent parakeet bowlers are

- able to think on their feet (claws)

- sponsored by well known pet food companies

- active only for five or six years

20.

history of parakeet bowling

- the sport began in the 15th century

- early bowlers used apples to knock down corn stalks

- first professional tour — 1932

Calling All Overachievers: Extra Practice with Electronic Media

The employee who created the slide presentation in Figure 12-1 slept through every single grammar lesson she ever had. Now it's up to you to correct her errors. You should find ten mistakes.

Figure 12-1: This presentation needs some grammatical help.

> ### Best careers for Parakeets; paper Shredder
>
> - Every bird earns a good salary
>
> - excellent working conditions
>
> - Each bird has an assistant and
>
> - the veterinary insurance plan has a low deductible
>
> - Seed breaks once an hour.

Answers to Electronic Media Problems

New forms of communication often bring new rules. See if you understand the grammar of electronic media by checking your answers here.

1 **Unacceptable.** No matter who your reader is, you should avoid incorrect spelling *(terible)*. Also, why lowercase the personal pronoun *I?* It's not much harder or time-consuming to add an apostrophe to *I'm.* Finally, you shouldn't repeat (delete one *ever*).

2 **Acceptable.** You don't have to write, "I met with the client, and the deal is okay with the client if we include shipping in the price we quoted. What do you think?" All those ideas come through in the shorter version.

3 **Acceptable.** The meaning is clear, and because the lobbyist wants to convince voters that his or her ideas are the product of an intelligent being, proper grammar and spelling are a plus.

4 **Unacceptable.** If Leo seriously wants to be excused for missing a homework assignment, he should unearth every bit of grammar knowledge he has. Here's a possible correction:

> Dear Mr. Smarva,
>
> I am sorry that I can't hand in my homework. I did the assignment, but my cat ate it. I'll hand in the work tomorrow.
>
> Sincerely,
>
> Leo

5 **Acceptable.** Good grammar is appropriate here, as the professional posting it wants to be taken seriously by the academic community — the most likely readers.

6 **Acceptable.** Surprised? Yes, I'd be happier with capitals for *dude* and *maybe,* with a period after *now.* But if you're writing to someone you know well enough to call *Dude* (or *dude*), the caps and periods don't really matter.

7 **Acceptable.** If you text a close friend, you probably know already that he or she will understand the abbreviations for "can't talk now" (ctn), "professor" (prof), and "talk to you later" (ttyl). Although this message is (in my opinion), hanging by its fingernails onto the cliff of acceptability, it does get the point across. Just be sure never to write something like this to someone who may misunderstand the abbreviations.

8 **Acceptable.** The punctuation is in the correct places, and the sentences make sense. Grandpa will be proud.

9 **Unacceptable.** If you want readers to heed your reviews, you need their respect. You can get away with this run-on sentence if you're a famous musician, but ordinary writers should try changing the comma after *screech* to a period, capitalizing *seriously,* and substituting a question mark for the period after *notes.*

10 **Unacceptable.** If you read the answer to Question 7, you may have assumed that a tweet to teens can include all sorts of abbreviations. But *tlion* is an abbreviation I made up. Inside my head. Just me! It means "the library is open now." Because no one could possibly know the meaning, the message isn't acceptable. Remember: Clarity is crucial.

11 **FYI: Lola in jail. Driving w/o a license. Needs $10K bail. Help!** The abbreviation *FYI* ("for your information") is standard, as is *w/o* ("without") and *K* ("thousand"). The last sentence is clearly a plea. Lola will probably make another plea when she sees the judge.

12 **Lawyer hopeful for probation + community service.** I wouldn't mind cutting the *for,* but with that word the message sounds a little more respectable (not like Lola). The plus sign could also be an ampersand (&) or the word *and.*

13 **Lulu to visit Lola asap, probably 12 p.m.** The standard abbreviation for "as soon as possible" is *ASAP,* but you don't really need the capital letters here. You could also cut *p.m.* from the message if you wish, as it's unlikely that a jail would allow visitors at midnight.

14 **Judge Saunders bad news for Lola b/c bitter about motorcycles after accident. Big penalty probable for L's motorcycle arrest.** The abbreviation *b/c* ("because") is standard, though you wouldn't use it for formal writing. Notice that I deleted the verbs because the meaning comes through without them. I also substituted *big penalty probable* for the longer *will probably throw the book at Lola.*

15 **Lola claimed license shredded in wash.** Isn't it fun to put your sentences on a diet? (Much more enjoyable than the other sort of diet.) Here you have all the information you need at half the length.

16 **Attend press conference on release?** This answer assumes that the reader knows you're writing about Lola. If not, more words are needed to clarify the situation. The question mark takes the place of *will you.*

17 **Capitalize *Parakeets.* Place a colon (:) at the end of the introductory statement.** Because the introductory statement is a complete sentence, it should begin with a capital letter and end with a colon, which indicates that a list follows.

18 **Capitalize *The* in the introductory statement. Change the bullet points so that each completes the sentence begun in the introductory statement.** The first word of the introductory statement needs a capital letter. No punctuation follows *have* because the statement isn't a complete sentence. In the original list each item is a complete sentence, so they don't combine well with the introductory statement. *The best bowling shoes for parakeets have they have room* . . . nope, I don't think so. The bullets should be *room for overgrown claws, bright colors, complimentary seed sticks,* and *clips rather than laces.*

19 **Capitalize *Most.*** Did I catch you with this one? No punctuation is needed because *are* doesn't complete the introductory sentence. Nor should you capitalize any of the bullet points, as they complete the sentence begun by the introductory statement. The only change is a capital *M* for the first word in the introductory sentence.

20 **Capitalize each word in the title except for *of*. Capitalize the first word of each bullet point and end each bullet point with a period. Change the last bullet point to a complete sentence.** This slide has a title, and titles need capital letters. The first two bullet points are complete sentences, so the third should match. One possible change: *The first professional tour took place in 1932.* Each bullet point should begin with a capital letter and end with a period.

21 — Best ~~c~~Careers for Parakeets~~:~~: ~~p~~Paper Shredder — 23
22 —

- Every bird earns a good salary~~.~~ — 24

- **All birds have** excellent working conditions~~.~~ — 26
25 —

- Each bird has an assistant~~.~~ ~~and~~ — 27

28 —
- ~~t~~The veterinary insurance plan has a low deductible~~.~~ — 29

30 —
- Seed breaks **are given** once an hour.

21 Capitalize the important words in a title. (See Chapter 8 for details.)

22 Separate a title from a subtitle with a colon (:).

23 Capitalize the first word of a subtitle.

24 Always place an endmark after a full-sentence bullet point; here a period is best.

25 The first bullet point is a complete sentence, so all the bullet points should also be complete sentences. (Alternate correction: Change all the bullet points to phrases.)

26 A complete sentence that makes a statement ends with a period.

27 One bullet point should not continue on to the next. Delete *and* and place a period at the end of this sentence.

28 This bullet point is a complete sentence, so it should begin with a capital letter.

29 This complete sentence needs an endmark — specifically, a period.

30 The original bullet point was not a complete sentence. To preserve uniformity, change this bullet point to a complete sentence by adding a verb.

Part IV
Upping the Interest: Describing and Comparing

The 5th Wave   By Rich Tennant

@RICHTENNANT

TECHNICAL DOCUMENTATION DEPT

"Hey, Al! Do we hyphenate 'Doo Hickey'?"

In this part . . .

Listen to a little kid and you hear language at its most basic: *Elizabeth want apple. Daddy go store? No nap!* These "sentences" — nouns and verbs and little else — communicate effectively, but everyone who's passed the sandbox stage needs a bit more. Enter descriptions and comparisons. Also enter complications, because quite a few common errors are associated with these elements.

In this part you can practice your navigation skills, steering around such pitfalls as the choice between adjectives, adverbs, and articles. (*Sweet* or *sweetly? Good* or *well? A* or *an?* Chapter 13 explains all.) This part also tackles the placement of descriptions (Chapter 14) and the proper way to form comparisons (Chapter 15). Mastering all these topics lifts you out of the sandbox and places you permanently on the highest grammatical level.

Chapter 13

Writing Good or Well: Adjectives and Adverbs

Do you write *good* or *well* — and what's the difference? Does your snack break feature *a apple* or *an apple* or even *the apple?* If you're stewing over these questions, you have problems . . . specifically, the problems in this chapter. Here you can practice choosing between two types of descriptions, adjectives and adverbs. This chapter also helps you figure out whether *a, an,* or *the* is appropriate in any given situation.

Putting Adjectives and Adverbs in Their Places

In your writing or speaking, of course, you don't need to stick labels on adjectives and adverbs. But you do need to send the right word to the right place in order to avoid arrest by the grammar police. A few wonderful words (*fast, short, last,* and *likely,* for example) function as both adjectives and adverbs, but for the most part, adjectives and adverbs are not interchangeable.

Adjectives describe nouns — words that name a person, thing, place, or idea. They also describe pronouns, which are words that stand in for nouns (*other, someone, they,* and similar words). Adjectives usually precede the word they describe, but not always. In the following sentence the adjectives are italicized:

> The *rubber* duck with his *lovely orange* bill sailed over the *murky bath* water. *(Rubber* describes *duck; lovely* and *orange* describe *bill; murky* and *bath* describe *water.)*

An adverb, on the other hand, describes a verb, usually telling how, where, when, or why an action took place. Adverbs also indicate the intensity of another descriptive word or add information about another description. In the following sentence the adverbs are italicized:

> The alligator snapped *furiously* as the duck *violently* flapped his wings. *(Furiously* describes *snapped; violently* describes *flapped.)*

Most adverbs end in *-ly*, but some adverbs vary, and adjectives can end with any letter in the alphabet, except maybe *q*. If you're not sure which form is an adjective and which is an adverb, check the dictionary. Most definitions include both forms with handy labels telling you what's what.

Here I hit you with a description dilemma: Which word is correct? The parentheses contain both an adjective and an adverb. Circle your selection.

0. The water level dropped (slow/slowly), but the (intense/intensely) alligator-duck quarrel went on and on.

A. **slowly, intense.** How did the water drop? The word you want from the first parentheses must describe an action, so the adverb *slowly* wins the prize. Next up is a description of a *quarrel,* a thing, so the adjective *intense* does the job.

1. The alligator, a (loyal/loyally) member of the Union of Fictional Creatures, (sure/surely) resented the duck's presence near the drainpipe.

2. "How dare you invade my (personal/personally) plumbing?" inquired the alligator (angry/ angrily).

3. "You don't have to be (nasty/nastily)!" replied the duck.

4. The two creatures (swift/swiftly) circled each other, both looking for a (clear/clearly) advantage.

5. "You are (extreme/extremely) territorial about these pipes," added the duck.

6. The alligator retreated (fearful/fearfully) as the duck quacked (sharp/sharply).

7. Just then a (poor/poorly) dressed figure appeared in the doorway.

8. The creature whipped out a bullhorn and a sword that was (near/nearly) five feet in length.

9. When he screamed into the bullhorn, the sound bounced (easy, easily) off the tiled walls.

10. "Listen!" he ordered (forceful/forcefully). "The alligator should retreat (quick/quickly) to the sewer and the duck to the shelf."

11. Having given this order, the (Abominable/Abominably) Snowman seemed (happy/happily).

12. The fight in the bathtub had made him (real/really) angry.

13. "You (sure/surely) can't deny that we imaginary creatures must stick together," explained the Snowman.

14. Recognizing the (accurate/accurately) statement, the duck apologized to the alligator.

15. The alligator retreated to the sewer, where he found a (lovely/lovingly) lizard with an urge to party.

16. "Come (quick/quickly)," the alligator shouted (loud/loudly) to the duck.

17. The duck left the tub (happy/happily) because he thought he had found a (new/newly) friend.

18. The alligator celebrated (noisy/noisily) because he had discovered an enemy (dumb/dumbly) enough to enter the sewer, the alligator's turf.

19. "Walk (safe/safely)," murmured the gator, as the duck entered a (particular/particularly) narrow tunnel.

20. The duck waddled (careful/carefully), beginning to suspect (serious/seriously) danger.

How's It Going? Choosing Between Good/Well and Bad/Badly

For some reason, the "judgment" adjective and adverb pairs (*good* and *well, bad* and *badly)* cause a lot of trouble. Here's a quick guide on how to use them. *Good* and *bad* are adjectives, so they have to describe nouns — people, places, things, or ideas. ("I gave a *good* report to the boss." The adjective *good* describes the noun *report.* "The *bad* dog snarfed up an entire bag of kibble this morning." The adjective *bad* describes the noun dog.) *Well* and *badly* are adverbs used to describe action. ("In my opinion, the report was particularly *well* written." The adverb *well* describes the verb *written.* "The dog slept *badly* after his kibble-fest.") The adverb *badly* describes the verb *slept.)* *Well* and *badly* also describe other descriptions. In the expression *a well-written essay,* for example, *well* describes *written,* which describes *essay.*

Well can be an adjective in one particular circumstance: health. When someone asks how you are, the answer (I hope) is "I am well" or "I feel well." You can also — and I hope you do — feel *good,* especially when you're talking about your mental state, though this usage is a bit more informal. Apart from health questions, however, *well* is a permanent member of the adverb team. In fact, if you can insert the word *healthy* in a particular spot, *well* works in the same spot also.

When a description follows a verb, danger lurks. You have to decide whether the description gives information about the verb or about the person/thing who is doing the action or is in the state of being. If the description describes the verb, go for an adverb. If it describes the person/thing (the subject, in grammatical terms), opt for the adjective.

Put on your judge's robes and circle the right word in each set of parentheses.

Q. The trainer works (good/well) with all types of dogs, especially those that don't outweigh him.

A. **well.** How does the trainer work? The word you need must be an adverb because you're giving information about an action (work), not a noun.

21. My dog Truffle barks when he's run (good/well) during his daily race with the letter carrier.

22. The letter carrier likes Truffle and feels (bad/badly) about beating him when they race.

23. Truffle tends to bite the poor guy whenever the race doesn't turn out (good/well).

24. Truffle's owner named him after a type of chocolate candy she thinks is (good/well).

25. The letter carrier thinks high-calorie snacks are (bad/badly).

26. He eats organic sprouts and wheat germ for lunch, though his meal tastes (bad/badly).

27. Truffle once caught a corner of a dog-food bag and chewed off a (good/well) bit.

28. Resisting the urge to barf, Truffle ate (bad/badly), according to his doggie standards.

29. Truffle, who didn't feel (good/well), barked quite a bit that day.

30. Tired of the din, his owner confiscated the kibble and screamed, "(Bad/Badly) dog!"

Mastering the Art of Articles

Three little words — *a, an,* and *the* — pop up in just about every English sentence. Sometimes (like my relatives) they show up where they shouldn't. Technically, these three words are adjectives, but they belong to the subcategory of articles. As always, forget about the terminology. Just know how to use them:

- ✔ *The* refers to something specific. When you say that you want *the book,* you're implying one particular text, even if you haven't named it. *The* attaches nicely to both singular and plural words.

- ✔ *A* and *an* are more general in meaning and work only with singular words. If you want *a book,* you're willing to read anything. *A* precedes words beginning with consonants, and *an* comes before words beginning with vowels *(a book, an encyclopedia). An* also precedes words that sound as if they begin with a vowel *(hour,* for example) because the initial consonant is silent.

If you want a general term but you're talking about a plural, try *some* or *any* instead of *a* or *an,* because these last two articles can't deal with plurals.

Write an article covering the finale of *Grammarian Idol* — oops, wrong type of article. Write the correct article in each blank in the sentences that follow.

Q. When Lulu asked to see _____ wedding pictures, she didn't expect Annie to put on _____ twelve-hour slide show.

A. **the, a.** In the first half of the sentence, Lulu is asking for something specific. Also, *wedding pictures* is a plural expression, so *a* and *an* are out of the question. In the second half of the sentence, something more general is appropriate. Because *twelve* begins with the consonant *t, a* is the article of choice.

31. Although Lulu was mostly bored out of her mind, she did like _____ picture of Annie's Uncle Fred snoring in the back of the church.

32. _____ nearby guest, one of several attempting to plug up their ears, can be seen poking Uncle Fred's ribs.

33. At Annie's wedding, Uncle Fred wore _____ antique bow tie that he bought in _____ department store next door to his apartment building.

34. _____ clerk who sold _____ tie to Uncle Fred secretly inserted _____ microphone and _____ miniature radio transmitter.

35. Uncle Fred's snores were broadcast by _____ obscure radio station that specializes in embarrassing moments.

36. Annie, who didn't want to invite Uncle Fred but was forced to do so by her mother, placed _____ buzzer under his seat.

37. Annie's plan was to zap him whenever he snored too loudly; unfortunately, Fred chose _____ different seat.

Hyphenating Descriptions

A hyphen (a short, horizontal line) links two or more words to make one description preceding the word being described (*second-base* error, *Hall-of-Fame* catcher). But when the first word in a multiword description ends in *-ly*, no hyphen appears (*completely ridiculous* umpire).

Hyphen rules vary. Before you decide whether to hyphenate or not, check with your Authority Figure (teacher, boss, judge, whatever) to determine the preferred style.

Are you in the mood to hyphenate? Circle the correct form from the parentheses.

0. The boss demanded a new (home plate/home-plate) umpire.

A. **home-plate.** The words *home* and *plate* combine to describe *umpire*.

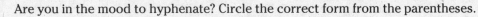

38. The (truly sorry/truly-sorry) player offered to practice a half hour more each day.

39. "I think (two thirds/two-thirds) of an hour is better," said the boss.

40. "My (player improvement/player-improvement) plan calls for increased practice," he added.

41. A (lost ball/lost-ball) mistake is common on sunny days.

42. A (stadium wide/stadium-wide) policy requires fans to wear protective helmets.

43. The (name brand/name-brand) helmets have (built in/built-in) radios tuned to the game.

44. Because of (poorly fielded/poorly-fielded) stray balls, fans must pay attention to the (on field/on-field) action.

Calling All Overachievers: Extra Practice with Descriptors

Show off the knowledge you gained from the sections in this chapter by finding the mistakes in this excerpt from a dress catalogue (see Figure 13-1). Twenty descriptive words are underlined, but only some of them are wrong. Look for adjectives trying to do an adverb's job (and vice versa), the wrong sort of articles, and descriptions that need to add or shed hyphens. When you find an error, correct it. If the description is okay, leave it alone.

Dollars' Clothing: Fashions That Work

A–D. <u>Surprising</u> <u>comfortably</u> suits for work and leisure. <u>Easily</u>-to-clean polyester in <u>real</u> varied colors goes from the <u>office</u> grind to the <u>extreme</u> <u>bright</u> club scene without a pause!

A. <u>Fast</u> <u>track</u> jacket. Stun your co-workers with <u>a</u> <u>astonishingly</u> elegance of <u>deeply</u> eggplant. <u>Gently</u> curves follow <u>an</u> <u>real</u> natural outline to accentuate your figure. The <u>silkily</u> lining, in <u>delightful</u> loud shades of orange, gives <u>a</u> <u>strong</u> message: I am woman! Hear me roar!

B. <u>Softly</u>, woven pants coordinate with <u>a</u> jacket described above — and with everything in your wardrobe. In eggplant, orange, or eggplant-orange plaid.

Figure 13-1:
Sample dress-catalogue exercise.

Answers to Adjective and Adverb Problems

I hope the challenging exercises in this short chapter on descriptive words didn't give you too much trouble. Find out how you did by comparing your work to the following answers.

1 **loyal, surely.** What kind of member is the alligator? A *loyal* member. Because you're describing a noun *(member)*, you need the adjective *loyal*. In the second part of the sentence, the adverb *surely* explains how the duck's presence was *resented*. *Resented* is a verb and must be described by an adverb.

2 **personal, angrily.** In the first part of the sentence, personal describes a thing *(plumbing)*. How did the alligator inquire? *Angrily*. The adverb tells about the verb, *inquire*.

3 **nasty.** The adjective *nasty* describes *you*. Of course I don't mean you, the reader. You earned my undying affection by buying this book. The *you* in the sentence is *nasty*!

4 **swiftly, clear.** The adverb *swiftly* describes the action of *circling*. The adjective *clear* explains what kind of *advantage* the creatures were seeking.

5 **extremely.** The adverb *extremely* clarifies the intensity of the descriptive word *territorial*. (If you absolutely have to know, *territorial* is an adjective describing you.)

6 **fearfully, sharply.** Both of these adverbs tell how the actions *(retreated* and *quacked)* were performed.

7 **poorly.** The adverb *poorly* gives information about the descriptive word *dressed*.

8 **nearly.** This was a tough question, and if you got it right, treat yourself to a spa day. The expression *five feet* is a description of the *sword*. The adverb *nearly* gives additional information about the description *five feet in length*.

9 **easily.** The adverb *easily* describes the verb *bounced*.

10 **forcefully, quickly.** The adverb *forcefully* tells how he *ordered,* a verb. The adverb *quickly* describes how the *alligator should retreat.*

11 **Abominable, happy.** You can cheat on the first part of this one just by knowing the name of the monster that supposedly stalks the Himalayas, but you can also figure out the answer using grammar. A *snowman* is a thing (or a person) and thus a noun. Adjectives describe nouns, so *abominable* does the trick. In the second half you need an adjective to describe the *snowman,* who was *happy*. You aren't describing the action of seeming, so an adverb isn't correct.

12 **really.** This sentence presents two commonly confused words. Because *angry* is an adjective, you need an adverb to indicate its intensity, and *really* fills the bill.

13 **surely.** That horse in the fifth race might be a *sure thing,* because *thing* is a noun and you need an adjective to describe it. But the verb *deny* must be described by an adverb, so *surely* is the one you want.

14 **accurate.** *Statement* is a noun that must be described by the adjective *accurate.*

15 **lovely.** A *lizard* is a noun, which may be described by the adjective *lovely* but not the adverb *lovingly*. Incidentally, *lovely* isn't an adverb, despite the fact that it ends with *-ly.*

16 **quickly, loudly.** The adverb *quickly* describes the verb *come,* and the adverb *loudly* describes the verb *shouted.*

17 **happy, new.** This sentence presents a puzzle. Are you talking about the duck's mood or the way in which he left the tub? The two are related, of course, but the mood is the primary meaning, so the adjective *happy* is the better choice to describe *duck*. The adjective *new* describes the noun *friend*.

18 **noisily, dumb.** The adverb *noisily* tells you how the alligator *celebrated*. Because *celebrated* is a verb, you need an adverb. The adjective *dumb* tells you about the noun *enemy*. Most, but not all, adjectives are in front of the words they describe, but in this case the adjective follows the noun.

19 **safely, particularly.** The adverb *safely* tells you about the verb *walk*. The second answer is also an adverb, because *particularly* explains how *narrow* the tunnel is.

20 **carefully, serious.** The adverb *carefully* explains how the duck *waddled,* and *waddled* is a verb. *Danger,* a noun, is described by the adjective *serious*.

21 **well.** The adverb *well* tells you how Truffle *has run.*

22 **bad.** This sentence illustrates a common mistake. The description doesn't tell you anything about the letter carrier's ability to *feel* (touching sensation). Instead, it tells you about his state of mind. Because the word is a description of a person, not of an action, you need an adjective, *bad. To feel badly* implies that you're wearing mittens and can't *feel* anything through the thick cloth.

23 **well.** The adverb *well* describes the action *to turn out* (to result).

24 **good.** What is her opinion of chocolate truffles? She *thinks* they are *good.* The adjective is needed because you're describing the noun *candy.*

25 **bad.** The description *bad* applies to the *snacks,* not to the verb *are.* Hence, an adjective is what you want.

26 **bad.** The description tells you about his *meal,* a noun. You need the adjective *bad.*

27 **good.** The adjective *(good)* is attached to a noun *(bit).*

28 **badly.** Now you're talking about the action *(ate),* so you need an adverb *(badly).*

29 **well.** The best response here is *well,* an adjective that works for health-status statements. *Good* will do in a pinch, but *good* is better for psychological or mood statements.

30 **Bad.** The adjective *bad* applies to the noun *dog.*

31 **the.** The sentence implies that one particular picture caught Lulu's fancy, so *the* works nicely here. If you chose *a,* no problem. The sentence would be a bit less specific but still acceptable. The only true clinker is *an,* which must precede words beginning with vowels — a group that doesn't include *picture.*

32 **A.** Because the sentence tells you that several guests are nearby, *the* doesn't fit here. The more general *a* is best.

33 **an or the, the.** In the first blank you may place either *an* (which must precede a word beginning with a vowel) or *the.* In the second blank, *the* is best because it's unlikely that Fred is surrounded by several department stores. *The* is more definitive, pointing out one particular store.

34 **The, the, a, a.** Lots of blanks in this one! The first two seem more particular (one *clerk,* one *tie*), so *the* fits well. The second two blanks imply that the clerk selected one from a group of many, not a particular microphone or transmitter. The more general article is *a,* which precedes words beginning with consonants.

35 **an.** Because the radio station is described as *obscure,* a word beginning with a vowel, you need *an,* not *a.* If you inserted *the,* don't cry. That article works here also.

36 **a.** The word *buzzer* doesn't begin with a vowel, so you have to go with *a,* not *an.* The more definite *the* could work, implying that the reader knows that you're talking about a particular buzzer, not just any buzzer.

37 **a.** He chose any old seat, not a particular one, so *a* is what you want.

38 **truly sorry.** These two words don't combine to form one, united description. Instead, *truly* tells you the intensity of *sorry.* Verdict: no hyphen here!

39 **two thirds.** Here's the deal on fractions: When they attach to a noun, they take a hyphen *(two-thirds majority).* When they precede *of,* they shouldn't be hyphenated. Hence your answer: *two thirds.*

40 **player-improvement.** These two words combine to form one description, so a hyphen is appropriate.

41 **lost-ball.** What kind of *mistake* is *common?* A *lost-ball mistake.* The combination works together, as the hyphen indicates.

42 **stadium-wide.** Here these two words indicate one sort of *policy,* and the hyphen unites them.

43 **name-brand, built-in.** You need hyphens here because the two words of each description combine to tell the reader one fact about the *helmets* and the *radios.*

44 **poorly fielded, on-field.** When the first word of a two-word description ends in *-ly,* you don't need a hyphen, so *poorly fielded* needs no punctuation. However, *on-field* is a different story. Those two words equal one description, so the hyphen is appropriate.

Dollars' Clothing: Fashions That Work

45/46 A–D. ~~Surprising~~ Surprisingly ~~comfortably~~ comfortable suits for work and leisure.

47/48 ~~Easily~~ Easy-to-clean polyester in ~~real~~ really varied colors goes from the

49/50/51 office grind to the ~~extreme~~ extremely bright club scene without a pause!

52/53 A. **Fast-track** jacket. Stun your co-workers with ~~a~~ the

54/55 ~~astonishingly~~ astonishing elegance of ~~deeply~~ deep eggplant.

56/58 ~~Gently~~ Gentle curves follow ~~an a~~ ~~real~~ really natural outline to accentuate your figure.

57/60 The ~~silkily~~ silky lining, in ~~delightful~~ delightfully loud shades of orange, gives

59/62 a strong message: I am woman! Hear me roar!

61

63/64 B. ~~Softly~~ Soft, woven pants coordinate with ~~a~~ the jacket described above — and with everything in your wardrobe. In eggplant, orange, or eggplant-orange plaid.

45 The description *comfortable* must be intensified by the adverb *surprisingly,* not by the adjective *surprising.*

46 The adjective *comfortable* describes the noun *suits.*

47 *Polyester* is a noun, so it must be described by an adjective, and *easy* fills the bill. Because you have a combo description, *easy-to-clean,* you need hyphens.

48 The description *varied* is intensified by the adverb *really.*

49 In this sentence *office* is an adjective describing *grind,* a noun here.

50 The adverb *extremely* intensifies the descriptive word *bright.*

51 The adjective *bright* describes the *club scene,* a noun.

52 That wonderful word *fast* may be either an adjective or an adverb. Here it combines with *track* to form a hyphenated adjective describing *jacket.*

53 A particular sort of elegance is being discussed, so the definitive *the* is called for.

54 *Elegance* is a noun, so the adjective *astonishing* is the best description.

55 *Eggplant* is a color, which is a thing and therefore a noun. To describe a noun, use the adjective *deep.*

56 To describe the noun *curves,* go for the adjective *gentle,* not the adverb *gently.*

57 *An* can precede only words beginning with vowels, and *real* begins with a consonant.

58 *Natural* is a descriptive word, so it must itself be described by an adverb, *really.*

59 The noun *lining* is described by the adjective *silky.*

60 The adverb *delightfully* describes another description, *loud.* Descriptions are always described by adverbs, not by adjectives.

61 The article *a* is the one you need to precede a word beginning with a consonant.

62 The adjective *strong* describes the noun *message.*

63 Did I fool you here? True, you may have thought that *softly* described *woven* in this sentence, but the meaning indicates otherwise. You're not talking about how the cloth was woven. Instead, you have two separate words (the comma is your clue) describing the noun *pants. Soft* is an adjective, appropriate for noun descriptions.

64 Clearly you're talking about one particular item, the extremely ugly jacket described as item A. Hence *the,* which goes well with particulars, is better than the more general *a.*

Chapter 14

Going on Location: Placing Descriptions Correctly

. . . .

In This Chapter

▶ Situating *even, only, almost,* and similar words

▶ Avoiding misplaced, dangling, or confusing descriptions

. . . .

The general principle guiding the placement of descriptions is simple: Descriptive words should clearly relate to what they describe. Some descriptions can wander a bit without changing meaning, but a few words require precision. In this chapter you can practice that precision and, like a real estate agent, concentrate on location, location, location.

Putting Descriptive Words in Their Place

The other day I saw a T-shirt that declared, "Grandma went to NYC and only bought me one lousy T-shirt." The misplaced *only* bugged me. The sentence as written means that Grandma did nothing at all in NYC except buy one T-shirt. Why? Because *only* — as well as *even, almost, just, nearly,* and *not* — should precede the word being described. The correct shirt should read, "Grandma went to NYC and bought me only one lousy T-shirt." Take a look at these examples:

> *Even* Mary knows that song. (Mary generally sticks to talk radio, but the song is so popular that she recognizes it.)

> Mary knows *even* that song. (Mary has 56,098 CDs. She knows every musical work ever written, including the one that the sentence is referring to.)

Got the idea? Now take a look at the following sentences. If you find a misplaced description, rewrite the sentence as it should be. If everything is fine and dandy, write "correct" in the blank.

Q. My Uncle Fred only pays taxes when he's in the mood or when the IRS serves an arrest warrant.

_____

_____

A. **My Uncle Fred pays taxes only when he's in the mood or when the IRS serves an arrest warrant.** The *only* has to move because it makes a comment on the conditions that make Fred pay up (his mood and the times when the IRS puts him in the mood). This description should precede the conditions it talks about. The *only* is not a comment on *pays,* so it's out of place in the original.

1. Because she was celebrating an important birthday, Ms. Jonge only gave us ten hours of homework.

   _____

   _____

2. The first task nearly seemed impossible: to write an essay about the benefits of getting older.

   _____

   _____

3. After I'd almost written two pages, my instant messenger beeped, and I put my pen down.

   _____

   _____

4. I even figured that Ms. Jonge, the meanest teacher on the planet, would understand the need to take a break.

   _____

   _____

5. I made a cup of coffee, but because I'm dieting, I only ate one doughnut and ignored the other three.

   _____

   _____

6. My friend Eloise nearly gained three pounds last week just from eating glazed doughnuts.

   _____

   _____

7. Eloise, my brother, and I love doughnuts, but all of us do not eat them; Eloise can't resist.

   _____

   _____

8. Eloise even draws the line somewhere, and she seldom munches more than three chocolate sprinkles a day.

   _____

   _____

9. After I had sent a text message to Eloise, I returned to my homework and found I only had five tasks left.

_____

_____

10. Not all the work was boring, and I actually liked the history assignment.

_____

_____

Relocating Misplaced Descriptions

If you're at a car dealership and want to buy a new car from a sales associate with snow tires, you're in the right place. Unfortunately, the description — *with snow tires* — is not, because its current placement attaches it to *sales associate* and thus indicates a car guy whose feet have been replaced by big round rubber things, not a vehicle you can drive confidently through a storm.

This section deals with long descriptions (for the grammar obsessed: prepositional phrases, verbals, and clauses) that sometimes stray from their appointed place. (I cover short descriptions — simple adjectives and adverbs — in Chapter 13.) To keep your descriptions legal, be sure that they're very close to the word they describe.

Except for a few place or time descriptions, nearly every multiword description directly follows the word it describes. The example in the first paragraph of this section should be "I want to buy a car *with snow tires* from a sales associate." In this version, the description *with snow tires* describes car.

When you move a misplaced description, take care not to make another error. For example, if I change "I placed a stone in my pocket that I found in the playground" to "I placed a stone that I found in the playground in my pocket," I have a problem. In the original sentence I found the *pocket* in the *playground*. In the changed sentence, I have a *playground* in my *pocket*. The solution is to place a description at the beginning of the sentence: "In my pocket I placed a stone that I found in the playground."

Check out the following sentences. If all the descriptions are where they should be, write "correct" in the blank. If anything is misplaced, rewrite the sentence in the blanks provided, dropping the description into the right spot. In addition to moving descriptions, you may have to reword here and there in order to create a sentence that makes sense.

Q. Even before she passed the road test, Julie bought a leather license holder that was given only twice a month.

_____

_____

A. Even before she passed the road test that was given only twice a month, Julie bought a leather license holder. The license holder is available all the time in a leather goods store, but the test shows up only twice a month. Move the description closer to *test* and you're all set.

11. Julie passed the eye examination administered by a very near-sighted clerk with flying colors.

_____

_____

12. The written test inquired about maneuvers for cars skidding on ice.

_____

_____

13. Another question inquired about defensive driving, which required an essay rather than a multiple-choice response.

_____

_____

14. About a week after the written portion of the exam, the Department of Motor Vehicles sent a letter giving Julie an appointment for the road test lacking sufficient postage.

_____

_____

15. Julie asked her sister to drive her to the testing site before the letter arrived.

_____

_____

16. Julie's examiner, a nervous man whose foot kept slamming onto an imaginary brake pedal, constantly wrote notes on an official form.

_____

_____

17. The first page contained details about Julie's turning technique, which was single-spaced.

_____

_____

18. Julie hit only two pedestrians and one tree in the middle of a crosswalk.

_____

_____

19. The examiner relaxed soon after Julie's road test in his aunt's house in Florida.

_____

_____

20. Julie wasn't surprised to hear that she had failed her first road test, but the pedestrians' lawsuit was a shock because the examiner had fainted when the speedometer hit 80.

_____

_____

Don't Leave Your Verbals Hanging: Dangling Descriptions

To spice up your writing, you may begin some sentences with introductory descriptions that resemble verbs but aren't actually verbs. (In official grammar terminology, they're _verbals_. Verbals can show up elsewhere in the sentence; in this section I'm just dealing with those that introduce sentences.) Usually a comma separates these introductory statements from the main portion of the sentence. When you begin a sentence this way, the introductory description must refer to the subject — the person or thing you're talking about in the sentence. In these examples, the introductory description is italicized:

> _Dazzled by Tiffany's new diamond ring,_ Lulu reached for her sunglasses. (The introductory description gives more information about _Lulu,_ the subject.)

> _To block out all visible light,_ Lulu's glasses have been coated with a special plastic film. (The introductory description gives more information about the subject, _glasses._)

A variation of this sort of introduction is a statement with an implied subject. Here you must be certain that the implied subject matches the stated subject in the main portion of the sentence:

> _While wearing these glasses,_ Lulu can see nothing at all and thus constantly walks into walls. (The implied statement is _While Lulu is wearing these glasses._)

A common error is to detach the introduction from the subject, resulting in a sentence with flawed logic, what grammarians call a _dangling modifier._ Standardized tests frequently include these errors for you to identify or correct. For example, you may see a sentence like this one: "Before buying them, the glasses carried a clear warning, which Lulu ignored." In this incorrect sentence, the meaning is "Before the glasses were buying them, the glasses carried a clear warning, which Lulu ignored." Illogical! To correct this sort of error, you often have to rewrite the sentence: "Before buying the glasses, Lulu read a warning about them and chose to ignore it."

Check out these sentences for danglers and rewrite if necessary. If everything is securely attached, write "correct" in the blank. Your rewritten sentence may differ from the suggested answer. No problem, as long as the introductory information refers to the subject.

0. After waiting for a green light, the crosswalk filled with people rushing to avoid Lulu and her speeding skateboard.

_____

_____

A. **After waiting for a green light, people rushed into the crosswalk to avoid Lulu and her speeding skateboard.** In the original sentence, the _crosswalk_ is _waiting for a green light_. The rewritten sentence has the people waiting for an escape hatch from the sidewalk, where Lulu is riding blind, thanks to her non-see-through sunglasses.

21. To skateboard safely, kneepads help.

_____

_____

22. Sliding swiftly across the sidewalk, a tree smashed into Lulu.

_____

_____

23. Although bleeding from a cut near her nose ring, a change of sunglasses was out of the question.

_____

_____

24. To look fashionable, a certain amount of sacrifice is necessary.

_____

_____

25. While designing her latest tattoo, a small camera attached to the frames of her glasses seemed like a good idea.

_____

_____

26. Covered in rhinestones, Lulu made a fashion statement with her glasses.

_____

_____

27. Discussed in the fashion press, many articles criticized Lulu's choice of eyewear.

_____

_____

28. Coming to the rescue, Tiffany swiped the offending glasses and lectured Lulu on the irrelevance of such fashion statements.

_____

_____

29. To pacify Tiffany and the pedestrians' lawyers, the glasses eventually went into the trash can.

_____

_____

30. Being reasonable, Lulu opted for a wraparound stainless steel helmet with UV protection.

_____

_____

31. When skateboarding, Lulu now takes care to avoid pedestrians.

_____

_____

32. Having hit no pedestrians for six months, a safety award seems appropriate for Lulu.

_____

_____

33. Knowing Lulu's tendency to place fashion over safety, shopping for new glasses was scheduled on a day when Tiffany was free.

_____

_____

34. To shop with Lulu, Tiffany canceled three appointments.

_____

_____

35. Hearing Tiffany's concerns, the rescheduled appointment was not a problem for her hairdresser.

_____

_____

Getting Caught in the Middle: Vague Descriptions

If you've read the previous sections in this chapter, you already know that the general rule governing descriptions is that they should be near the word they're describing. If you place a description an equal distance from two words it may describe, however, you present a puzzle to your reader. Not a good idea! Consider this sentence: "Protesting successfully scares politicians." Which word does *successfully* describe? *Protesting* or *scares?* You can't tell. The writer may be saying, "Successful protests scare politicians." Or, the meaning may be that "protests scare politicians successfully." The moral of the story: clarity is crucial.

Exam writers prize clarity, so take care to place your descriptions where they belong when you face a standardized test.

Check out the following sentences and decide whether they're clear or unclear. If they're clear, write "correct" in the blanks. If not, rewrite them. *Note:* The fact that a sentence is vague means that more than one correction is possible. In the answer key I provide two possible fixes. Your answer may differ. No problem! Just be sure the meaning is clear.

0. The senator speaking last week voted against the Clarity Bill.

_____

_____

A. **The senator speaking voted against the Clarity Bill last week.** Or, **The senator who spoke last week is the one who voted against the Clarity Bill.** You may find still other variations. As long as your sentence indicates whether *last week* is attached to *speaking* or *voted,* you're fine.

36. Running a red light once earned a stiff fine.

_____

_____

37. Backing away from the traffic cop swiftly caused a reaction.

_____

_____

38. The ticket he got last summer was a blot on his spotless driving record.

_____

_____

39. The judge said when the case came to trial he would punish the drivers severely.

_____

_____

40. The warden of the driving-infraction division soon arrived on the scene.

_____

_____

Calling All Overachievers: Extra Practice Placing Descriptions

As you breathe deeply, check out this yoga instruction manual (see Figure 14-1), which, my lawyer begs me to mention, does *not* describe real postures that a normal human body can achieve. Do *not* try these positions at home, but *do* look for ten errors caused by vague, misplaced, or dangling descriptions. After you find the clunkers, correct them. Cross out misplaced words, insert words by using carats, and revise sentences in the margins of this book. The errors have several possible corrections, but in the answers section, I show only one correction for each error. If your answer is clear, you're fine.

Yoga and Y'all: An Excerpt

If you only learn one yoga posture, this should be it. Beginners can even do it. To form the "Greeting Turtle Posture," the mat should extend from knees to armpits freshly laundered and dried to fluffiness. While bending the right knee up to the nose, the left ankle relaxes. You should almost bend the knee for a minute before straightening it again. Throw your head back now extending each muscle to its fullest, only breathing two or three times before returning the head to its original position. Tucking the chin close to the collarbone, the nose should wiggle. Finally, raise the arms to the sky and bless the yoga posture that is blue.

Figure 14-1: Sample instruction manual exercise.

Answers to Description Placement Problems

Now that you've had a chance to practice your description placement skills, check your work with the following answers.

1 **Because she was celebrating an important birthday, Ms. Jonge gave us only ten hours of homework.** The implication of this sentence is that she could have given twenty hours. Because the number of hours is the issue, the *only* belongs in front of *ten hours,* not in front of *gave.*

2 **The first task seemed nearly impossible: to write an essay about the benefits of getting older.** If it *nearly seemed,* it did not *seem* — just approached that state. But that's not what you're trying to say here. Instead, the task approached *impossible* but stopped just short, still in the realm of possibility. Thus the *nearly* describes *impossible* and should precede that word.

3 **After I'd written almost two pages, my instant messenger beeped, and I put my pen down.** How many pages did you write? That's what the sentence discusses. When the *almost* is in the right place, you have about a page and a half or a bit more. In the original sentence you have nothing at all on paper because the sentence says that the speaker *had almost written* (had approached the action of writing but then stopped).

4 **I figured that even Ms. Jonge, the meanest teacher on the planet, would understand the need to take a break.** Clearly the sentence compares this particular teacher with all others, so the *even* belongs in front of her name.

5 **I made a cup of coffee, but because I'm dieting, I ate only one doughnut and ignored the other three.** This sentence compares the number of doughnuts eaten (one) with the number available (four). The *only* belongs in front of the number, not in front of the action (ate).

6 **My friend Eloise gained nearly three pounds last week just from eating glazed doughnuts.** One word — *just* — is in the appropriate place, but *nearly* must be moved. The *nearly* tells you that the gain was a bit less than three, and the *just* tells you the reason (snarfing down doughnuts).

7 **Eloise, my brother, and I love doughnuts, but not all of us eat them; Eloise can't resist.** To correct this sentence you have to play around with the verb a little, because you don't need the *do* in the new sentence. Here's the logic: If Eloise eats the doughnuts and the rest keep their lips zipped, *not all* but *some* eat doughnuts. The original sentence illogically states that no one eats and then goes on to discuss Eloise's gobbling.

8 **Even Eloise draws the line somewhere, and she seldom munches more than three chocolate sprinkles a day.** The *even* shouldn't precede *draws* because two actions aren't being compared. Instead, *Eloise* is being singled out.

9 **After I had sent a text message to Eloise, I returned to my homework and found I had only five tasks left.** The sentence comments on the amount of remaining homework (*only five tasks,* not six or seven). Hence the *only* properly precedes *five tasks.*

10 **Correct.** Some work made you yawn and some didn't. Logic tells you that *not all* is what you want.

11 **With flying colors, Julie passed the eye examination administered by a very near-sighted clerk.** You can easily see what's wrong with the original sentence. Fixing it can be tricky. If you move *with flying colors* so that it follows *examination,* you solve one problem and create another because then the *colors* are *administered by a very near-sighted clerk.* You can place *with flying colors,* as I have, at the beginning of the sentence or, if you wish, after *passed.* In either spot the description is close enough to the verb to tell you how *Julie passed,* and that's the meaning you want.

12 **Correct.** The two descriptions, *written* and *for cars skidding on ice,* are close to the words they describe. *Written* describes *test* and *for cars skidding on ice* describes *maneuvers.*

13 **Another question, which required an essay rather than a multiple-choice response, inquired about defensive driving.** Defensive-driving techniques don't include essays, but test questions do. The description belongs after *question* because that's the word being described.

14 **About a week after the written portion of the exam, the Department of Motor Vehicles sent a letter lacking sufficient postage and giving Julie an appointment for the road test.** The *letter* is described by *lacking sufficient postage,* so that description must follow *letter.* I inserted *and* after *postage* to clarify that the letter, not the postage, gave Julie her appointment. The *and* attaches both expressions *(lacking sufficient postage, giving Julie an appointment for the road test)* to the same word, *letter.* Another possible correction drops *lacking sufficient postage* and inserts *postage-due* before *letter.*

15 **Before the letter arrived, Julie asked her sister to drive her to the testing site.** This sentence mentions two actions: *asked* and *drive.* The time element, *before the letter arrived,* tells you when Julie asked, not when she wanted her sister to drive. The description should be closer to *asked* than to *drive* because *asked* is the word it describes.

16 **Correct.** The description is where it should be. The information about the examiner's foot is near *nervous man,* and he's the one with the fidgety foot.

17 **The first page, which was single-spaced, contained details about Julie's turning technique.** The *page* is described by *single-spaced,* not Julie's three-point turn.

18 **Julie hit only two pedestrians in the middle of a crosswalk and one tree.** Common sense tells you that the tree isn't in the crosswalk, but the pedestrians are. The description *in the middle of a crosswalk* should follow the word it describes, in this case, *pedestrians.*

19 **The examiner relaxed in his aunt's house in Florida soon after Julie's road test.** The relaxing took place *in his aunt's house in Florida.* The road test took place on Route 9. Move the description closer to the word it describes.

20 **Because the examiner had fainted when the speedometer hit 80, Julie wasn't surprised to hear that she had failed her first road test, but the pedestrians' lawsuit was a shock.** The *because* statement should be closer to *was not surprised,* as that expression is being described. You may have been tempted to move *because the examiner had fainted when the speedometer hit 80* to the spot after *test.* Bad idea! If you put the *because* information after test, it looks as if she failed *because the examiner had fainted.* Yes, the examiner fainted, but the *because* information relates to Julie's lack of surprise and thus needs to be near *was not surprised.*

21 **To skateboard safely, you may find kneepads helpful.** In the original sentence, no one is skateboarding. A person must be inserted into the sentence. I've chosen *you,* but *skaters, people,* and other terms are also okay, as long as some sort of potential skater is in the sentence.

22 **Sliding swiftly across the sidewalk, Lulu smashed into a tree.** Lulu should be the one doing the *sliding,* not the tree, but the original sentence has the tree sliding across the sidewalk.

23 **Although Lulu was bleeding from a cut near her nose ring, a change of sunglasses was out of the question.** The original sentence has *a change of sunglasses bleeding.* The easiest way to correct a sentence with the wrong implied subject is to insert the real subject, which is *Lulu.* Another correct revision: **Although bleeding from a cut near her nose ring, Lulu said that a change of sunglasses was out of the question.** Now Lulu is doing the bleeding, a common state for her.

24 **To look fashionable, one must sacrifice a certain amount.** Who is looking fashionable? In the original sentence, no one. Add a person: *one, you, everybody,* or something similar.

25 **While designing her latest tattoo, Lulu thought it would be a good idea to attach a small camera to the frames of her glasses.** Lulu has to be doing the designing, but in the original sentence, *a small camera is designing her latest tattoo.* Another way to correct this sentence is to insert *Lulu* into the first part of the sentence, making her the subject. Now the sentence begins *While Lulu was designing. . . .*

26 **Covered in rhinestones, Lulu's glasses made a fashion statement.** Lulu's glasses are covered in rhinestones, not Lulu herself. *Lulu's glasses* must be the subject of the sentence.

27 **Discussed in the fashion press, Lulu's choice of eyewear was criticized in many articles.** What was discussed? The *eyewear,* not the *articles.*

28 **Correct.** Tiffany's *coming to the rescue,* so the sentence is fine.

29 **To pacify Tiffany and the pedestrians' lawyers, Lulu eventually threw the glasses into the trash can.** The *glasses* can't pacify, but *Lulu* can.

30 **Correct.** Okay, it's a stretch to see *Lulu* as *reasonable,* not to mention the discomfort of a *stainless steel helmet,* but grammatically this sentence is correct.

31 **Correct.** *Lulu* is the stated subject, and she makes sense as the implied subject also *(When Lulu is skateboarding . . .).*

32 **Having hit no pedestrians for six months, Lulu deserves a safety award.** In the original, the *award* hasn't hit any pedestrians. Yikes! Not exactly what you're trying to say. In the revised sentence, *Lulu* hasn't hit anybody — not with her skateboard, anyway.

33 **Knowing Lulu's tendency to place fashion over safety, Tiffany scheduled shopping for glasses on a free day.** Who's scheduling? *Tiffany* or *shopping? Tiffany,* of course, so she must be the subject.

34 **Correct.** This sentence is legal because Tiffany performs both actions in the sentence, expressed by *to shop* and *canceled.*

35 **Hearing Tiffany's concerns, the hairdresser had no problem with the rescheduled appointment.** The *appointment* can't hear anything, but the *hairdresser* can. Therefore, the *hairdresser* must be the subject of the sentence.

36 **A single red-light infraction earned a stiff fine.** Or, **Running a red light earned a stiff fine at one time.** The problem is *once*, which must be clearly attached to either *running* or *earned*. Here you have to reword and drop the *once* in order to be perfectly clear whether you're talking about *at one time* or a *single time*, both of which are meanings of *once*.

37 **Backing swiftly away from the traffic cop caused a reaction.** Or, **Backing away from the traffic cop caused a swift reaction.** Here *swiftly* causes problems. You can move it closer to *backing*, or you can change it to *swift* to describe *reaction*.

38 **Correct.** It's hard to imagine that anyone would hear this sentence and attach *last summer* to *was*. This one passes the clarity test.

39 **When the case came to trial, the judge said that he would punish the drivers severely.** Or, **The judge said that he would punish the drivers severely when the case came to trial.** The problem with the original is subtle but nevertheless worthy of attention. The expression *when the case came to trial* may be when the judge made his statement or when the judge intended to wallop the drivers. Move the expression and clarity reigns.

40 **Correct.** The description *soon* can describe only *arrived*. The word preceding the description, *division*, doesn't logically attach to a time element, so the sentence is okay as written.

Yoga and Y'all: An Excerpt

If you ~~only~~ learn **only** one yoga posture, this should be it. **Even B**~~b~~eginners can ~~even~~ do it. To form the "Greeting Turtle Posture," ~~the mat should extend from knees to armpits freshly laundered and dried to fluffiness~~ from knees to armpits extend the **mat, which has been freshly laundered and dried to fluffiness**. While bending the right knee up to the nose, **relax** the left ankle ~~relaxes~~. You should ~~almost~~ bend the knee for **almost** a minute before straightening it again. **Now T**~~t~~hrow your head back, ~~now~~ extending each muscle to its fullest, ~~only~~ breathing **only** two or three times before returning the head to its original position. Tucking the chin close to the collarbone, ~~the nose should~~ wiggle **the nose**. Finally, raise the arms to the sky **that is blue** and bless the yoga posture ~~that is blue~~.

(with labels 41, 42, 43, 44, 45, 46, 47, 48, 49, 50)

---

41 The description *only* applies to the number, not to the act of learning.

42 The description *even* is attached to *beginners* to show how easy this posture is.

43 The sentence begins with a verb form *(To form the "Greeting Turtle Posture"),* so the subject of the sentence must be the person who is supposed to do this ridiculous exercise. In the corrected sentence, an understood "you" fills that need.

44 The laundry description belongs to *mat,* not to *armpits,* though I do think fluffy armpits are nice.

45 In the original sentence the subject of *bending* is implied, not stated, so by default, the other subject in the sentence *(the left ankle)* takes that role. But the *left ankle* can't bend the right knee, so the logic is flawed. Changing the second half of the sentence to "relax the left ankle" makes the subject you (understood), and "you" works as the understood subject you want for the first half of the sentence. Another possible solution: Change the first half of the sentence to "While you are bending. . . ."

46 The description *almost* applies to *minute,* not to bending.

47 In the original sentence *now* is equidistant from *throw* and *extending,* creating a vague statement. Moving the description clarifies the meaning. After you move *now,* add a comma between *back* and *extending* to help the reader separate these two actions.

48 The description *only* applies to the number of times one should breathe, not to the number of actions one should be doing.

49 The introductory verb form must be an action done by the subject, and the *nose* can't *tuck the chin.* The understood subject *you* can *tuck the chin.*

50 The color description belongs to *sky,* not to *yoga posture.* Another, more concise correction is to delete *that is blue* and simply say, *blue sky.*

Chapter 15

For Better or Worse: Forming Comparisons

Does Nell have a *bigger* or *the biggest* ice cream cone? Is your cold *worse* or *more bad?* Can you say that Robert Pattinson is *more attractive?* Are you (grammatically) correct in stating that Obama is *taller* than any President of the United States? If human beings weren't so tempted to compare their situations with others', life (and grammar) would be a lot easier.

But don't despair. In this chapter I tell you everything you need to know about creating comparisons, whether they show up as one word *(higher, farthest),* two words *(more beautiful, least sensible),* or many words *(fastest texter in the Midwest* or *as much water as Niagara Falls).* I help you steer away from incomplete or illogical comparisons so your meaning will come through easy and clear. (Oops. What I meant was *more easily and more clearly!*)

Visiting the -ER (And the -EST): One- or Two-Word Comparisons

Adjectives (words that describe people, places, things, or ideas — in other words, nouns and pronouns) and *adverbs* (describing actions, states of being, or other descriptions — verbs, adjectives, and adverbs, in grammar terms) may help create comparisons. Regular unadorned adjectives and adverbs are the base upon which two types of comparisons may be made: the *comparative* and the *superlative.* Comparatives *(dumber, smarter, neater, more interesting, less available,* and the like) deal with only two elements. *Superlatives (dumbest, smartest, neatest, most interesting, least available,* and so forth) identify the extreme in a group of three or more. To create simple comparisons, follow these guidelines:

▸ **Tack -er onto the end of a one-syllable descriptive word to create a positive comparative form.** When I say *positive,* I mean that the first term of the comparison comes out on top, as in "parakeets are noisier than canaries," a statement that gives more volume to *parakeets.* Occasionally a two-syllable word forms a comparative this way also *(lovelier,* for example).

✔ **To make the comparative forms of a word with more than one syllable, you gener-ally use *more* or *less*, not *-er*.** This guideline doesn't hold true for every word in the dictionary, but it's valid for most. Therefore, you'd say that "canaries are more popular than parakeets," not "canaries are popularer." Just to be clear: *popularer* isn't a word!

✔ **Glue *-est* to one-syllable words to make a positive superlative.** A positive superlative gives the advantage to the element cited in the comparison. For example, *canaries* have the edge in "canaries are the finest singers in the bird world." Also, a few two-syllable words use *-est* to create a superlative (such as *loneliest*).

✔ **Add *most* or *least* to longer words to create a superlative.** Again, the definition of *longer* isn't set in stone, but a word containing two or more syllables, such as *beautiful*, generally qualifies as long. The superlative forms are *most beautiful* or *least beautiful*.

✔ **Negative comparative and superlative forms always rely on two words.** If you want to state that something is *less* or *least*, you have to use those words and not a tacked-on syllable. Therefore, "the canary's song is *less pretty* when he has a head cold," and "my parakeets are *least annoying* when they're sleeping."

✔ **Check the dictionary if you're not sure of the correct form.** The entry for the plain adjective or adverb normally includes the comparative and superlative forms, if they're single words. If you don't see a listing for another form of the word, take the *less/more, least/most* option.

A few comparatives and superlatives are irregular. I discuss these in the next section, "Going from Bad to Worse (And Good to Better): Irregular Comparisons."

Never add *-er* or *-est* AND *less/more* or *least/most*. These forms together are not correct.

Ready for some comparison shopping? Insert the comparative or superlative form as needed into the blanks for each question. The base word is in parentheses at the end of the sentence.

0. Helen is the _____ of all the women living in Troy, New York. *(beautiful)*

A. **most beautiful.** The sentence compares *Helen* to other women in Troy, New York. Comparing more than two elements requires the superlative form. Because *beautiful* is a long word, *most* creates a positive comparison. (*Least beautiful* is the negative version.)

1. Helen, who manages the billing for an auto parts company, is hoping for a transfer to the Paris office, where the salaries are _____ than in New York but the night life is _____. *(low, lively)*

2. Helen's boss claims that she is the _____ and _____ of all his employees. *(efficient, valuable)*

3. His secretary, however, has measured everyone's output of P-345 forms and concluded that Helen is _____ and _____ than Natalie, Helen's assis-tant. *(slow, accurate)*

4. Natalie prefers to type her P-345s because she thinks the result is _____ and _____ than handwritten work. *(neat, professional)*

5. Helen notes that everyone else in the office writes _____ than Natalie, whose penmanship has been compared to random scratches from a blind chicken; however, Natalie types _____. *(legibly, fast)*

6. Helen has been angry with Natalie ever since her assistant declared that Helen's coffee was _____ and _____ than the tea that Natalie brought to the office. *(drinkable, tasty)*

7. Helen countered with the claim that Natalie brewed tea _____ than the office rules allow, a practice that makes her _____ than Helen. *(frequently, productive)*

8. Other workers are trying to stay out of the feud; they know that both women are capable of making the work day _____ and _____ than it is now. *(long, boring)*

9. The _____ moment in the argument came when Natalie claimed that Helen's toy duck "squawked _____ than Helen herself." *(petty, annoyingly)*

10. That duck was the _____ and _____ toy in the entire store! *(expensive, cute)*

11. Knowing about Helen's transfer request, I selected a duck that sounded _____ and _____ than the average American rubber duck. *(international, interesting)*

12. The clerk told me my request was the _____ he had ever encountered, but because he holds himself to the _____ standards of customer service, he did not laugh at me. *(silly, high)*

13. I replied that I preferred to deal with store clerks who were _____ and _____ than he. *(snobby, knowledgeable)*

14. Anyway, Helen's transfer wasn't approved, and she is in the _____ mood imaginable, even _____ than she was when her desk caught fire. *(nasty, annoyed)*

15. We all skirt Natalie's desk _____ than Helen's, because Natalie is even _____ than Helen about the refusal. *(widely, upset)*

16. Natalie, who considers herself the _____ person in the company, wanted a promotion to Helen's rank or an even _____ job. *(essential, important)*

17. Larry is sure that he would have gotten the promotion because he is the _____ and _____ of all of us in his donations to the Party Fund. *(generous, creative)*

18. "Natalie bakes a couple of cupcakes," he commented _____ than a boxing champion, "and the boss thinks she's executive material." *(forcefully)*

19. "I, on the other hand, am the _____ of the three clerks in my office," he continued, "and I am absent _____ than everyone else." *(professional, often)*

20. When I left the office, Natalie and Larry were arm wrestling to see who was _____, and Helen was surfing Internet job sites _____ than usual. *(strong, carefully)*

Going from Bad to Worse (And Good to Better): Irregular Comparisons

A couple of basic descriptions form comparisons irregularly. Irregulars don't add *-er* or *more/less* to create the comparative form, a comparison between two elements. Nor do irregulars tack on *-est* or *most/least* to point out the top or bottom of a group of more than two, also known as the superlative form of comparisons. (See the preceding section, "Visiting the *-ER* (And the *-EST*)," for more information on comparatives and superlatives.) Instead, irregular comparisons follow their own strange path, as you can see in Table 15-1.

Table 15-1	Forms of Irregular Comparisons	
Description	*Comparative*	*Superlative*
Good or well	Better	Best
Bad or ill	Worse	Worst
Much or many	More	Most

Take a stab at this section's practice exercises, but don't go to the *-ER* if your aim is faulty and you put the wrong form of the description (which you find in parentheses at the end of each sentence) in the blank. Just read the explanation in the answers section of the chapter and move on.

Q. Edgar's scrapbook, which contains souvenirs from his trip to Watch Repair Camp, is the _____ example of a boring book that I have ever seen. *(good)*

A. **best.** Once you mention the top or bottom experience of a lifetime, you're in the superlative column. Because *goodest* isn't a word, *best* is the one you want.

21. Edgar explains his souvenirs in _____ detail than anyone would ever want to hear. *(much)*

22. Bored listeners believe that the _____ item in his scrapbook is a set of gears, each of which Edgar can discuss for hours. *(bad)*

23. On the bright side, everyone knows that Edgar's watch repair skills are _____ than the jewelers' downtown. *(good)*

24. When he has the flu, Edgar actually feels _____ when he hears about a broken watch. *(bad)*

25. Although he is only nine years old, Edgar has the _____ timepieces of anyone in his fourth grade class, including the teacher. *(many)*

26. The classroom clock functions fairly well, but Ms. Appleby relies on Edgar to make it run even _____. *(well)*

27. Edgar's scrapbook also contains three samples of watch oil; Edgar thinks Time-Ola Oil is the _____ choice. *(good)*

28. Unfortunately, last week Edgar let a little oil drip onto his lunch and became sick; a few hours later he felt _____ and had to call the doctor. *(ill)*

29. "Time-Ola Oil is the _____ of all the poisons," cried the doctor. *(bad)*

30. "But it's the _____ for watches," whispered Edgar. *(good)*

Letting Absolute Words Stand Alone

Because you bought this book, I'm assuming that you (like me) are *perfect*. Therefore you can't be compared to anything or anyone else because the word *perfect* — as well as *unique, round, circular, right, mistaken,* and a few other terms — is an absolute. Logic, which pops up from time to time in English grammar, is the basis for this rule. If you reach an absolute state, you can't be more or less absolute. Therefore an expression such as *more circular* or *really unique* is a no-no. You can, however, approach an absolute, being, for example, *nearly perfect* (okay, I admit that's a better term for me) or *almost round*.

Words for direction and shape tend to be absolutes. You can turn *left* but not *lefter* or *more left.* Nor can you be the *squarest* or *most square* of them all, at least when you're discussing a four-sided figure.

Check out the following sentences, in which pairs of one or more words appear in parentheses. Circle the correct element from each parenthesis. Just to keep you awake, I throw in some pairs in which both elements are wrong or both elements are right. (For those sentences, circle both answers or write "neither" in the margin.)

0. The vase is (unique/quite unique), and I expect to pay big bucks for it.

A. **unique.** The vase is either one-of-a-kind or not, so *unique* is an absolute. If you want anything less than *unique,* use *rare, unusual,* or *uncommon.*

31. The base of your vase is round, and mine is (almost round/rounder).

32. The antiques dealer said that the top of the vase is (circular/nearly circular), but he's probably mistaken.

33. To find a better antiques dealer, drive (west/more west) for about an hour.

34. That dealer sells Victorian-era buttons that are some of the (most unusual/most unique) gift items you can imagine.

35. The (reasonably circular/very circular) shape of the buttons is surprising, given that the buttons are so old.

36. The dealer obtained the buttons from an (extremely elderly/elderly) widow.

37. The widow claimed that she would sell her antiques only when the time was (very right/just right).

38. Last week I bought a button that was (almost perfect/surprisingly perfect).

39. I thought I could sell it over the Internet for a huge profit, but my plans were (more wrong than I had assumed/very wrong).

40. My sister confiscated the button, claiming that it was (uniquely suited/uncommonly suited) to her personal style.

Completing Half-Finished Comparisons

By definition, a comparison discusses two elements in relation to each other or singles out the extreme in a group and explains exactly what form the extremism takes. For example, "She throws more pies than I do" or "Of all the clowns, she throws the most pies." A comparison may also examine something in relation to a standard, as in "Her comment was so sugary that I had to take an extra shot of insulin." A comparison may be any of these things, but what it may not be is partially absent. If someone says, "The snapper is not *as* fresh" or "The sea bass is *most* musical," you're at sea. *As fresh* as what? *Most musical* in comparison to whom? You have no way of knowing.

Of course, in context these sentences may be perfectly all right. If I say, "I considered the snapper but in the end went with the flounder. The snapper is not as fresh," you know that the second sentence is a continuation of the first. Also, some words in a comparison may be implied, without loss of meaning. I may write, "The snapper makes fewer snotty comments than a large-mouth bass *does*." The italicized word in the preceding sentence may be left out — and frequently is — without confusing anyone. And that's the key: The reader must have enough information to understand the comparison.

One very common incomplete comparison involves *so. So* may mean *therefore,* but that meaning isn't a problem. In comparisons, *so* is supposed to pair with *that,* as in "I was so hungry that I ate the frozen hamburger." In informal speech, *so* may be used alone as the equivalent of *very,* as in "I was so tired." In formal English, however, *so* should be paired with *that* when it creates a comparison.

Incomplete comparisons appear on many standardized tests. Watch for them!

Read the following sentences; see whether you can catch an incomplete comparison. If the sentence is correct, write "correct" in the blank. If not, rewrite the sentence to complete the comparison. You may come up with thousands of possible answers, a further illustration of why incomplete comparisons make for poor communication. I give two suggested answers for the example, but only one suggested answer for the exercises that follow, because I can't cover everything. Check your answer by determining whether your comparison is clear and complete.

Q. "There are more fish in the sea," commented the grouper as she searched for her posse.

A. **"There are more fish in the sea than you know,"** **commented the grouper as she searched for her posse.** Or, **"There are more fish in the sea than on a restaurant menu,"** **commented the grouper as she searched for her posse.** The key here is to define the term *more. More than* what? If you answer that question, you're fine.

41. The trout, who is wealthier, spends a lot of money on smartphone apps.

_____

_____

42. The octopus plays more video games, often opposing himself with different arms.

_____

_____

43. Mermaids are the most adept at financial planning, in my experience.

_____

_____

44. On the other hand, mermaids are less competent at purchasing shoes.

_____

_____

45. Not many people realize that mermaid tail fins are so sensitive.

_____

_____

46. Whales are as fashion-challenged at shoe and accessory selection.

_____

_____

47. This whole under-the-sea theme has become more boring.

_____

_____

48. The marine jokes are so uninteresting.

_____

_____

49. I will work harder at formulating new ideas.

_____

_____

50. You can always boycott this chapter if you find the comedy less than satisfying.

_____

_____

51. I hear the jokes are better in Chapter 16 than they are here.

_____

_____

52. Fortunately, comparisons are the most interesting topic.

_____

_____

53. Compared to verb tense, comparisons are easier.

_____

_____

Being Smarter Than Yourself: Illogical Comparisons

If I say that Babe Ruth was a better slugger than any Yankee, I'm making an error that's almost as bad as a wild throw into the stands. Why? Because the Babe was a Yankee! According to the logic of my original statement, the Babe would have to outslug himself. I don't think so! The solution is simple. Insert _other_ or _else_ or a similar expression into the sentence. Then the Babe becomes "a better slugger than any other Yankee" or "better than anyone else who has ever played for the Yankees."

Don't insert _other_ or _else_ if the comparison is between someone in the group and someone outside the group. I can correctly say, for example, that "the current Yankee shortstop, Derek Jeter, is cuter than all the Mets" — in terms of grammar, at least. You can check the team photos and decide the cuteness levels for yourself.

Standardized-test writers love to test your powers of logic, so carefully check every comparison you encounter.

Time for some comparison shopping. Check out the following sentences. If the comparison is logical, write "correct" in the blank. If the comparison is faulty, rewrite the sentence in the space provided. Because some sentences may be corrected in more than one way, your answer may differ from mine. Just be sure that your answers are logical.

0. The average pigeon is smarter than any animal in New York City.

_____

_____

A. **The average pigeon is smarter than any other animal in New York City.** Pigeons are animals, and pigeons flap all over New York. (I've even seen them on subway cars, where they wait politely for the next stop before waddling onto the platform.) Without the word *other,* pigeons are smarter than themselves. Penalty box! The insertion of *other* repairs the logic.

54. Except for the fact that they don't pay the fare, subway pigeons are no worse than any rider.

_____

_____

55. Spotting a pigeon waiting for the subway door to open is no odder than anything you see on an average day in New York.

_____

_____

56. On a Midtown corner I once saw a woman shampooing her hair in the rain, an experience that was weirder than anything else I've seen in New York City.

_____

_____

57. Singing a shower song with a thick New York accent, she appeared saner than city residents.

_____

_____

58. A tourist gawking through the window of a sightseeing bus was more surprised than New Yorkers on the street.

_____

_____

59. Is this story less believable than what you read in this book?

_____

_____

60. You may be surprised to know that it is more firmly fact-based than the material in this chapter.

_____

_____

61. Tourists to New York probably go home with stranger stories than visitors to big cities.

_____

_____

62. New Yorkers themselves, of course, make worse tourists than travelers from large metropolitan areas.

_____

_____

63. New Yorkers are more likely to become impatient than residents of small towns.

_____

_____

64. New Yorkers also talk faster than people who live in large American cities.

_____

_____

65. Can you believe that the Empire State Building, with 102 floors, is taller than any skyscraper?

_____

_____

Calling All Overachievers: Extra Practice with Comparisons

Political campaign literature is heavy with comparisons — Why Seymour and not Sally or Oliver? — but not all the comparisons are correct. (I'm talking grammar here, not politics.) Run your eyeballs over the campaign leaflet in Figure 15-1. It's for a completely fictitious race between some fifth-graders hoping to become president of grade six. Locate and correct 15 errors in comparisons. To correct the errors, you may have to rewrite an entire sentence or phrase.

Vote for Sally!

Sally will be the most unique president our grade has ever had for these reasons:

✔ Our cafeteria is dirtier than the cafeterias of the six schools in District 2.

✔ Sally is more good at organizing school events than her opponents.

✔ Sally will collect dues most efficiently, compared to Seymour.

✔ Oliver was very wrong when he said that Sally spent class money on herself.

✔ The principal thinks Sally is more competent than any candidate.

✔ Seymour is absent frequentlier than Sally, and Sally is so committed to school events.

✔ Sally's plan for the school field will make it more square and add the best bleachers.

✔ Oliver and Seymour are more funnier, but Sally is more smarter than anyone in our class.

✔ The school paper endorses Sally as "a very perfect candidate."

✔ Of all the candidates, Sally gives less boring and shorter speeches.

Figure 15-1:
Faux political campaign literature riddled with errors.

Answers to Comparison Problems

How does this chapter compare to the others you've worked on? Was it harder than the last one you did, or was it the easiest of all the chapters in the book? See how your answers compare to mine.

1 **lower, livelier.** The comparative form is the way to go because two cities, Paris and New York, are compared. One-syllable words such as *low* form comparatives with the addition of *-er*. Most two-syllable words rely on *more* or *less,* but *lively* is an exception.

2 **most efficient, most valuable.** In choosing the top or bottom rank from a group of three or more, go for superlative. *Efficient and valuable,* both long words, take *most* or *least.* In the context of this sentence, *most* makes sense.

3 **slower, less accurate.** Comparing two elements, in this case *Helen* and *Natalie,* calls for comparative form. The one-syllable word takes *-er,* and the longer word relies on *less.*

4 **neater, more professional.** Here the sentence compares typing to handwriting, two elements, so the comparative is correct. The one-syllable word becomes comparative with the addition of *-er,* and the two-syllable word turns into a two-word comparison.

5 **more legibly, faster.** After you read the word *everyone,* you may have thought that superlative (the form that deals with comparisons of three or more) was needed. However, this sentence actually compares two elements (Natalie and the group composed of everyone else). *Legibly* has three syllables, so *more* creates the comparative form. Because *fast* is a single syllable, *-er* does the job.

6 **less drinkable, less tasty.** In comparing *coffee* and *tea,* go for the comparative form. Both *more drinkable* and *less drinkable* are correct grammatically, but Helen's anger more logically flows from a comment about her coffee's inferiority. Negative comparisons always require two words; here, *less tasty* does the job.

7 **more frequently, less productive.** The fight's getting serious now, isn't it? Charges and countercharges! Speaking solely of grammar and forgetting about office politics, each description in this sentence is set up in comparison to one other element (how many times Natalie brews tea versus how many times the rules say she can brew tea, Natalie's productivity versus Helen's). Because you're comparing two elements and the descriptions have more than one syllable, go for a two-word comparative.

8 **longer, more boring.** When you compare two things (how long and boring the day is now and how long and boring it will be if Natalie and Helen get angry), go for the comparative, with *-er* for the short word and *more* for the two-syllable word.

9 **pettiest, more annoyingly** or **less annoyingly.** The argument had more than two moments, so superlative is what you want. The adjective *petty* has two syllables, but *-est* is still appropriate, with the letter *y* of *petty* changing to *i* before the *-est.* The second blank compares two (the duck and Helen) and thus takes the comparative. I'll let you decide whether Natalie was insulting Helen or the duck. Grammatically, either form is correct.

10 **most expensive, cutest.** A store has lots of toys, so to choose the one that has the highest price (the meaning that fits the sentence), go for superlative. Because *expensive* has three syllables, tacking on *most* is the way to go. The superlative for a single-syllable word, *cute,* is formed by adding *-est.*

11 **more international, more interesting.** Comparing two items (the sound of the duck you want to buy and the sound of the "average American rubber duck") calls for comparative, which is created with *more* because of the length of the adjectives *international* and *interesting.*

12 **silliest, highest.** Out of all the requests, this one is on the top rung. Go for superlative, which is created by changing the *y* to *i* and adding *-est (resulting in silliest) and adding -est* to *high,* a one-syllable word.

13 **less snobby, more knowledgeable.** Two elements (*he* and *a group of store clerks,* with the group counting as a single item) are being compared here, so comparative is needed. The add-on *less* does the job for the first answer; *more* is what you want for the second comparison.

14 **nastiest, more annoyed.** I can imagine many moods, so the extreme in the group calls for the superlative. The final *y* changes to *i* before the *-est to create nastiest; in the second blank, more creates a two-word comparative form.*

15 **more widely, more upset.** Employee habits concerning two individuals (Natalie and Helen) are discussed here; comparative does the job.

16 **most essential, more important.** Natalie is singled out as the extreme in a large group. Hence superlative is the one that fits the first blank. Three-syllable words need *most* to form the superlative *most essential.* In the second blank, two jobs are compared — one of Helen's rank and one that is *more important,* the comparative form of a long word.

17 **most generous, most creative.** *All* includes more than two (*both* is the preferred term for two), so superlative rules. Go for the two-word form because *generous* and *creative* are three-syllable words.

18 **more forcefully.** This sentence compares his force to that of a boxer. Two things in one comparison give you comparative form, which is created by *more.*

19 **most professional, less often.** Choosing one out of three in the first part of the sentence calls for superlative. In the second part of the sentence, the speaker is comparing himself to every other employee, one at a time. Therefore, comparative is appropriate. Because the speaker is bragging, *less often* makes sense.

20 **stronger, more carefully.** Natalie and Larry are locked in a fight to the death (okay, to the strained elbow). In the first part of the sentence, the comparison of two elements requires comparative. Because *strong* is a single syllable, tacking on *-er* does the trick. The second part of the sentence also compares two elements — the way Natalie usually surfs job sites and the way she surfs in this situation. Go for *more carefully,* the comparative form.

21 **more.** Two elements are being compared here: the amount of detail Edgar uses and the amount of detail people want. When comparing two elements, the comparative form rules.

22 **worst.** The superlative form singles out the extreme (in this case the most boring) item in the scrapbook.

23 **better.** The sentence pits Edgar's skills against the skills of one group *(the downtown jewelers).* Even though the group has several members, the comparison is between two elements — Edgar and the group — so comparative form is what you want.

24 **worse.** Two states of being are in comparison in this sentence, Edgar's health before and after he hears about a broken watch. In comparing two things, go for comparative form.

25 **most.** The superlative form singles out the extreme, in this case Edgar's timepiece collection, which included a raw-potato clock until it rotted.

26 **better.** The comparative deals with two states — how the clock runs before Edgar gets his hands on it and how it runs after.

27 **best.** To single out the top or bottom rank from a group of more than two, go for superlative form.

28 **worse.** The sentence compares Edgar's health at two points (immediately after eating the oil spill and a few hours after that culinary adventure). Comparative form works for two elements.

29 **worst.** The very large group of poisons has two extremes, and Time-Ola is one of them, so superlative form is best.

30 **best.** The group of watch oils also has two extremes, and Time-Ola is one of them, so once again you need superlative.

31 **almost round.** Because *round* is absolute, it can be approached *(almost round)* but not compared. Therefore, the term *rounder* isn't Standard English.

32 **circular** and **nearly circular.** The absolute in question here *(circular)* can be stated simply, or the sentence can explain how closely the object comes to the absolute, as in *nearly circular.* Thus, both choices work.

33 **west.** You can't go *more west.* The direction is absolute.

34 **most unusual.** Because *unique* is an absolute term, *most unique* is illogical. *Unusual,* on the other hand, isn't absolute, so *most* may be attached.

35 **Neither.** The shape is either *circular* or not. The *reasonably* and the *very* don't work, because absolutes can't be compared.

36 **extremely elderly** and **elderly.** I tried to trick you here by sneaking in a non-absolute, *elderly.* You can be *very, extremely, really,* and *not-so elderly,* depending upon your birth certificate and your degree of truthfulness.

37 **just right.** *Right* is an absolute, so you're either *right* or *wrong,* not *very right* or *wronger.* You can, however, be *just right,* implying that you have reached the absolute state.

38 **almost perfect** and **surprisingly perfect.** *Perfect* is an absolute, but *almost* expresses an approach to the absolute (legal) and *surprisingly* deals with the opinion of the speaker, not with a degree of perfection (also legal).

39 **Neither.** *Wrong* is an absolute, so *more* and *very* are wrong.

40 **uniquely suited** and **uncommonly suited.** If the button is *uniquely suited,* nothing else in the universe is *suited* in the same way. No problem. *Uncommonly* means that more than one item may be suited, but this button fits to a rare degree. Also no problem.

41 **The trout, who is wealthier than the president of a Swiss bank, spends a lot of money on smartphone apps.** The problem with the original is that you can't tell what or who is being compared to the trout. The missing element of the comparison must be supplied.

42 **The octopus plays more video games than the shark, often opposing himself with different arms.** The original sentence begins the comparison nicely *(more video games than)* and then flubs the ending *(than* what? *than* who?). Supply an ending and you're fine.

43 **Mermaids are the most adept at financial planning of all marine mammals, in my experience.** The original comparison doesn't specify the group in which mermaids excel. Your answer must provide context.

44 **On the other hand, mermaids are less competent at purchasing shoes than other mammals.** In the original the reader is left to wonder about the basis of comparison. In the corrected sentence the mermaids are compared to other mammals. Now the comparison is complete.

45 **Not many people realize that mermaid tail fins are so sensitive that special tail-protection is a must.** In common speech, *so* is often used as an intensifier, the equivalent of *very*. In proper English, however, *so* begins a comparison. The original sentence contains an incomplete comparison. *So sensitive* that what? Who knows? The suggested answer finishes the comparison by supplying another idea.

46 **Whales are as fashion-challenged at shoe and accessory selection as mermaids.** It doesn't matter how you finish the comparison so long as you finish it. In the suggested answer I plugged in *mermaids,* but I could just as easily have placed something else in the blank.

47 **This whole under-the-sea theme has become more boring than a lecture on the economics of toenail clippers.** Finish the comparison with your favorite example of excruciating boredom.

48 **The marine jokes are so uninteresting that I may never go to the beach again.** The *so* statement must be completed by some sort of *that* statement.

49 **Correct.** Normally a comparison *(harder,* in this sentence) must be placed in context. In this sentence, however, the context is implied *(harder* than I did before).

50 **Correct.** The phrase *less than satisfying* compares the comedy to an ideal state (satisfying). The comparison is complete.

51 **Correct.** Two locations, Chapters 15 and 16, are compared, giving you a complete and correct comparison.

52 **Fortunately, comparisons are the most interesting topic in the book.** To complete this comparison, you need to define the group in which comparisons are *most interesting*.

53 **Correct.** Because you have a basis for comparison *(Compared to verb tense),* the comparison is complete.

54 **Except for the fact that they don't pay the fare, subway pigeons are no worse than any other rider.** The context makes clear that pigeons sometimes ride the subways. (I'm not kidding about this one, honest! I have seen the little feathered guys on my train.) Without the *other,* pigeons are no worse than themselves, an impossible situation.

55 **Spotting a pigeon waiting for the subway door to open is no odder than anything else you see on an average day in New York.** The *else* serves an important purpose in this sentence; it shows the reader that the pigeon waiting for the subway is being compared to *other* events in New York City. Without the *else,* the sentence is irrational because then the sentence means that seeing pigeons in New York is no odder than what you see in New York.

56 **Correct.** The *else* creates a logical comparison between this event (also true!) and other strange things I've seen in New York City.

57 **Singing a shower song with a thick New York accent, she appeared saner than other city residents.** If she's got a New York accent, she's a city resident. Without the word *other,* you're saying that she's saner than herself. Not possible!

58 **Correct.** The tourist isn't a city resident, so he or she may be compared to *New Yorkers on the street* without the word *other.*

59 **Is this story less believable than the rest of what you read in this book?** The story is in the book, and it can't be compared to itself. The phrase *the rest of* differentiates the story but preserves the logic. You may also correct this one by writing *less believable than others you read in this book.*

60 **You may be surprised to know that it is more firmly fact-based than the other material in this chapter.** Your correction must indicate, in any of several ways, that this story is being compared to the rest of the dumb jokes I placed in this chapter. The expressions *other, rest,* or *anything else* can do the job.

61 **Tourists to New York probably go home with stranger stories than visitors to other big cities.** New York is a big city, but the original sentence implies otherwise. The insertion of *other* solves the problem.

62 **New Yorkers themselves, of course, make worse tourists than travelers from other large metropolitan areas.** New York is a *large metropolitan area,* and the original indicates that it isn't. Trouble! Insert *other* and you're all set.

63 **Correct.** New Yorkers are compared to *residents of small towns,* and that comparison is legal.

64 **New Yorkers also talk faster than people who live in other large American cities.** The addition of *other* changes the sentence from illogical (New Yorkers *do live* in a large American city) to logical.

65 **Can you believe that the Empire State Building, with 102 floors, is taller than any other skyscraper?** Without *other,* you're making an illogical statement in which the Empire State Building, clearly a skyscraper, is compared to itself.

Vote for Sally!

66 Sally will be the most ~~unique~~ **unusual** president our grade has ever had for these reasons:

✔ **67** Our cafeteria is ~~dirtier than~~ **the dirtiest of** the cafeterias of the six schools in District 2.

✔ **68** Sally is ~~more good~~ **better** at organizing school events than her opponents.

✔ **69** Sally will collect dues ~~most~~ **more** efficiently, compared to Seymour.

✔ Oliver was ~~very~~ wrong when he said that Sally spent class money on herself. **70**

✔ The principal thinks Sally is more competent than any **other** candidate. **71**

✔ **72** Seymour is absent ~~frequentlier~~ **more frequently** than Sally, and Sally is so committed to school events **that she hardly ever misses any**. **73**

✔ Sally's plan for the school field will make it more **nearly** square and add the best bleachers **in the district**. **74**

✔ **75** Oliver and Seymour are ~~more~~ funnier, but Sally is ~~more~~ smarter than anyone **else** in our class. **76** **77**

✔ **78** The school paper endorses Sally as "a ~~very~~ perfect candidate." **79**

✔ Of all the candidates, Sally gives ~~less~~ **the least** boring and ~~shorter~~ **shortest** speeches. **81**

80

---

66 *Unique* is an absolute and can't be compared. You can say that Sally is *unique* or that she is *most unusual,* but not *most unique.*

67 In comparing more than two elements, use the superlative *(dirtiest).*

68 *Better* is an irregular comparison. *More good* isn't proper English.

69 In comparing two items (the way Sally gets the money from her classmates and the way Seymour does), go for comparative, not superlative form.

70 *Wrong* is an absolute and may not be compared.

71 Sally is a candidate, so to make the comparison logical, add *other*.

72 *Frequently* is a three-syllable word and can't become comparative with just a tacked-on syllable.

73 Your answer may differ; just be sure that you've completed the comparison begun by *so.*

74 The absolute term *square* may be approached with *nearly* but not be compared.

75 The *best bleachers* in the school? The town? The universe? Who knows? The comparison must be finished in some way.

76 You can't combine *more* and *-er*.

77 Because you can add *-er* to the end of a one-syllable word, you don't need *more*.

78 To make the comparison logical, add *else*.

79 *Perfect* is an absolute, so it can't be intensified by *very*.

80 Because three candidates are in the race, the superlative is appropriate here.

81 The extreme in a group of three or more takes the superlative.

Part V
Improving Your Writing Style

The 5th Wave   By Rich Tennant

"Brian Foley, you know perfectly well when I said I wanted 'holly' hung over the door I was talking about an object, not a person!"

In this part . . .

Completing the exercises in this part is the equivalent of creating clothes for one of those reality shows that identify the best and most stylish designers. If you can make it through this material, you've arrived at the top. The topics in this part include more than grammar; and when you master them, your writing will be as stylish as a supermodel.

Chapter 16 tackles *parallelism,* the grammar term for order and balance in a sentence — and a standardized-test favorite. (In fashion terms, parallelism means not wearing rain boots with an evening gown.) Chapter 17 lets you practice adding variety to sentences, so you don't end up wearing the same outfit . . . er, structuring every sentence the same way. This chapter also shows you how to trim your sentences so they're clear and concise (another frequent flier on college-entrance exams). Chapter 18 concerns the little errors (commonly confused words, for example) that can sabotage your writing.

Chapter 16

Staying on Track: Parallel Writing

In This Chapter

▶ Ensuring that parts of a sentence are balanced

▶ Avoiding shifts in tense, person, and voice

▶ Deciphering rules for paired conjunctions (*either/or, not only/but also,* and the like)

In the world of grammar, *parallelism* refers to order and balance, the quality a sentence has when it flows smoothly. No parallel sentence starts out in one direction (toward, say, Grandma's house) only to veer suddenly off the road (perhaps to a tattoo parlor two states away). This chapter provides a road map and some practice drives to keep your sentences on track.

Combining Geometry and English: Making Sentences Parallel

When a sentence is parallel, everything performing the same function in the sentence has the same grammatical identity. If you have two subjects, for example, and one is an infinitive *(to ski),* the other one must be an infinitive also *(to fracture).* You can't mix and match; *to ski and fracturing* shouldn't show up as paired (or part of tripled or quadrupled or whatever) subjects. Check out these sentences:

▶ **Nonparallel:** Roberta didn't enjoy paying full price for a lift ticket and that the cashier treated her rudely.

▶ **Parallel:** Roberta didn't enjoy paying full price for a lift ticket and being treated rudely by the cashier.

In checking for parallelism, don't worry about terminology. Just read the sentence aloud and listen: Parallel sentences sound balanced, but nonparallel sentences sound lopsided.

You may see parallelism issues in error-recognition or sentence-revision questions on standardized tests. Let your ear be your guide as you listen to the voice inside your head, reading the sentence "aloud." (Of course, if you actually read the sentence aloud, you'll be thrown out of the exam room.)

Keep your balance while you check out the following sentences. Decide whether or not they're parallel. If they are, write "correct" in the blank after each sentence. If they're nonparallel, correct the sentence in the blanks provided. *Note:* When you check your answers, your correction may not match mine. No problem, as long as the elements of your sentence match.

O. Speeding down Thunder Mountain, spraying snow across his rival's face, and to get the best seat in the ski lodge were Robert's goals for the afternoon.

_____

_____

A. **Speeding down Thunder Mountain, spraying snow across his rival's face, and getting the best seat in the ski lodge were Robert's goals for the afternoon.** The sentence has three subjects. The first two subjects are verb forms ending in *-ing* (gerunds, in official grammar terminology), but the third is an *infinitive* (the *to* form of a verb). Mismatch! My suggested answer makes all three subjects into gerunds. Here's another possibility: "To speed down Thunder Mountain, to spray snow across his rival's face, and to get the best seat in the ski lodge were Robert's goals for the afternoon." Now all are infinitives, and the sentence is parallel.

1. The ski pants that Robert favors are green, skintight, and made of stretch fabric.

_____

_____

2. When he eases into those pants and zipping up with force, Robert feels cool.

_____

_____

3. In this ski outfit, Robert can breathe only with great difficulty and loudly.

_____

_____

4. The sacrifice for the sake of fashion is worth the trouble and how he feels uncomfortable, Robert says.

_____

_____

5. Besides, sliding down the mountain and coasting to a full stop is easier in clothing that resembles a second skin.

_____

_____

6. Robert has often been known to object to secondhand clothing and how some equipment is used.

_____

_____

7. "With a good parka or wearing a warm face mask I'm ready for anything," he says.

_____

_____

8. He adds, "The face mask is useful on the slopes and doing double duty in bank robberies."

_____

_____

9. The ski pants can also be recycled, if they are ripless and without stains.

_____

_____

10. However, robbing a bank and to mug someone is more difficult in ski pants.

_____

_____

11. Robbers need speed and to be private, but they also need pockets.

_____

_____

12. Stashing stolen money and where to put an unwanted ski mask are important issues.

_____

_____

13. Robert, who is actually quite honest and not having the inclination to rob anyone, nevertheless thinks about crime and fashion.

_____

_____

14. He once wrote and had even edited a newsletter called _Crimes of Fashion._

_____

_____

15. Skiing and to pursue a career in law enforcement are Robert's dreams.

_____

_____

16. Robert should have no trouble achieving his goals because he is smart and energetic and not without ambition.

_____

_____

17. When Robert applied to the Police Academy, he first asked his mother's permission and that she pay his tuition.

_____

_____

18. Old-fashioned in manners and up-to-date in clothing design — that's Robert!

_____

_____

19. The Alpine Patrol, founded in 1888 and increasing in importance every year, has recruited Robert.

_____

_____

20. Robert had a few questions for the recruiter about uniforms and whether he'd have to work with a St. Bernard dog.

_____

_____

Finishing What You Start: Avoiding Unnecessary Shifts

My driving instructor (my husband) explained to me at least a thousand times that shifting at the wrong time was bad for (a) the engine and (b) his nerves. I did my best, though the grinding noise echoing through the car wasn't always my teeth.

Sentences should stay in gear also, unless the meaning requires a shift. Every sentence has _tense_ (the time of the action or state of being), _person_ (who's talking or being talked about), and _voice_ (active or passive). A sentence has a parallelism problem when one of those qualities shifts unnecessarily from, say, present to past tense, or from first person (the *I* form) to third (the *he* or *they* form). Nor should a sentence drift from singular to plural without good reason. For help with verb tense, check out Chapters 1 and 10. Pronoun tips appear in Chapters 3 and 9.

Some shifts are crucial to the meaning of the sentence. If "I hit you" and then "he hits me," the shift from one person to another is part of what I'm trying to say. That sort of sentence is fine. What's not parallel is a statement like "I hit him because you always want to be aggressive in tight situations," where the *you* is a stand-in for *I* or *everyone.*

Standardized tests often ask you to recognize or correct an illegal shift.

Hop in for a test ride. Check out the following sentences. If everything's okay, write "correct" in the blank after each sentence. Rewrite the nonparallel sentences to eliminate improper shifts.

0. Miranda read her introduction, and then the slides of our trip to Morocco were shown by me.

_____

_____

A. **Miranda read her introduction, and then I showed the slides of our trip to Morocco.** The original sentence unwisely shifts from active voice *(Miranda read)* to passive *(slides . . . were shown).* Verdict: Stripped gears, caused by a lack of parallelism.

21. If anyone has studied biology, you know that a person must learn the names of hundreds, if not thousands, of organisms.

_____

_____

22. Who gave those names, and why?

_____

_____

23. The Amoeba Family provides a good example of the process, so its name will be explained.

_____

_____

24. You may not know that the first example of this single-celled organism would have the name Amy.

_____

_____

25. When you split them in half, the new organisms name themselves.

_____

_____

26. The right half of Amy was still called Amy by herself, but the left half now called herself Bea.

_____

_____

27. The next time Amy and Bea split, you have four new organisms.

_____

_____

28. No one could imagine a conference between four single-celled organisms unless they witnessed it.

_____

_____

29. Amy Right Half favored a name that people will notice.

_____

_____

30. Amy Left Half thought about the choice for so long that her swimming was neglected.

_____

_____

31. Bea Right Half opted for "Amy-Bea," because she wants to honor both her parents.

_____

_____

32. Everyone always pronounced "Amy-Bea" very fast, and soon "Amoeba" was their preferred spelling.

_____

_____

33. Single-celled organisms should have simple names that can be remembered by biology students.

_____

_____

34. Bea Left Half, by the way, will change her name to Amy-Bea when she reached the age of seventeen days.

_____

_____

35. You know what a teenager is like; they always have to assert their identities.

_____

_____

36. A person forms an identity when you have some experience.

_____

_____

37. For amoebas, these experiences include sitting under a microscope or having had a chance to swim in a large pond.

_____

_____

38. The wise amoeba meets as many other organisms as possible, and phone numbers are also given freely.

_____

_____

Following Special Rules for VIPs: Very Important Pairs

Some words that join ideas (*conjunctions,* in grammar-speak) arrive in pairs. Specifically, *either/or, neither/nor, not only/but also,* and *both/and* work as teams. Your job is to check that the elements being linked by these words have the same grammatical identity (two nouns, two noun-verb combos, two adjectives, or two whatevers). If they don't, your sentence has a parallelism problem. Check out the following examples, in which the linked elements are underlined and the conjunctions are italicized:

> ✔ **Nonparallel:** Gertrude was *not only* <u>anxious</u> to achieve fame *but also* <u>she wanted</u> to make a lot of money. *Either* <u>by going to the moon</u> *or* <u>to swim across the Pacific Ocean</u> will make Gertrude famous.

> ✔ **Parallel:** Gertrude was *not only* <u>anxious to achieve fame</u> *but also* <u>eager to make a lot of money</u>. *Either* <u>going to the moon</u> *or* <u>swimming the Pacific Ocean</u> will make Gertrude famous.

The linked elements in the first parallel example are both adjectives and infinitives. In the second parallel example, the linked elements are nouns created from the *-ing* form of a verb — in grammar terminology, a gerund. (You don't really need to know the grammatical terms.) If you say the underlined sections aloud, your ear tells you that they match. In the first nonparallel sentence, the first element is just a description, but the second contains a subject/verb combo (a clause). Nope! Grammar crime! In the second nonparallel sentence, the first element is a gerund and the second an infinitive (*to* plus a verb). Grammar jail for you!

If you see a conjunction pair on a standardized test, check the joined elements. Parallelism is a big deal on these exams. A good tactic is to underline the elements, as I did in the examples. Then you can see whether or not they match. Keep your eye out for *not only . . . but also*. That construction is especially popular with test writers.

Parallel or nonparallel? Take a look at the following sentences. If they're parallel, write "correct" in the blanks. If they aren't, correct them.

Q. The bird both swooping over my head and the surprise in the garbage pail startled me.

_____

_____

A. **Both the bird that swooped over my head and the surprise that I found in the garbage pail startled me.** In the original sentence, *swooping over my head* and *surprise in the garbage pail* don't match. The first element has a verb form *(swooping),* and the second doesn't. The corrected version matches *bird that swooped* to *surprise that I found.* By the way, your correction may differ from mine. So long as the paired conjunctions join the same grammatical elements, you're fine.

39. When she traveled to the biker convention, Lola intended to show off both her new Harley and to display her new tattoo.

_____

_____

40. Either Lulu would accompany Lola or stay home to work on a screenplay about bikers.

_____

_____

41. Neither Lulu plans ahead nor Lola.

_____

_____

42. Lola not only writes screenplays about bikers but about alien invasions also.

_____

_____

43. Lulu both is jealous of Lola's writing talent and the award for "best cycle" on Lola's trophy wall.

_____

_____

44. Lola scorns not only awards but also refuses to enter most contests.

_____

_____

45. Neither the cycling award nor the trophy for largest tattoo has significance for Lola.

_____

_____

46. Lulu, on the other hand, both wants the cycling award and the trophy.

_____

_____

47. Not only did Lulu bribe the judges, but also ran a full-page ad bragging about herself.

_____

_____

48. The judges were either unimpressed with Lulu's efforts or liked Lola better.

_____

_____

49. Neither the television crew's opinion nor that the audience preferred Lulu influenced the judges.

_____

_____

50. Not only did the judges ignore the fans' applause, but they also didn't read the tweets supporting Lulu.

_____

_____

Calling All Overachievers: Extra Practice with Parallels

Look for any parallelism problems in this letter to an elected official from an unfortunate citizen (see Figure 16-1). You should find ten mistakes in parallelism, various shifts, and conjunction pairs. When you find a mistake, correct it.

Dear Mr. Mayor:

I do not like complaining or to be a nuisance, but if a person is persecuted, they should be heard. As you know, the proposed new highway not only runs through my living room but also into my swimming pool. When I spoke to the Department of Highways, the clerk was rude, and that he took my complaint lightly. He said I should either be glad the road didn't touch the breakfast nook or the kitchen. I demand that the issue be taken seriously by you. I have written to you three times already, and you will say that you are "working on the problem." I am angry and in the mood to take legal action. Moving the highway or to cancel it entirely is the only solution. I expect you to cooperate and that you will fire the clerk.

Sincerely,

Joshua Hickman

Figure 16-1:
A disgruntled citizen writes a letter with unparalleled problems.

Answers to Parallelism Problems

Writing parallel sentences doesn't require the stars to be aligned; it just takes some practice. See how you did on the questions in this chapter by checking your answers here.

1 **The ski pants that Robert favors are green, skintight, and stretchy.** The original sentence links two adjectives (*green* and *skintight*) with a verb form (*made of stretch fabric*). Two adjectives + one verb form = penalty box. The corrected version relies on three adjectives (*green, skintight,* and *stretchy*) to describe Robert's favorite pants.

2 **When he eases into those pants and zips up with force, Robert feels cool.** The original sentence isn't parallel because the *and* joins two verbs (*eases* and *zipping*) that don't match. In the corrected version, *and* links *eases* and *zips*. Another possible correction: *Easing into those pants and zipping up with great difficulty, Robert feels cool.* Now *easing* parallels *zipping*.

3 **In this ski outfit, Robert can breathe only with great difficulty and loudness.** The original sentence matches up *difficulty* (a noun) and *loudly* (a description). These two are headed for the divorce court. The correction pairs two nouns (*difficulty* and *loudness*).

4 **The sacrifice for the sake of fashion is worth the trouble and discomfort, Robert says.** The original sentence joins a noun, *trouble,* and a whole clause (that's the grammar term for a statement with a subject/verb combo), *how he feels uncomfortable.* Not parallel! The correction links two nouns, *trouble* and *discomfort.*

5 **Correct.** The sentence yokes two -*ing* forms (*sliding* and *coasting*). Verdict: legal.

6 **Robert has often been known to object to secondhand clothing and used equipment.** You're okay with two nouns (*clothing* and *equipment*). You're not okay with a noun (*clothing*) and a clause (*how some equipment is used*), which is what you had in the original sentence.

7 **"With a good parka or a warm face mask, I'm ready for anything," he says.** The *or* in the original sentence links *with a good parka* and *wearing a warm face mask.* The second term includes a verb form (*wearing*), and the first doesn't, so you know that the parallelism is off. In the correction, *parka* and *face mask* are linked. Because they're both nouns, the parallelism works.

8 **He adds, "The face mask is useful on the slopes and does double duty in bank robberies."** The original sentence isn't parallel because *is useful* and *doing* don't match. The corrected sentence pairs *is* and *does,* two verbs.

9 **The ski pants can also be recycled, if they are ripless and clean.** *Ripless* is an adjective, but *without stains* is a phrase. Penalty box! The corrected version has two adjectives (*ripless* and *clean*).

10 **However, bank robbery and mugging are more difficult in ski pants.** In the correction I match two nouns (*robbery* and *mugging*), but you could also go for two infinitives (*to rob a bank* and *to mug someone*). Just be sure the two subjects have the same grammatical identity.

11 **Robbers need speed and privacy, but they also need pockets.** The original sentence falls off the parallel tracks because *speed* is a noun and *to be private* is an infinitive. The correction joins two nouns, *speed* and *privacy.*

12 **How to stash stolen money and where to put an unwanted ski mask are important issues.** In the correction, the subjects are both clauses; that is, they're both expressions containing subjects and verbs. (Think of a clause as a mini-sentence that can sometimes, but not always, stand alone.) Two clauses = legal pairing. The original sentence derails because the first subject (*stashing stolen money*) is a gerund, and the second is based on an infinitive *(to put)*.

13 **Robert, who is actually quite honest and not inclined to rob anyone, nevertheless thinks about crime and fashion.** The original sentence links a plain-vanilla-no-sprinkles description *(honest)* with an *-ing* verb form *(not having the inclination to rob anyone)*. No sale. The answer matches two descriptions, *honest* and *inclined*.

14 **He once wrote and even edited a newsletter called *Crimes of Fashion*.** The answer matches two past tense verbs, *wrote* and *edited*. The original matched a past *(wrote)* and a past perfect *(had edited)* without any valid reason for a different tense, so it wasn't parallel.

15 **To ski and to pursue a career in law enforcement are Robert's dreams.** Pair two infinitives *(to ski* and *to pursue)* and you're fine. Another option is to pair *skiing* and *pursuing* for an alternate correct answer.

16 **Robert should have no trouble achieving his goals because he is smart, energetic, and ambitious.** Three descriptions are listed in the original sentence, but two are adjectives *(smart, energetic)* and one is a prepositional phrase *(not without ambition)*. In the corrected version, all three adjectives match.

17 **When Robert applied to the Police Academy, he first asked that his mother give her permission and that she pay his tuition.** In the original sentence, Robert requests a noun *(permission)* and a clause *(that his mother pay his tuition)*. A noun and a clause — a subject/verb combo — aren't parallel. To fix the error, change the noun to a clause *(that his mother give her permission)*.

18 **Correct.** The sentence begins with two descriptions *(old-fashioned, up-to-date)*, so it's parallel.

19 **Correct.** The subject of the sentence *(Alpine Patrol)* is followed by two descriptions created by verbs. The verbs are in different tenses: *founded* in past tense, *increasing* in present tense. However, the meaning justifies two tenses, so the sentence is fine.

20 **Robert had a few questions about wearing a uniform and working with a St. Bernard dog.** *Wearing* and *working* are a match, replacing the mismatched *about uniforms* (a prepositional phrase) and *whether he'd have to work with a St. Bernard dog* (a subject/verb combo, also known as a clause).

21 **If you've studied biology, you know that a person must learn the names of hundreds, if not thousands, of organisms.** The original sentence shifts from *anyone* (third person) to *you* (second person). The correction stays in second. Another possible fix pairs *anyone* with *he or she knows* — all third-person forms. Be careful not to pair *anyone* with *they*. *Anyone* is singular, and *they* is plural. Mismatch!

22 **Correct.** Two questions. No shifts, no problem.

23 **The Amoeba Family provides a good example of the process, so I will explain its name.** The original sentence shifts unnecessarily from active *(provides)* to passive *(will be explained)*. The corrected sentence stays in active voice. True, it contains a shift from third person (talking about the Amoeba Family) to first, but that shift is justified by meaning.

24 **You may not know that the first example of this single-celled organism was named Amy.** The original sentence shifts inappropriately from present tense *(may not know)* to conditional *(would have)*. The tenses in the correction make more sense; the first part is present and the second past, because you *may not know* right now about something that happened previously. The shift is there, but it's justified by meaning. The correction has another shift, also justified, from active *(may not know)* to passive *(was named)*. Because the person giving the name is unknown, the passive is correct.

25 **When they split in half, the new organisms name themselves.** The question sentence is non-parallel because it moves from the second person *you* to the third person *organisms*. The correction stays in third person (talking about someone), with *they* and *organisms*.

26 **The right half of Amy still called herself Amy, but the left half now called herself Bea.** In the original, the extra *by* in the first half of the sentence unbalances the sentence. The correction eliminates the problem by making both parts of the sentence active.

27 **The next time Amy and Bea split, they formed four new organisms.** Parallel statements should stay in one person, in this case third person, talking about *Amy, Bea,* and *they*.

28 **No one could imagine a conference between four single-celled organisms unless he or she witnessed it.** The issue here is singular/plural pronouns. The original sentence begins with the singular *no one* and then shifts illegally to *they,* a plural. The correction begins with singular *(no one* again) and stays singular *(he or she)*.

29 **Amy Right Half favored a name that people would notice.** The first verb in the original is past, but the second shifts illogically to the future. Penalty box. In the correction, the past tense *favored* is matched with a conditional *(would notice),* but that change is logical because Amy is attaching a condition to her choice of name.

30 **Amy Left Half thought about the choice for so long that she neglected her swimming.** Why change from active *(thought)* to passive *(was neglected)?* Two actives work better.

31 **Bea Right Half opted for "Amy-Bea," because she wanted to honor both her parents.** The original sentence has a meaningless tense shift, from past *(opted)* to present *(wants)*. The correction stays in past tense *(opted, wanted)*.

32 **Everyone always pronounced "Amy-Bea" very fast, and soon "Amoeba" was the preferred spelling.** The original sentence shifts from singular *(everyone)* to plural *(their)*. The answer avoids the problem by dropping the second pronoun entirely.

33 **Single-celled organisms should have simple names that biology students can remember.** The shift from active in the original *(should have)* to passive *(can be remembered)* isn't a good idea. The verbs in the correction *(should have, can remember)* stay active, jogging at least an hour a day.

34 **Bea Left Half, by the way, will change her name to Amy-Bea when she reaches the age of seventeen days.** The original contains an illogical tense shift. The first verb is future *(will change)* and the second is past *(reached),* placing the sentence in some sort of time warp and out of the realm of parallel structure. In the correction, both actions are in the future *(will change, when she reaches)*.

35 **You know what teenagers are like; they always have to assert their identities.** The corrected sentence stays in plural *(teenagers, they)*, but the original improperly shifts from singular *(a teenager)* to plural *(they)*.

36 **You form an identity when you have some experience.** The problem with the original is a change from third person (talking about *a person*) to second (talking to *you*). Change both to second, as I did here, or both to third, in which case *a person* matches *he or she has*.

37 **For amoebas, these experiences include sitting under a microscope or having a chance to swim in a large pond.** *Sitting* is parallel to *having*, but the original paired *sitting* with *having had* — an unnecessary change in tense.

38 **The wise amoeba meets as many other organisms as possible and gives phone numbers freely.** The original sentence shifts from active voice *(meets)* to passive *(are given)*. Nope. Go for two active verbs to create a parallel sentence.

39 **When she traveled to the biker convention, Lola intended both to show off her new Harley and to display her new tattoo.** The paired conjunction here is *both/and*. The correction matches two infinitives *(to show* and *to display)*, in contrast to the original sentence, which joins a noun *(Harley)* and an infinitive *(to display)*.

40 **Lulu would either accompany Lola or stay home to work on a screenplay about bikers.** The elements joined by *either/or* in the original sentence don't match. One is a subject-verb combo *(Lulu would accompany)* and the other just a verb *(stay)*. The new version links two verbs *(accompany and stay)*.

41 **Neither Lulu nor Lola plans ahead.** The corrected sentence links two nouns *(Lulu, Lola)* with the *neither/nor* conjunction pair. The original sentence fails the parallelism test because it links a subject-verb *(Lulu plans)* with a noun *(Lola)*.

42 **Lola writes screenplays not only about bikers but also about alien invasions.** The original isn't parallel because the first element joined by *not only/but also* includes a verb *(writes)* but the second doesn't. The new version joins two prepositional phrases.

43 **Lulu is jealous of both Lola's writing talent and the award for "best cycle" on Lola's trophy wall.** Here you're working with *both/and*. In the original sentence *both* precedes *is*, a verb, but no verb follows the *and*. In the correction, each half of the conjunction pair precedes a noun *(talent, award)*.

44 **Lola not only scorns awards but also refuses to enter most contests.** The conjunction pair, *not only/but also,* links two verbs in the answer sentence *(scorns, refuses)*. The original sentence joins a noun, *awards,* to a verb, *scorns*. Mismatch!

45 **Correct.** The *neither/nor* combo precedes two nouns in the sentence *(award, trophy)*. Verdict: parallel.

46 **Lulu, on the other hand, wants both the cycling award and the trophy.** In the original sentence, *both* comes before a verb *(wants)*, but *and* precedes a noun *(trophy)*. No dice! The new version does better, linking two nouns *(award, trophy)*.

47 **Not only did Lulu bribe the judges, but she also ran a full-page ad bragging about herself.** The two conjunctions *(not only/but also)* link subject-verb combos in the corrected version *(did Lulu bribe, she ran)*, but in the original these conjunctions improperly link a subject-verb and a verb *(did Lulu bribe, ran)*.

48 **Either the judges were unimpressed with Lulu's efforts or they liked Lola better.** The *either/or* pair in the corrected sentence connects two complete sentences *(the judges were unimpressed* and *they liked Lola better)*. In the original, a description *(unimpressed)* incorrectly follows *either,* but a verb *(liked)* follows *or.*

49 **Neither the television crew's opinion nor the audience's preference influenced the judges.** After *neither* you have a noun *(opinion),* but in the original sentence *nor* is followed by a subject/verb combo *(that the audience preferred Lulu).* Change the combo to a noun *(preference)* and you're parallel.

50 **Correct.** The conjunction pair, *not only/but also,* links two complete sentences. Parallelism rules!

Dear Mr. Mayor:

51 I do not like ~~complaining~~ to complain or to be a nuisance, but if a person is

52 persecuted, ~~they~~ he or she should be heard. As you know, the proposed new

highway ~~not only~~ runs **not only** through my living room but also into my swimming **53**

pool. When I spoke to the Department of Highways, the clerk was rude, and

54 ~~that~~ he took my complaint lightly. He said I should ~~either~~ be glad the road didn't

55 touch **either** the breakfast nook or the kitchen. I demand that ~~the issue be taken~~

56 ~~seriously by you~~ you take the issue seriously. I have written to you three times

57 already, and you ~~will say~~ said that you are "working on the problem." I am angry

58 and ~~in the mood~~ ready to take legal action. ~~Moving the highway~~ To move the

highway or to cancel it entirely is the only solution. I expect you to cooperate and **59**

60 ~~that you will~~ to fire the clerk.

Sincerely,

Joshua Hickman

---

51 You may change *complaining* to *to complain,* as I did, or you may change *to be* to *being.* Either change makes a parallel sentence.

52 *A person* is singular, but *they* is plural. I change *they* to the singular *he or she,* but if you want to keep *they,* you may scrap *a person* and insert *people* instead.

53 Each part of the *not only/but also* pair should precede a prepositional phrase.

54 The *and* may link *was* and *took,* two verbs, but not a verb *(was)* and a subject-verb combo *(he took).* Another way to correct this sentence is to select an adjective to replace *he took my complaint lightly — dismissive, flippant, disrespectful,* or a similar word. Then the verb *was* precedes two adjectives, *rude* and *dismissive,* perhaps.

55 After the correction, each half of the conjunction pair *either/or* precedes a noun. In the original, the *either* comes before a verb *(be)* and the *or* before a noun.

56 The original sentence switches from active *(I demand)* to passive *(be taken . . . by you)*. The corrected version avoids the shift.

57 The original shifts from present perfect tense *(have written)* to future *(will say)* for no good reason. The correction is in past tense, but that tense is justified by the meaning of the sentence.

58 *Angry* is an adjective, but *in the mood* is a phrase. *Ready,* an adjective, makes the sentence parallel.

59 Either two infinitives (my correction) or two *-ing* forms *(Moving and canceling)* are acceptable here, but not one of each.

60 Two infinitives *(to cooperate, to fire)* are legal, as are two subject-verb combinations *(that you will cooperate* and *that you will fire)* but not one of each.

Chapter 17

The Writing Diet: Adding Spice and Cutting Fat from Your Sentences

"As I write this, the rain beats down on my window. How glad I am not to be outside! Smiling, I type away, dry and cozy." Compare the preceding sentences to these: "I am writing. The rain beats down on my window. I am glad that I am not outside. I am smiling. I type away. I am dry and cozy." Okay, admit it. The first version is better. Why? Because variety is not only the spice of life but the spice of writing as well. In this chapter you practice adding variety to your sentences by altering the underlying structure and combining ideas. You also get some scissor practice by cutting repetition — a favorite topic on standardized tests.

Starting Off Strong: Introductory Elements

The spine of most English sentences is subject-verb: *Mary walks, Oliver opens,* and so forth. Most sentences also have some sort of completion, what grammarians call a complement or an object: *Mary walks the dog, Oliver opens the peanut butter jar.* Even when you throw in some descriptions, this basic skeleton is boring if it's the only structure you ever use. The easiest and most effective way to change the basic pattern is to add an introductory element, which is italicized in the following examples:

Sticking her finger in the jar, Agnes stirred the peanut butter. (The introductory verb form tells something Agnes did.)

Despite the new polish on her nails, Agnes was willing to eat without a fork. (The introductory phrase gives information about Agnes's eating habits.)

When she was full, Agnes closed the jar. (The introductory statement has a subject and a verb, she was, and in grammar terms is a clause. Once again, you get more information about Agnes.)

As always in grammar, you don't need to clutter your mind with definitions. Simply try some of the patterns, but be sure to avoid a common error: The subject of the main part of the sentence must be the one doing the action or in the state of being described by the introductory verb form. Check out Chapter 14 for more information on this sort of error.

The skills you practice in this section help you in paragraph- or sentence-revision questions on college entrance tests, such as the SAT and the ACT.

Put boredom behind you by combining the two statements in each question, making one of the statements an introductory element. *Note:* Several answers are possible for each exercise. Your answer may differ from the one I provide in the answers section and still be correct. Check to see that you express the same ideas as the original statements and that the action or state of being expressed by the introductory verb form relates to the subject of the main portion of the sentence.

0. The boss wants the memo immediately. Jesse stops cleaning his teeth and starts typing.

_____

_____

A. Realizing that the boss wants the memo immediately, Jesse stops cleaning his teeth and starts typing. This is just one of many possibilities. You may also begin with a statement like **Now that Jesse knows that the boss wants the memo immediately, he stops cleaning his teeth and starts typing.**

1. Jesse is considering retirement. Jesse's mortgage holder thinks that Jesse should work at least 100 more years.

_____

_____

2. The bank wants Jesse to work hard. Jesse's debt is quite large.

_____

_____

3. Jesse wants to drink martinis on a tropical island. Jesse also wants to keep his house.

_____

_____

4. Jesse's entire plan is impractical. An especially unrealistic part lets Jesse drink martinis all day.

_____

_____

5. The bank manager speaks to Jesse in a loud voice. She points out that Jesse has $0.02 in his savings account.

_____

_____

6. The bank manager angers easily. Jesse brings out the worst in her.

_____

_____

7. Jesse considered robbing the bank. Jesse is an honest man.

_____

_____

8. The bank manager eventually decided to rob the bank. She drank martinis on a tropical island.

_____

_____

9. Jesse joined the FBI. He searched for the bank manager and arrested her.

_____

_____

10. Jesse received a $10 million reward. Jesse retired to the tropical island.

_____

_____

Making Short Sentences Work Together

In grammar, the term *subordinate* doesn't refer to the poor slob who has to make coffee for the boss. Instead, a *subordinate clause* is the part of the sentence that, while still containing a subject and a verb, occupies a position of lesser importance in relation to the rest of the sentence. Subordinate clauses may fall at the beginning, middle, or end of the sentence. Here are some examples, with the subordinate in italics:

The box, *which Ellen was told never to open,* practically screamed, "Look inside!"

After she had pried up the lid, Ellen ran screaming down the hall.

Ellen is planning to repair *whatever was damaged.*

As you see, subordination tucks one idea into another, making your writing less choppy by eliminating a series of short sentences.

Take a shot at inserting ideas. Combine the ideas in these exercises into one sentence per question, using subordinate clauses.

0. Ellen's boss held a press conference. The boss issued a statement about "the incident."

_____

_____

A. **Ellen's boss held a press conference at which he issued a statement about "the incident."** More than one answer is possible here. Here's another: **Ellen's boss, who held a press conference, issued a statement about "the incident."**

11. Joseph Schmo is a prize-winning reporter. He asked the boss a number of questions.

_____

_____

12. The boss asked Joe to sit down and be quiet. Joe refused. He was still looking for information about "the incident."

_____

_____

13. The CIA became interested in the case. The agency sent several agents to investigate.

_____

_____

14. Ellen didn't want to talk to the agents. Her boss said that her job was in jeopardy.

_____

_____

15. Ellen bought a bus ticket. She slipped out of the office.

_____

_____

16. The CIA may track her down. They will deal with her harshly.

_____

_____

17. Ellen is away. The boss is trying to manage the news media.

_____

_____

18. Ellen has offered her story to an independent film company. The film company is tentatively interested.

_____

_____

19. Ellen wrote about "the incident" on 100 pieces of paper. She put her manuscript in a box.

_____

_____

20. The box has been placed in a bank vault. The vault has a titanium door.

_____

_____

21. Ellen's closest friends know the location of the box. Those people are in danger.

_____

_____

22. The film will come out next summer. Then the whole world will know about "the incident."

_____

_____

Shedding and Discarding Redundancy

Don't you hate listening to the same thing twice? I hate listening to the same thing twice. You probably hate listening . . . okay, I'm sure you get the point by now! Repetition is boring. You should avoid it in your writing, regardless of the form it takes — and it does take many forms, including doubled adjectives _(calm and serene)_, extra phrases _(six feet tall in height)_, or just plain saying the same thing two different ways _(in my opinion I think)_.

Teachers hate grading papers, so they come down hard on redundancy. Test takers, take note!

Rewrite the following sentences, eliminating the extra words (if any) to avoid redundancy.

0. Anxious and extremely tense, Susannah approached the starting line where the race would begin.

_____

_____

A. **Extremely tense, Susannah approached the starting line.** I chose *extremely tense,* but you could cut those words and stay with *anxious.* Don't use both *tense* and *anxious* because they say pretty much the same thing. The other cut *(where the race would begin)* is justified because that's what a *starting line* is.

23. Susannah's new and innovative idea for racing strategy was to cut away quickly from the crowd and separate herself.

_____

_____

24. I believe, in my view, that Susannah has a great chance of winning and finishing in first place.

_____

_____

25. The spikes that she installed and put on her tire rims should easily and without much effort cut her opponents' tires.

_____

_____

26. Bethany thinks that Susannah scattered tacks and little nails over the left side of the course, where her chief and most important rival rides.

_____

_____

27. There are two sides to every story, of course; Susannah and Bethany have different ideas about what is fair and unfair in a motorcycle race.

_____

_____

28. A little tack can alter the outcome of the race in an important and significant way.

_____

_____

29. Susannah says that in future days to come she will win legally or not at all.

_____

_____

30. Such honesty and integrity are commendable now in these current times.

_____

_____

Calling All Overachievers: Extra Practice Honing Your Sentences

PRACTICE

In Figure 17-1 is a short story excerpt that could use some major help. Revise it as you see fit, paying attention to varied sentence patterns, unnecessary words, and choppiness. *Note:* You can revise in a thousand different ways. In the answer section I provide some possible changes. Your revision may differ. In fact, it may be better than mine! Check for variety and conciseness when you evaluate your work.

Figure 17-1:
Sample
short story
excerpt
with horrid
sentence
structures.

> Darla fainted. Darla was lying on the floor in a heap. Her legs were bent under her. She breathed in quick pants at a rapid rate. Henry came. He ran as fast as he could. He neared Darla and gasped. "My angel," he said. His heart was beating. His cardiologist would be worried about the fast rate. Henry did not care. Henry cared only about Darla. She was the love of his life. She was unconscious. He said, "Angel Pie, you don't have to pawn your engagement ring." He knelt next to her.

Answers to Sentence Improvement Problems

The best writing uses different sentence lengths and structures while still being grammatically correct. Check your rewritten sentences with the ones I suggest here.

1. **Despite the fact that Jesse is considering retirement, his mortgage holder thinks that Jesse should work at least 100 more years.** My answer begins with a prepositional phrase. You may also start with *Although Jesse is . . .* or *Contrary to Jesse's desire to. . . .*

2. **Because Jesse's debt is quite large, the bank wants him to work hard.** The first time I show this sentence structure to my students, they often protest that "you can't begin a sentence with *because.*" Yes, you can, as long as you have a complete thought in the sentence.

3. **In addition to his desire to drink martinis on a tropical island, Jesse also wants to keep his house.** I start here with a prepositional phrase, but a clause (*Even though Jesse wants to drink martinis on a tropical island*) would also be a good beginning, pairing nicely with the rest of the sentence (*Jesse also wants to keep his house*).

4. **Impractical in every way, the plan is especially unrealistic in letting Jesse drink martinis all day.** The introduction here is just another way to describe *plan,* the subject of the main part of the sentence.

5. **Speaking to Jesse in a loud voice, the bank manager points out that Jesse has $.02 in his savings account.** How the bank manager speaks is expressed by an introductory verb form now, not by a separate sentence.

6. **Angering easily, the bank manager admits that Jesse brings out the worst in her.** I added admits so that *the bank manager* is the subject of the sentence. A dangler (an error I explain in Chapter 14) would be created by leaving *Jesse* as the subject and beginning with *angering* or a similar expression. In such a sentence, *Jesse* would be the one *angering easily* — not the meaning you want to convey. Another possible correction: *Bringing out the worst in the bank manager, Jesse angered her easily.*

7. **Even though he is an honest man, Jesse considered robbing the bank.** The first part of the sentence is a clause because it has a subject and a verb, but it depends upon the statement in the second part of the sentence to complete the thought.

8. **With martinis on a tropical island in her future, the bank manager eventually decided to rob the bank.** Here a set of prepositional phrases packs an opening punch.

9. **Having joined the FBI, Jesse searched for the bank manager and arrested her.** I started with a verb form, but you can also attach a *clause* (a statement containing a subject and a verb) such as *After Jesse joined the FBI, he searched. . . .*

10. **Receiving a $10 million reward, Jesse retired to the tropical island.** Here the reward information comes across in an introductory verb form.

11. **Joseph Schmo, a prize-winning reporter, asked the boss a number of questions.** The *appositive* (a grammar term for an "equivalent" noun or pronoun) tells you more about Joseph Schmo — specifically, that he's a prize-winning reporter.

12. **Although the boss asked Joe to sit down and be quiet, Joe refused, as he was still looking for information about "the incident."** This sentence relies on two *subordinate clauses* (subject/verb statements that convey information that's less important in relation to the main idea of

the sentence). Here, *Joe refused* is the most important part of the statement. The clauses beginning with *Although* and *as he was* are subordinate.

13 **The CIA, which was interested in the case, sent several agents to investigate.** The pronoun *which* stands in for the CIA and introduces extra information about that secretive agency.

14 **Ellen didn't want to talk to the agents, because her boss said that her job was in jeopardy.** The new, combined sentence has a cause-and-effect structure introduced by the word *because.*

15 **When she slipped out of the office, Ellen bought a bus ticket.** The word *when* ties the information about slipping out to the reason for Ellen's actions.

16 **If the CIA tracks her down, they will deal with her harshly.** Ignoring the CIA isn't a good idea. Nor is writing choppy sentences! *If* expresses a possibility, as does the verb *may* in the original.

17 **While Ellen is away, the boss is trying to manage the news media.** A time expression works nicely here, tying Ellen's absence to the boss's press conference.

18 **Ellen has offered her story to an independent film company that is tentatively interested.** When you use *that* to introduce an idea, a comma is seldom necessary.

19 **After writing about the incident on 100 pieces of paper, Ellen put her manuscript in a box.** The introductory statement gives you more information about Ellen's manuscript.

20 **The box has been placed in a bank vault that has a titanium door.** Sounds like the plot of a new TV series, doesn't it? When you're tucking ideas into your sentences, don't forget *that* — a very useful little connective word!

21 **Ellen's closest friends, who know the location of the box, are in danger.** The *who* ties the information to *friends* efficiently.

22 **When the film comes out next summer, the whole world will know about "the incident."** A time statement just begs for a subordinate position, introduced by *when.*

23 **Susannah's new idea for racing strategy was to cut away quickly from the crowd.** You may cut *new* and leave *innovative,* but don't use both. Also, you may drop to *cut away quickly from the crowd* and leave *separate herself.* With that option, you may want to move *quickly* to the end of the sentence, just to retain the idea of speed.

24 **Susannah has a great chance of winning.** Why say *I believe* or *in my view*? If you're saying that Susannah has a chance, the listener or reader knows that's what you think. *Winning* and *finishing in first place* are the same; choose either one.

25 **The spikes that she installed on her tire rims should easily cut her opponents' tires.** More doubles: *installed* and *put in* match, as do *easily* and *without much effort.* Choose one of each, but not both.

26 **Bethany thinks that Susannah scattered tacks over the left side of the course, where her chief rival rides.** I imagine that a hardware specialist could explain the difference between *tacks* and *little nails,* but to the general reader, the distinction is irrelevant. Ditto for *chief* and *most important.*

27 **Susannah and Bethany have different ideas about what is fair in a motorcycle race.** The whole first part of the sentence is unnecessary. Of course differing points of view exist, and because the sentence moves to specifics, the general statement is a waste of words. Also, if the bikers can't agree on what's fair, by definition they also don't agree on what's unfair, so that part of the statement may also be cut.

28 **A little tack can alter the outcome of the race in an important way.** If you prefer, drop *important* and keep *significant*. Don't use the two together.

29 **Susannah says that in the future she will win legally or not at all.** Is there a future in the past? Or somewhere else in time? Once you say *future,* you don't have to add *days to come.* (If you'd rather keep *days to come,* go for it and drop *future.*)

30 **Such honesty is commendable in these current times.** The original has two doubles — *honesty, integrity* and *now, in these current times.* I chose one from each pair, but if you chose the other word, no problem. Notice that the plural verb *are* changes to the singular *is* when you drop one subject.

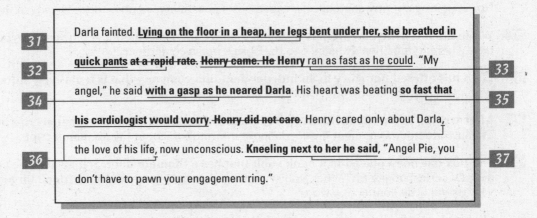

Darla fainted. **Lying on the floor in a heap, her legs bent under her, she breathed in** — **31**

32 — quick pants ~~at a rapid rate~~. ~~Henry came. He~~ Henry ran as fast as he could. "My — **33**

34 — angel," he said **with a gasp as he neared Darla**. His heart was beating **so fast that** — **35**

his cardiologist would worry. ~~Henry did not care~~. Henry cared only about Darla,

36 — the love of his life, now unconscious. **Kneeling next to her he said**, "Angel Pie, you — **37**

don't have to pawn your engagement ring."

31 Three sentences — *Darla was lying on the floor in a heap, Her legs were bent under her,* and *She breathed in quick pants* — may be easily combined. The ideas in the first two sentences are turned into introductory elements, with the last of the three sentences as the main idea. If you add an introductory element with a verb form, be sure that the subject of the main section of the sentence is the person or thing doing the action or in the state of being mentioned in the introduction. Another possible combination: *After Darla fainted, she was lying on the floor in a heap. With her legs under her, she breathed in quick pants.*

32 The revision cuts repetition; *rapid* and *quick* are the same.

33 Two sentences combine and retain *Henry* as the subject.

34 Two sentences — *He neared Darla and gasped. "My angel," he said.* — have been combined. The new version is more concise and more interesting.

35 A subordinate clause *(that his cardiologist would worry)* tucks an idea from one sentence into another.

36 The original story ends with several short, choppy sentences. The revision combines all but the last sentence.

37 The last two sentences of the original combine with an introductory verb form, *kneeling.* If you begin with *kneeling,* be sure that *he* or *Henry* is the subject of the main part of the sentence. You can also revise this section in this way: *"Angel Pie, you don't have to pawn your engagement ring," he said as he knelt next to her.*

Chapter 18

Steering Clear of Tricky Word Traps

In This Chapter

▶ Distinguishing between similar words

▶ Clarifying what measurement words you can count on

▶ Eliminating nonstandard words and expressions from your writing

▶ Figuring out when you sit/set and when you'd rather lay/lie down

Because little things mean a lot, as the saying goes, this chapter puts your writing under a microscope. The tiny errors that can sink you — such as a nonstandard expression, a faulty irregular verb, or the wrong word from a pair of similar words — are in focus here. Peer through the lens and raise your writing to the highest level.

Telling Word-Twins Apart: Commonly Confused Words

Do you know any twins who resemble each other but have completely different personalities? If so, you already understand that each half of a similar-looking pair may function differently, and woe to the writer who sends one to do the other's job. This section helps you employ word-twins properly.

> **Affect** usually expresses action: Mallory's tantrum did not *affect* her mother's decision to leave the candy aisle.
> **Effect** is most often used as a noun and means "result": One *effect* of Mallory's sweet tooth was a truly impressive dental bill.

> Both *affect* and *effect* may be used in other ways, though much less frequently. *Affect* as a noun means "the way someone displays emotions." *Effect* as a verb means "to bring about a change in the face of opposition." In this chapter, though, I concentrate on the more common usage for each.

> **Farther** refers to distance: Mallory runs *farther* than anyone else when a candy bar is at stake.
> **Further** refers to just about everything but distance (intensity, degree, time, and so forth): When Mallory thought *further* about the matter, she decided that artificial sweetener was not a good choice.

Like expresses similarity, but it may not be attached to a subject/verb combo: She jumps *like* Mike.

As expresses similarity too, but it's the one you want in front of a subject/verb: She jumps *as* Mike does, but she gets paid less for her leaps.

Such as introduces examples: Mallory's cupboard is stocked with sweets *such as* pie filling, pudding mix, and chocolate.

Imply is "to hint": Mallory never actually asked for a gumdrop, but she strongly *implied* that one would be welcome.

Infer is "to figure something out that has been implied": Hearing Mallory's "Ode on a Gumdrop," I *inferred* that the bag of candy would probably be empty after Mallory's visit.

Can you tell the following twins and triplets apart? Circle the best word or phrase in each set of parentheses.

0. Fueled by the caffeine in two double lattes, Jake drove (farther/further) than anyone else.

A. **Farther.** If you're dealing with distance, *farther* is the one you want.

1. The judge insisted on (farther/further) proof that the cop's speed gun was broken.

2. I gave the judge tons of proof, (like/as/such as) a photo of my car, a statement from my girlfriend about how I always drive slowly, and a perfect-attendance award I earned in second grade.

3. Waving my wallet vigorously at the judge, I (implied/inferred) that it was empty and paying the fine was out of the question.

4. (Like/As) judges often do, Judge Crater stubbornly refused to hear my side of the story.

5. "Don't go any (farther/further) with your testimony," he snarled.

6. (Like/As) a statue, I shut up and sat as still as a stone.

7. The judge, unfortunately, (implied/inferred) from my behavior that I was silently protesting his ruling.

8. The (affect/effect) of this decision was disastrous.

9. Nothing I said, when I started talking again, (affected/effected) the judge's ruling.

10. Financial setbacks (like/as/such as) speeding tickets completely wreck my budget.

11. I can't convince my romantic partner to spend (farther/further) time with me without reservations at an expensive restaurant.

12. High-priced food, in my experience, (affects/effects) the way a potential date reacts; if I plan a bowling evening, my date will (imply/infer) that I'm poor and dump me.

Counting and Measuring Grammatically

Lost in the fog of the history of English is the reason why different words are used to describe singulars and plurals when you're counting or measuring:

More than, many, and **fewer** work for plurals: *more than* 19 witnesses, *many* problems, *fewer* than 50 coffee cups. These words work well with things you can count.
Less, much, and **over** take you into singular territory: *less* interest in the sport, *much* unrest, *over* an hour. These words are best with things you can measure but not count.

The word *over* is frequently misused in place of *more* or *more than*.

Amount is appropriate when the item you're discussing is singular: the *amount* of enthusiasm.
Number applies to plurals: the *number* of bowties.

Between is the word you want when you're talking about two people or things: I'm having trouble choosing *between* pistachio and chocolate chip.
Among is for groups of three or more: *Among* the twelve candidates for mayor, Shirley stands out.

Uncover your toes (in case you need to count higher than ten) and take a stab at these sentences. Circle the correct word in each set of parentheses.

0. Just (between/among) you and me, do you think he needs a dye job?

A. **between.** *You* plus *me* equals two, and *between* is the word for couples. *Among* comes into play for three or more, as in *among the five of us.*

13. The boss sent (more than/over) 300 memos describing when and how we can order paper for the copy machine.

14. We employees, all 4,546 of us, discussed the memo (between/among) ourselves, and despite (many/much) difference of opinion, we eventually agreed on one thing.

15. We decided that e-mail uses (fewer/less) paper and is easier to ignore.

16. The boss's (many/much) memos scold us for the (number/amount) of paper we waste.

17. Recently, the boss's secretary collected (more than/over) 5,000 sheets of paper from our desks, all of them memos sent by the boss.

18. Surely it takes (fewer/less) energy to shelve the issue altogether.

19. (More than/over) a year ago the boss caught "shredding fever."

20. The (number/amount) of important material he shredded is impossible to determine.

21. Personally, in a contest (between/among) him and his dog, the dog would win the award for "Best Boss."

22. The dog would fire (fewer/less) employees.

23. With the dog in charge, the (amount/number) of barking would also decrease.

24. (Among/between) the other candidates for a replacement boss that I would consider are all the inhabitants of New York City.

Banishing Bogus Expressions

English *should of* been easier, I *cannot help but* think. *Being that* English is difficult to learn, I'm going to *try and* spend more time studying it. *Irregardless*, I'll still have time to fold origami, a hobby which I *can't hardly* resist because it does *not* have *no* stress attached to it. *Alright,* I admit that this hobby has *alot* of relaxing qualities.

By now I'm sure you've figured out that the italicized words in the preceding paragraph are all problematic. In proper English, they don't exist. If you're using any made-up expressions, it's time to remove them from your speech and writing and substitute the correct words, which you can see in Table 18-1.

Table 18-1	Correcting Made-Up Words
Wrong	*Right*
Should of	Should have, should've
Would of	Would have, would've
Could of	Could have, could've
Cannot help but	Cannot help [insert the *-ing* form of the verb]
Not . . . no	Not *or* no (not both)
Being that	Because
Try and	Try to
Alot	A lot
Alright	All right
Irregardless	Regardless
Can't hardly	Can hardly

Here's your challenge: Rewrite the following sentences, substituting proper English for any nonstandard terms. I throw a few correct sentences into the mix, so when you find one, simply write "correct" in the blank.

Q. I can't help but think that your questions about the final exam are extremely annoying.

_____

_____

A. **I can't help thinking that your questions about the final exam are extremely annoying.** The expressions *can't help but* and *cannot help but* are double negatives. English, not always the most logical language in the universe, is logical in this instance: The two negatives (*not* and *but*) cancel each other and express a positive meaning. Thus the original sentence means that you can stop thinking this way if you want to do so.

25. Irregardless of the teacher's views on having alot of technology in the classroom, Mark sends an instant message to his brother.

_____

_____

26. Kevin doesn't answer immediately, being that he's in the middle of the sandbox and feels that everything is alright.

_____

_____

27. "I'll try and answer Mark after snack," he thinks.

_____

_____

28. The teacher doesn't want no distraction from the peanut butter cookies she has prepared, so she confiscates Kevin's smartphone, with which Kevin tweets alot of information to his followers.

_____

_____

29. Kevin should of hidden his smartphone until nap time, but he thought it would be alright to use it openly.

_____

_____

30. Mark can't hardly believe some of the stories Kevin tells about kindergarten.

_____

_____

31. Mark remembers his own days in finger-paint land, which he should of treasured.

_____

_____

32. Because the third-grade room is near the kindergarten, Mark could of walked out of the classroom and spoken directly to Kevin.

_____

_____

33. Kevin can't help thinking about his smartphone, which now resides on the teacher's desk.

_____

_____

34. Being that the day is almost over, Kevin asks the teacher to return the phone.

_____

_____

35. "Being in kindergarten is really annoying sometimes," Kevin thinks.

_____

_____

36. "I can't hardly wait until I'm in first grade," he remarks with alot of enthusiasm.

_____

_____

Setting Aside Time to Lay into Tricky Verbs

Sit (not _set_) yourself down for some practice with four headache-inducing verbs. Afterward you can _lie_ (not _lay_) down for a rest.

To **lie** is "to rest or recline the body." (Yes, it also means that you aren't telling the truth, but that definition isn't a problem.) The past tense of _lie_ is _lay_. The form of the verb _lie_ that combines with _has, have,_ or _had_ is _lain_.
To **lay** is "to place something" or "to put." The past tense of _lay_ is _laid_. For _lay_, the form that combines with _has, have,_ or _had_ is _laid_.

To **sit** is "to bend your knees and put your bottom on some sort of surface." The past tense and the combo form are both _sat_.
To **set** is "to place, to put something somewhere." The past tense and combo forms are also _set_.

To tell the difference between these two pairs of verbs, think of *lie* and *sit* as actions that a person does to himself or herself: I *lie* down, I *sit* in the chair. *Lay* and *set,* on the other hand, are actions that a person does to something else: I *lay* the check on the desk, I *set* the vase down on the piano.

Don't set down your pen until you try the following questions. Circle the correct form of the verb in the parentheses.

0. Yesterday Alice was so tired that she (lie/lay/lied/laid/lain) down for a nap even though her favorite soap opera was on television.

A. **lay.** The meaning in this sentence is "to rest or to recline," so the verb you want is *to lie,* and the past tense of *to lie* is *lay.*

37. The main character in Alice's favorite show (lies/lays) in bed, comatose.

38. In the world of soaps, the rule is that the doctor must (sit/set) by the bed every day with a look of concern and love on his or her face.

39. In yesterday's episode, the doctor (sit/sat/set) a bouquet of flowers on the nightstand.

40. When the nurse told the doctor to go home and (lie/lay) down, the doctor replied that she would "(sit/set) down for a while."

41. Last week the doctor (lay/laid) a wreath on a mysterious tomb.

42. The viewers think the wreath that (lies/lays) there is a sign that the tomb contains the body of the doctor's long lost lover.

43. During sweeps week, the long lost lover will show up and (sit/set) next to the doctor in the cafeteria.

44. The final show will reveal that the long lost lover has (lain/laid) in a bed, comatose too.

45. While the doctor (sits/sets) there gobbling tuna salad, the lover will explain what happened to the evil twin.

Calling All Overachievers: Extra Practice with Tricky Words

In Figure 18-1 check out an obituary that (never, I assure you) appeared in a local paper. Whenever you encounter a misused word, correct the clunker. You should find ten mistakes.

Lloyd Demos Dies at 81: Specialized in Ancient Egypt

Lloyd Demos died yesterday as he was pursuing farther study in ancient Egyptian culture. Demos, who effected the lives of many residents of our town, had alot of varied interests. Demos should of been famous, but he was very shy. He knew 12 languages, including ancient Egyptian. Being that he spent much time studying Egyptian grammar, his writing was always alright. Demos had just set down to supper when the Grim Reaper appeared at his door. Irregardless, Demos insisted on finishing his mashed potatoes, though he was heard to say, "I would like to lay down for a while." Demos, who wrote over 50 books, will be fondly remembered.

Figure 18-1:
Mock
obituary
filled with
errors.

Answers to Tricky Word Problems

Keeping tricky words straight takes a lot of effort. Use the answers below to check your work on the practice exercises.

1 **further.** In this sentence you want a word that indicates a greater degree, so *further* fills the bill.

2 **such as.** The word must introduce a list of examples, so *such as* is the best choice.

3 **implied.** The speaker in this sentence is hinting that his finances are in bad shape, and *to imply* is "to hint."

4 **As.** In front of a subject/verb combo, *as* is the only appropriate choice.

5 **further.** The verb *go* makes you think of distance (and *farther* is the word you want for distance), but testimony is not a road that can be measured. Instead, the judge is referring to time, and *further* does the job.

6 **Like.** The speaker resembles a statue, and *like* expresses similarity. Because no verb follows, *like* is better than *as*.

7 **inferred.** Picking up on subtle hints, the judge *inferred* that the speaker was annoyed with the speeding ticket.

8 **effect.** The sentence calls for a noun meaning *result*. Bingo: *effect* wins.

9 **affected.** Here you're looking for a verb that's the same as *influence*. *Affect* is that verb.

10 **such as.** The tickets are presented as an example of budget-wreckers, and *such as* introduces examples.

11 **further.** Once you're talking about time, *farther* isn't an option, because *farther* refers to distance.

12 **affects, infer.** Substitute the verb *influences* and the sentence makes sense. *Affect* is a verb meaning "influence." In the second part of the sentence, the date will "figure out," or *infer* the poverty.

13 **more than.** *Memos,* a plural, calls for *more than.*

14 **among, much.** Because more than two employees are talking, *among* is the one you want. *Between* works for couples, not mobs. In the second parentheses, *much* is the choice because *difference* is singular.

15 **less.** The word *paper* is singular, so *less* is appropriate.

16   **many, amount.** *Many* works for plurals, and *memos* is a plural word. In the second parentheses, the singular *paper* is the issue. *Number* works with plurals, but *amount* is for singular expressions.

17   **more than.** When you're talking about *sheets,* you're in plural land. Use *more than.*

18   **less.** It may take *fewer* employees to shelve the issue, but it takes *less* energy, because *energy* is singular.

19   **over.** One year calls for *over,* the term for singulars.

20   **amount.** The word *material* is singular, even though the term may refer to a ton of stuff, as in *the material in my file cabinet that I don't want to work on.* Singular takes *amount.*

21   **between.** In comparing two potential candidates for leadership awards, *between* is best.

22   **fewer.** *Employees* is a plural, so *fewer* does the job.

23   **amount.** Here you're talking about *barking* (yes, the boss barks too), so *amount* is needed for the singular term.

24   **Among.** If you're looking at *all the inhabitants of New York City,* you're talking about more than two people. Hence, *among.*

25   **Regardless of the teacher's views on having a lot of technology in the classroom, Mark sends an instant message to his brother.** *Irregardless* is the Loch Ness Monster of formal English; it doesn't exist. Substitute *regardless. A lot* is always written as two words.

26   **Kevin doesn't answer immediately, because he is in the middle of the sandbox and feels that everything is all right.** Another nonexistent expression is *being that.* Use *because* or *as.* To express an A-OK situation, opt for *all right.* The single-word version *(alright)* is all wrong.

27   **"I'll try to answer Mark after snack," he thinks.** The expression *try and* says that the speaker is going to do two things: *try* and *answer.* But the real meaning of the sentence is "try to answer."

28   **The teacher doesn't want any distraction from the peanut butter cookies she has prepared, so she confiscates Kevin's smartphone, with which Kevin tweets a lot of information to his followers.** Double negatives are a no-no. Change *doesn't want no* to *doesn't want any.* The two-word expression, *a lot,* is acceptable. The single-word *(alot)* is a no-no.

29   **Kevin should have hidden his smartphone until nap time, but he thought it would be all right to use it openly.** The expression *should of* sounds like *should've,* but *should've* is the contraction of *should have,* not *should of.* The other correction eliminates a single word *(alright)* that's common but always incorrect. Go for two: *all right.*

30 **Mark can hardly believe some of the stories Kevin tells about kindergarten.** *Can't hardly* is a double negative, which reverses the intended meaning of the sentence. Go with *can hardly,* which means that Mark thinks Kevin is exaggerating.

31 **Mark remembers his own days in finger-paint land, which he should've treasured.** The contraction *should've* is the short form of *should have.*

32 **Because the third-grade room is near the kindergarten, Mark could have walked out of the classroom and spoken directly to Kevin.** Either *could have* or *could've* is fine, but stay away from *could of.*

33 **Correct.** The expression *can't help* is fine when it precedes the *-ing* form of the verb. Just don't place it with *but,* because then you'll have a double negative.

34 **Because the day is almost over, Kevin asks the teacher to return the phone.** Delete *being that* wherever you find it; send in *because* instead.

35 **Correct.** In this sentence *being* is fine because it's not used as a faulty substitute for *because.* Instead, it's a gerund — a fancy grammatical term for an *-ing* verb form functioning as a noun.

36 **"I can hardly wait until I'm in first grade," he remarks with a lot of enthusiasm.** *Can't hardly,* a double negative, flips your meaning. *Can hardly* says that waiting is a tough task. Remember that *a lot* is always written as two separate words.

37 **lies.** The character, in suitably pale makeup, rests in bed, so *lies* is correct.

38 **sit.** The doctor isn't placing something else on the bed but instead is making a lap. Go for *sit.*

39 **set.** To place something somewhere calls for the verb *set.*

40 **lie, sit.** Both of these spots call for personal body movements, not the placement of something else. *To lie* and *to sit* deal with plopping in bed, on the couch, or in a chair.

41 **laid.** Because the doctor placed the wreath, the verb of choice is *to lay,* and the past tense of *to lay* is *laid.*

42 **lies.** This one is a bit tricky. The doctor *lays* the wreath, but the wreath itself just *lies* (rests) there.

43 **sit.** The lover will pull out a chair and *sit* in it, not place an object somewhere.

44 **lain.** The lover has been stretched out in a bed, in the traditional soapy coma, so the verb must be a form of *lie.* The combo form of *lie* is *lain.*

45 **sits.** The doctor isn't placing something, just staying in a chair, eating. The verb is *to sit,* and the form that matches *doctor* is *sits.*

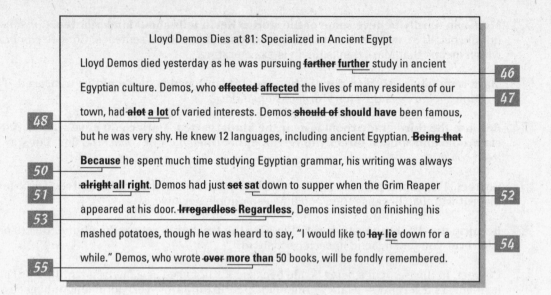

46 — Lloyd Demos died yesterday as he was pursuing ~~farther~~ **further** study in ancient Egyptian culture.

47 — Demos, who ~~effected~~ **affected** the lives of many residents of our town

48 — had ~~alot~~ **a lot** of varied interests.

49 — Demos ~~should of~~ **should have** been famous, but he was very shy. He knew 12 languages, including ancient Egyptian.

50 — ~~Being that~~ **Because** he spent much time studying Egyptian grammar, his writing was always

51 — ~~alright~~ **all right**.

52 — Demos had just ~~set~~ **sat** down to supper when the Grim Reaper appeared at his door.

53 — ~~Irregardless~~ **Regardless**, Demos insisted on finishing his mashed potatoes,

54 — though he was heard to say, "I would like to ~~lay~~ **lie** down for a while."

55 — Demos, who wrote ~~over~~ **more than** 50 books, will be fondly remembered.

46 *Farther* refers to distance; *further* is for time, intensity, or duration.

47 *Effected* can be a verb, but as such it means "to be the sole agent of change." In this sentence "influenced" is the more likely meaning, so *affected* is the one you want.

48 *A lot* is always written as two words.

49 *Should of* isn't proper English. Go for *should have* or *should've.*

50 *Being that* isn't proper English. Opt for *because.*

51 *All right* is always two words, never one.

52 *Sat* is the past tense of *sit,* which is the verb you want for plopping your body in a chair. *Set* is to place something else somewhere else.

53 *Irregardless* doesn't exist, but *regardless* expresses the same idea.

54 *Lie* is to rest or recline; *lay* (in the present tense) is to put something down somewhere. Demos wants to rest, so *lie* is appropriate.

55 *Fifty books* is plural, so *more than* comes into play. *Over* is for singular terms.

Part VI
The Part of Tens

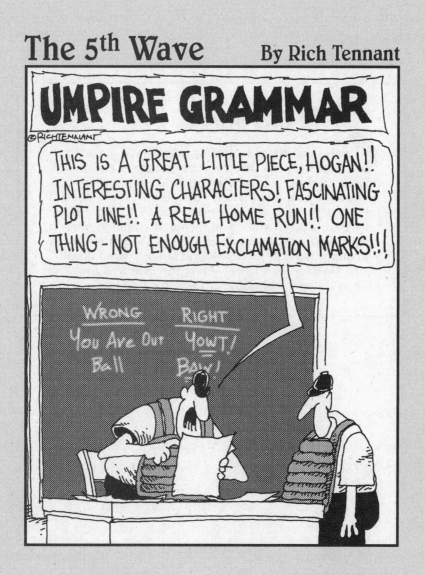

The 5th Wave   By Rich Tennant

In this part . . .

Confession time: This book may be dangerous. Why? Because when you begin to pay attention to proper English, you may be tempted to overcorrect, throwing *whom* into all sorts of spots where it doesn't belong or writing sentences that sound stilted. Never fear: In this part I show you the most common over-corrections so you can steer clear of them. I also warn you about ten ugly mistakes you should avoid at all costs. No exercises here — only the best tips for improving your speaking and writing. Read on.

Chapter 19

Ten Overcorrections

● ●

In This Chapter
▶ Resisting the urge to complicate your sentences
▶ Putting the brakes on unnecessary changes

● ●

*E*nglish teachers recognize a certain tone of voice that comes into play the minute people learn that they're talking to a grammarian. All of a sudden the eyes glaze over, the chin lifts, and the grammar/style portion of the brain goes into overdrive. *Me* becomes *I* for no reason at all. Verb tenses tangle up, and *had* is suddenly as common as tweets from a celebrity. Sadly, what I call "overcorrection" is as bad an error as whatever mistake it's designed to remedy. Here's how to identify these grammar and style potholes so you can avoid them.

Substituting "Whom" for "Who"

True, some uneducated people never utter the word *whom,* even when it's needed in a sentence. But throwing *whom* into every situation isn't a good idea either. Sentences requiring *whom* are actually quite rare. In fact, you need *whom* only when the sentence calls for an object of some sort. (Check out Chapter 9 for more information on *who* and *whom.*)

Objects receive the action of the verb, as in "Whom did you call?" In this sentence, *whom* receives the action of the verb *did call.* (*You,* in case you were wondering, is the subject.) The problem with *whom* is that when it does show up, it's often in a sentence containing other thoughts, so you have to sort out the various threads. One common error: "Whom shall I say is calling?" Sounds nice, right? But it's wrong. Untangling shows you why: "I shall say whom is calling." "Whom is calling?" Nope. "Who is calling."

Inserting "Had" Unnecessarily

As a helping verb, *had* is very good (hangs out in all the best clubs, does community service without a court order, and so on). But it shouldn't be overused. *Had* places an action in the past before another action in the past, as in this sentence: "Archie had already shaved when the aerosol can exploded." On a timeline, the *shaving* precedes the *exploding,* and both precede the present moment. Jackpot. The *shaving* part of the sentence gets the *had.* Overcorrection comes when people sprinkle in a *had had* here and there, without rhyme or reason: "Archie had already shaved when the aerosol can had exploded."

Overusing "Have"

Another helping verb, *have,* shows up where it has no business, I suspect because it makes the sentence sound more complicated and therefore somehow more sophisticated. Like the purple and blue hair I saw yesterday on the bus, an unnecessary *have* stands out, but not in a good way. The *have* error I hear the most is "Nice to have met you." Oh really? The *have* places the meeting in the past, before another action occurring in the present. So "nice to have met you" implies some sort of deadline, as in "nice to have met you before our wedding" or "nice to have met you before it was time for me to clip your toenails." The better expression is "nice to meet you" (now, in the present, as we talk).

Sometimes, when you're texting or tweeting and you're cutting unnecessary words, even a correct use of *have* may be too much. "Gone home" tells your reader just as much as "I have gone home," assuming the reader knows that you're writing about yourself.

Sending "I" to Do a "Me" Job

Me sounds childlike, doesn't it? It conjures up memories of "Me Tarzan!" and similar statements. But *I* isn't the personal pronoun for every spot in a sentence. *I* is a subject pronoun, so it belongs in a subject role or after a linking verb — and nowhere else. An error that pops up frequently is *I* as the object of a preposition: "between you and I" or "except you and I." Penalty box! The correct phrases are "between you and me" and "except you and me."

Speaking or Writing Passively

The government, in my humble opinion, is to blame for this particular overcorrection. Official forms tend to throw passive verbs all over the place, perhaps because passive voice allows the writer to omit the subject — the doer, and therefore the one responsible for the action. How much safer it must feel to write "the taxes were tripled yesterday" rather than "I tripled your taxes yesterday; now please vote for me." But passive voice comes across as stilted. Unless you need it (perhaps because you truly don't know who did the action or because the subject isn't the point of the sentence), opt for active voice. An added bonus pops up when you have a tight word limit (while texting or tweeting, for example): Active voice sentences tend to be shorter. "Fred needs help" has fewer characters than "help is needed by Fred."

Making Sentence Structure Too Complicated

Hey, I can handle complications. I live in New York, where buying an apartment involves a three-inch pile of official forms, each of which must be signed in triplicate. But complicated sentences (which abound in the pile of forms I just mentioned) don't make your writing look more mature. They just make your writing awkward. Stay away from sentences like "It was this treaty that ended the war" and substitute "This treaty ended the war." Run from "That which he discovered yesterday is the invention which will make his fortune" and toward

"The invention he discovered yesterday will make his fortune." As you've probably guessed, unnecessary complications eat up more space than straightforward writing, so avoiding this mistake is a plus when you're instant messaging or tweeting.

Beginning All Your Sentences with Descriptions

Description is good, especially when you're agreeing to a blind date with someone you've never met. (Think of the sentence "Howie is pleasantly plump," in which *pleasantly plump* tells you something important about *Howie*.) Descriptions containing verb forms are good too, because they provide even more information: "Howie, howling at the moon as he does every evening, is happy to double date." The description *howling at the moon as he does every evening* is certainly an eye-opener, giving you a lot of information about *Howie*. Descriptions in the beginning of a sentence are especially good because they vary the usual, boring sentence pattern: "Running with his friend Wolfie, Howie often stays out all night." The description *running with his friend Wolfie* tells you something about *Howie* that you probably should know.

But — and this is a big *but* — don't overuse the introductory description, or you'll simply create a new, but immediately boring, sentence pattern. Also, be sure that the introductory description applies to the subject — the first person or thing mentioned in the sentence. If not, you have a dangler, a truly big no-no.

Becoming Allergic to "They" and "Their"

For some writers, the pronouns *they* and *their* seem to be radioactive. Because many writers make the mistake of pairing the plural *their* with something singular (say, *a person* or *everybody*), overcorrectors do the opposite. Even when a plural is justified, these writers send in *he or she* and similar phrases. Bad idea! Plurals (*the guys, three grapefruits, both, several, a few,* and so on) match with other plurals (*they* and *their*). So don't write "The kids blew off his or her homework and blamed the dog." Instead, keep the plurals together: "The kids blew off their homework and blamed the dog."

Being Formal in Friendly Situations

Compare these messages:

> MESSAGE #1: I am free during period E. I should do my calculus homework, but I am willing to defer it to my evening leisure hours. Shall we meet at the coffee shop?

> MESSAGE #2: I'm free E. Will blow off calc HW if you will. Coffee shop?

Which message would you like to see on your phone? The second one, I bet. It's more appealing in a friend-to-friend situation. Also, it's acceptable even to a grumpy grammarian (like me, for instance). The level of formality in your written and spoken English isn't a constant. Rather, the level adjusts according to the situation. (For a longer discussion of this point, turn to Chapter 12.) Being less formal than you need to be is not a good idea, but being more formal may also be a problem.

Not Knowing When Enough Is Enough

I'm a writing teacher, and as much as anyone else in the field, I'm guilty of asking for more, more, and did I mention I want to see more detail? So when some poor kid hands me a paper about an apple, I'm there with my red pen (teachers' revenge color), writing "What color is the apple? How many seeds does it have?" In the real world, however, I'm not particularly interested in reading 15 sentences about an apple when all I want to know is who threw it at my head when I was returning graded essays. The cure for underexplaining isn't overexplaining. The best path is to provide interesting and relevant details and nothing more. And if your readers wander around wondering how many seeds were in that apple, that's their problem.

Chapter 20

Ten Errors to Avoid at All Costs

. . . .

In This Chapter

▶ Reviewing some mistakes that will ruin your writing

▶ Remembering not to rely too heavily on computers

. . . .

*W*hat did you forget? Your lunch? A parachute? I ask these questions to point out that some mistakes are worse than others. If the plane is going down, I personally am willing to forgo the peanut butter and jelly, but not that handy little life-saving device.

Your writing can crash also, especially if you err in a few specific ways. Ten ways, actually, which I explain here. Everyone makes mistakes, but this chapter shows you how to avoid the big ones.

Writing Incomplete Sentences

Unless, of course, you want to make a style point. I pause to acknowledge that the preceding sentence is incomplete. That's my attempt at irony and also my way of pointing out that sometimes breaking the rules is a good thing. Yes, you heard me correctly. I, a grammarian, believe that chopping some required elements out of your sentences is not only acceptable but also sometimes advisable.

Think about electronic communication — texts, instant messages, tweets, and the like. Depending on the device and format, you may be writing with a fixed character limit. (The number of characters is the sum of all letters, numbers, symbols, and spaces in your text.) Or you may simply have thumb fatigue from typing on a microscopic keyboard. In such situations a subject or a verb may sometimes be omitted, so long as your reader can understand the meaning. (For more information on the interaction between grammar and electronic media, see Chapter 12.)

Even in more traditional situations (words that you actually see on a piece of paper), an occasional incomplete statement sprouting inside a forest of complete sentences calls attention to an important point. Take care, though, not to write an entire forest of incomplete sentences. Then you're not making a style point; you're employing poor English and calling into question whether you know how to fashion a complete sentence (a bad impression to give your reader).

Bottom line: Without a good reason to write an incomplete sentence, be sure that each of your sentences has a subject-verb pair, an endmark, and a complete thought. (For more information on complete sentences, take a look at Chapter 4.)

Letting Sentences Run On and On

A run-on sentence is actually two or more sentences stuck together without any legal "glue" — a word such as *and* or a semicolon. An especially annoying form of run-on is what grammarians call a *comma splice,* in which a comma attempts (and fails) to attach one complete sentence to another. Be especially careful with words that resemble legal joiners (*consequently, however, therefore, nevertheless,* and so forth). Use them for the meaning, but not for glue. (Chapter 4 explains run-ons in greater detail.)

A word here about electronic media: I've received plenty of text messages and tweets with no punctuation at all, and some of them puzzle me. Where does one thought end and another begin? I'm all for adapting grammar to tiny keyboards and messages sent in haste (see the preceding section, as well as Chapter 12), but the nanosecond it takes to insert a period to clarify your meaning is worth your time.

Forgetting to Capitalize "I"

I know, I know. Creating a capital letter on a smartphone or anything else with a minuscule keyboard is a real pain. But you risk alienating the reader by breaking this basic rule: The personal pronoun *I* is always capped. Period.

One more thing: If you place a little circle or heart atop a lowercase, handwritten *i,* you may appear cute to someone who already thinks you're adorable (your grandma, for example). In the professional or academic world, however, you're unlikely to make a good impression on your reader if you fiddle with the basic shapes of letters. Use a dot!

Being Stingy with Quotation Marks

Whether you're writing for school, work, or personal reasons, honesty requires you to credit your sources. Lifting someone else's words, dropping them into your own writing, and failing to use quotation marks is as dishonest as passing the teller a note demanding all the money. In school, such practices earn "F" grades; in work or public life, you may be fired or even sued. The solution is simple. If the words aren't yours, credit the source, as I have in this example, in which I cite a nonexistent author: *As Martin Sherman writes, "Plagiarism is a fatal wound to the body of knowledge."*

Don't forget to acknowledge electronic sources, even if the author isn't named. Someone created the writing on a Web site. If that someone is you, fine. No citation or credit is necessary, though you should probably explain that you're the author. If you aren't the author, you still need to insert quotation marks and to explain where the material appeared, as in this (nonexistent) example: *According to the Toe-Fungus Society Web page, "The good health of the nation's pinky toes is everyone's responsibility."*

Using Pronouns Incorrectly

Pronouns — noun substitutes such as *he, they, all, other, neither,* and the like — are governed by more rules than the citizens of a fanatical tyrant. Even if you don't know every fine point, you should never neglect the basics: Pronouns should replace only nouns or other pronouns, and the word the pronoun refers to should be clearly identifiable. Don't use an object pronoun in a subject-pronoun spot. Singular pronouns should replace singular nouns, and plurals match with plurals. (Check out Chapters 3 and 9 for details on these issues.)

Placing New Words in the Wrong Context

New words seep into your vocabulary gradually. First, they begin to look familiar when they show up in something you're reading. Later, you recognize them as old friends. Later still, you feel comfortable using them in your own sentences. Don't skip any of these stages! Every teacher, including me, has received papers from someone who memorized the "100 words most likely to appear on standardized tests" and who is determined to get as much mileage out of them as possible. The problem is that the nuances of a word's meaning are hard to grasp from a list or a couple of encounters.

Premature use of vocabulary can be *really* embarrassing. You may find yourself, as one of my students did, writing about "New York City's government *suppository* of documents." (**Hint:** A *suppository* is a medicine put inside the body without a needle, a spoon, or a glass of water. Look it up.) What the writer meant to say was *depository* — a storage facility.

Letting Slang Seep into Your Speech

It ain't that slang is always sketchy. In fact, slang can be sick — the real bee's knees. But if you don't have the 411, you may miss the boat.

That paragraph contains a mixture of slang from several different eras. You may have recognized one of the slang expressions and missed another. Therein lies the problem. Slang changes fast — so fast that no one can possibly keep up. If your reader understands that *sick* in the sentence above is slang for "good," fine. But the reader who grasps that concept may not realize that *bee's knees* is a term for the latest, best fashion. By the way, *411* means "information." *Ain't* is a corruption of "isn't," and *sketchy* conveys danger. Bottom line: A writer who uses slang risks confusion. Also, slang sounds informal; if you want to impress a boss or a teacher, it's not the best vocabulary to employ.

Forgetting to Proofread

Even if you finished the paper or project only ten minutes before you have to cram it into the mailbox, take the time to proofread your work. Yo maye ffind tat som latters are nut where they sould be, not to mentione. punctuation, (Translation: You may find that some letters are not where they should be, not to mention punctuation.)

And yes, you should proofread e-mail, texts, tweets, and instant messages before you hit Send. Why? Because using electronic media doesn't give you a get-out-of-grammar-jail-free card. In fact, because writing with electronic media tends to be concise, mistakes stand out as if they were written in fluorescent pink. (For more information on grammar shortcuts you *can* use when writing with electronic media, turn to Chapter 12.)

Relying on Computer Checks for Grammar and Spelling

You can't cash them in, but computer checks are popular anyway, and you should remember to glance at them as you write. (I'm referring to the red and green lines that show up on the screen to alert you to a possible mistake.) I have to admit that sometimes they actually help, but they're not 100 percent accurate. First of all, plenty of eras slip through. (See what I mean? That last sentence should read *plenty of errors.*) Secondly, the computer often identifies a mistake when the sentence is actually correct. I get little wavy lines lots of times, and as you have figured out by now, I'm prefect. Er . . . perfect.

Repeating Yourself or Cutting Essential Words

In conclusion, at the end of this chapter, I would like to state and declare that saying the same thing more than once repetitively is a real drag, an annoyance, and a pain. Don't — do not — repeat, because repetition isn't a fun or enjoyable way to pass the time. Repetition will send your reader away fast and quickly, not to mention rapidly. Shall I reiterate the point? Once is enough.

At the other end of the spectrum is writing that is too concise — so clipped that the reader has to puzzle out what you probably meant. If you type "fired" and press the send button, the recipient may think (1) I lost my job! or (2) You lost your job! or (3) Someone we were talking about earlier lost a job! Each of these situations is different, and adding an extra word or two for the sake of clarity is crucial.

Appendix

Grabbing Grammar Goofs

● ●

*H*ow sharp are your eyes? This appendix is the grammatical equivalent of an optometrist's chart. If you can see it with 20/20 vision, you'll spot 30 mistakes in each of the first six exercises. Of course, after you spot the errors, your mission is to correct them. The errors may involve faulty structure or word choice, punctuation, capitalization, and anything else the *English Grammar Workbook For Dummies* covers.

Spotting and correcting errors prepares you for standardized writing tests. The last two exercises in this chapter go even further by mimicking a common format. If you're preparing for one of those tortures — sorry, *exams* — these exercises will help. Even if you aren't sharpening No. 2 pencils for the SAT, the ACT, or a similar challenge, you can still improve your grammar and writing style by working through exercises seven and eight.

Exercise One

Sneak a peek at the college catalogue (from a university that exists only in my mind) in Figure A-1. This course description has many faults — 30, by my count. Your count may differ slightly depending on how you group your answers. Don't worry about numbers — your mission is to search and destroy the mistakes.

6901 World Domination (3 credits): Professor Peck, Mr. Lapham, Ms. Austin. One two-hour lecture period per week is required. Three periods of fieldwork per week is also required.

This course on world domination and dictatorship involve both lecture and that they put into practice what students will learn. A student will report to their faculty advisors once a month. Everyone must keep a journal of revolutions started, governments overthrown, and peasants' oppressed. Readings include Karl and Groucho Marx's masterful essay, "Laughing All The Way to The Throne", and Chairman Mayo's autobiography, *Hold the Bacon.* This is sure to interest students who's career plans are to be an emperor; tsar; dictator; or reality-show winner. By the time the course concludes, students have gathered all necessary information about what it takes to rule the world. We will be discussing topics like propaganda, media manipulation, and telegenic coronation clothes (including crown-jewel selection). Working in the field, spy networks will be set up, this will count as a quarter of the grade. The students's task is to outmaneuver everyone in the course by becoming the first to conquer a hostile country that is required for graduation. Exams also emphasizes real practical skills, and theoretical ideas. Students only write two papers.

Admission to this course and it's sequel (Universal Domination) are by permission of the Department of Politically Science Irregardless of age or class rank, applicants should be as motivated than the average freshman and should try and visit the departmental office for an interview.

Figure A-1: A scary sample course description that needs some work (in more ways than one).

Exercise Two

This letter from a made-up publisher, in Figure A-2, is full of errors. Try your hand at correcting all 30.

Higgen Publishing Company

459 elm Avenue

Bronxton, VT 05599

October 31, 2010

Mr. Chester Slonton

33 Warwickville Road

Alaistair, CA 90990

Dear Mr. Slonton:

Thank you for sending us your novel, "The Lily Droops at Dawn." To read over 1,000 pages about a love affair between plants is a very unique experience. In your talented hands, both of the plants becomes characters that are well-rounded and of great interest to the reader. Before Mr. Higgen, whom you know is our founder, commits to publishing this masterpiece, I must ask for some real minor changes.

Most of the editors, including Mr. Higgen, was confused about the names. You are absolutely right in stating that each of the lovers are in the lily family, scientifically they have similar characteristics. Calling the lovers Lila and Lyle would not of been a problem if the characters were distinguished from one another in personality or habits or appearance. Unfortunately, your main characters resembles each other in petal color and height. True, one of the lilies is said to be smartest, but the reader doesnt know which.

A second problem are the love scenes. You mention in your cover letter that you can make them more lengthier. Mr. Higgen feels, and I agree, that you write vivid; nevertheless, we think you could cut them alot without losing the reader's attention. After all, once a person has read one flower proposal, he or she has essentially read them all.

Finally, the ending needs work. When the lily droops, the book ended. Are you comfortable with a tiny change. Market research shows that books with happy endings appeal to the readers, whoever he or she may be. These volumes sell good. Instead of drooping, perhaps the lily could spread it's petals and welcome the dawn. Or become a rose.

Higgen Publishing would like this novel for their fall list. I hope that you are open to the changes I had outlined in this letter. I cannot help but mention that Higgen Publishing is probably the only publisher with experience in plant romance volumes I look forward to having talked with you about the editing process.

Sincerely,

Cynthia Higgen

Figure A-2: A sample letter from a publisher (with a lot of mistakes, so you know it must be fake).

Exercise Three

Try your hand at editing the newspaper article in Figure A-3. You should find 30 errors, including some in the quoted material. (If you're quoting someone who makes a grammar error, you may usually leave the error in the quotation in order to convey the speaker's style or personality. For the purposes of this exercise, however, correct every mistake.)

Hold the Tights: a Former Television Star Plays Shakespeare

Silver, the actor that played a talking horse on the Emmy-winning series *Mr. Said* is now starring in the Royal Theater production of "Hamlet." The handsome blond recently agreed to discuss his approach to acting. It were never about talking, in Silvers' view. As he had munched oats and sipped delicately from a water pail, the colt explained that he learned to talk at the age of one. Him talking was not fulfilling enough, only acting met his need for recognition.

"I started by reciting monologues for whomever would listen," he said. Then one day I got a call from a Hollywood agent offering me the part of Mr. Said." Tossing his mane in the air, Silver continued, "I plays that role for nine seasons. You get typecast. Nobody want to take a chance on your dramatic ability if they can find someone else for the role." He added, "Sitting by the phone one day, it rang, and my agent told me that I had a audition." That audition resulted in him getting the part. Silver is the only horse that have ever played Hamlet, as far as he knows.

The actor has all ready began rehearsals. His costume includes a traditionally velvet coat but no tights. "Between you and I," he whispered, "the tights snag on my fur." Director Ed Walketers asked Silver to consider shaving, and he also tried several types of material for the tights. Even Silver's wife got involved in this key costuming decision. "No one tried harder than her to find tights I could wear," Silver said. Nothing was suitable for this extremely unique situation.

Silver is equally as involved with the role itself. "I relate to Hamlet's problems," he explained. "Us horses often find it hard to take action and being decisive." The role is also exhausting; Silver lays down for a quickly nap every day before having gone onstage as Hamlet.

Figure A-3:
A sample newspaper article with a plethora of errors.

Exercise Four

Don't you hate computer manuals? The one in Figure A-4 is even worse than the usual techno-babble because it contains 30 mistakes. Correct them!

Installing You're New Widget Wheel

To install the widget wheel, a computer should first be turned off, then follow these simple steps.

Important: If you have an A4019 or a newest model, please discard this manual. You must have sent for manual number 218B, or, in the case of a computer that previously has a widget, for manual number 330B. Being that your computer is not covered in this manual, discard it. Faulty directions have been responsible for explosions and that software crashed.

1. Unpack the widget wheel which looks like a sharks tooth.

2. Unpack the two disk poles. Grasp the disk pole that is more circular. Lining up the teeth with the teeth on the widget. *Note:* Teeth should be brushed alot with a WidgetBrush. see the enclosed order form for more information.

3. After the teeth are tight clenched, a person should insert the widget disk into slot C. However, if the widget disk has a blue strip, in which case it should be inserted into slot D. Don't mix up the slots as the computer will catch fire. Neither of these slots are open when the computer is standing upright. Sit the computer on its side before beginning this step.

4. Turn on the computer. If the screen is blank call the service specialist at 914-555-5039. If the screen blinks rapid from red to green (or from blue to yellow in model 2W4T), run further from the screen. This means the widget was installed improper, the computer is altogether unusable.

5. You are almost ready to enjoy your new widget!! Place a hand on the mouse that is not wearing any rings, including wedding rings. Depending upon the model number, either press firmly or softly. Some widgets can work good no matter what the pressure.

Figure A-4: The world's biggest headache inducer: A sample of a poorly written computer manual.

Exercise Five

A memo to the boss should be perfect. The one in Figure A-5, a report on a fictional construction project, is far from ideal. Improve this employee's chances for promotion — or, at the very least, job retention — by editing out 30 mistakes.

"Memorandum"

To: Eliot Simpson

From: Nina Winter

Date: september 23, 2020

Re: Bid for Hacker' Wallpaper Factory

This morning Jenna Pamek and myself met with Oscar Hacker, President of Hacker Wallpaper. We presented our bid to renovate his wallpaper factory, that has been located on the corner of 71st Street and Alexander Avenue. The two of us, who Mr. Hacker will have praised for our work on the paste factory, set down to try and go over the financial aspects of the project. Although mathematics were hard for me when I took it in college, I explained the numbers real well. When I had left, I was convinced that Mr. Hacker would give the job to this fine company of ours'.

No matter what Jenna will have said, everyone were satisfied with their gift basket. It is totally a lie and not true at all that one of the gift baskets were filled with money. Mr. Hacker objects to me bribing him. Jenna was just upset; because she had to listen to Mr. Hacker explain that a square had four sides, and the "square" in our design has five. "You should of studied geometry"! Mr. Hacker exclaimed.

Jenna, whom everyone thinks is close friends with Mrs. Hacker, was very wrong when she said that I stapled her hair to the table. Pulling out the staple, the table was damaged and that it will need repairs. Either Mr. Hacker or his assistants is willing to testify that I never touched the stapler. Mr. Hacker awarded the contract to our competitor because our bid was too high and for no other reason.

Figure A-5:
A memo from an employee to his supervisor. Both the employee and the memo have many problems!

Exercise Six

Here's a particularly bad set of PowerPoint-style presentation slides. Make some changes (30, to be exact) to Figure A-6 to make this presentation conform to grammar rules.

Slide #1

> Marketing potential for Pierced-Elbow Rings
>
> The target buyer is:
>
> - 21–92 years old
>
> - has two piercings already in other body parts
>
> - Concerned about their appearance and what they look like

Slide #2

> Specifications of Pierced-Elbow Rings
>
> - they dont pinch the elbow's skin
>
> - Manufacturing cost are minimal.
>
> - Karen Oleson the designer specifies allergy free metal.
>
> - Some of the rings is made of plastic.

Slide #3

> Themes And Holiday Promotions include the following
>
> - greased rings for Labor day in honor of the "elbow grease" a person uses when you are working
>
> - back to school rings that looks like rings in binders
>
> - Telephone rings with alot of ring tones (purchasing separately)
>
> - engagement rings decorated with wedding bells laying over clasped hands

Slide #4

> Marketing challenges will have been
>
> - Long sleeved shirts cover the rings.
>
> - When catching on cloth, antiseptic that kills germs must be applied.
>
> - You only have two elbows, and we can't hardly sell more than two rings per person.

Figure A-6: Presentation slides with a powerful number of errors.

Exercise Seven

If you're a high school student, sooner or later you're likely to encounter a reading passage that tests your grammar skills. Standardized tests, such as the SAT and the ACT, hit you with multiple-choice questions about a paragraph desperately in need of revision. If your school days are in the rear-view mirror, you can still sharpen your editing skills with this exercise, which resembles what you may encounter in standardized testing (but with a little humor thrown in).

Directions: Following this student essay are six questions. Choose the best answer.

⎡1⎤ Being a teenager, a large part of my life takes place at school. ⎡2⎤ I love most of the academic experience. ⎡3⎤ But one aspect of school is frowned upon by me: tests. ⎡4⎤ Every year the school board, college admissions offices, and my personal teachers give more and more tests. ⎡5⎤ Sometimes I spend more time explaining what I know than I do having relaxed in the cafeteria.

⎡6⎤ Last year the arts curriculum included a unit on technology. ⎡7⎤ Acquiring knowledge and relaxing with friends should be the primary reason for school. ⎡8⎤ I created a great movie script, cast the roles, and built the sets. ⎡9⎤ I only filmed one scene. ⎡10⎤ Why? ⎡11⎤ I was spending the days filling in little bubbles with a pencil. ⎡12⎤ When I offered my movie as an alternative to boring exams, the school board said no.

⎡13⎤ Students should be able to skip their tests if they have another way to show how much they have learned. ⎡14⎤ The student will be happier, and the alternative assessment will be more valuable (Hollywood pays a lot) and exams create stress.

181. Which of the following is the best revision of Sentence 1?

(A) No change.

(B) Being a teenager, most of my life happens at school.

(C) Being a teenager, I spend a large part of my life at school.

(D) Because of being a teenager, a large part of my life begins at school.

(E) A large portion of every teenager's life takes place at school.

182. How may Sentences 2 and 3 be combined most effectively?

(A) No change.

(B) I love most of the academic experience, but tests are frowned upon by me.

(C) I love most of the academic experience; one aspect, tests, is really frowned upon by me.

(D) Accept for tests, I love most of the academic experience.

(E) I love most of the academic experience, but I frown upon tests.

183. How should Sentence 5 be revised?

(A) No change.

(B) Sometimes I spend more time explaining what I know, than I do having relaxed in the cafeteria.

(C) Sometimes I spend more time explaining what I know than relaxing in the cafeteria.

(D) Sometimes I spend more time having explained what I know than I do having relaxed in the cafeteria.

(E) Sometimes I spend more time explaining what I know than I relax in the cafeteria.

184. Sentence 7 should

(A) remain where it is

(B) be placed between Sentences 3 and 4

(C) be deleted

(D) be moved to the end of the second paragraph

(E) be moved to the end of the third paragraph

185. Which of the following is the best revision of Sentence 9?

(A) No change.

(B) I filmed only one scene.

(C) Only I filmed one scene.

(D) I did film only one scene.

(E) I had only filmed one scene.

186. To improve this essay, what should be done with the third paragraph (Sentences 13 and 14)?

(A) No change.

(B) Delete Sentence 14.

(C) Reverse the order, so Sentence 13 follows Sentence 14.

(D) Add an additional example of a useless test.

(E) State that this essay represents the author's opinion.

Exercise Eight

If you plan to fill little ovals with pencil lead anytime soon — or even if you don't — you can hone your writing skills with this exercise, which is set up in the same format you may meet on a standardized test. Read the essay and answer the questions that follow. *Note:* This essay is a little silly in terms of subject matter, but the questions are serious. And so are the SATs and ACTs and the rest of the "alphabet soup" of exams!

Directions: Following this student essay are six questions. Choose the best answer.

[1] A wise man once said that, "You may as well be yourself because being someone else requires too much makeup." [2] Being yourself isn't as easy as you may think. [3] First, you have to figure out who you are. [4] And who you are is defined in many ways. [5] Your family gives you one definition. [6] The society in which you live in this current time also gives you a definition. [7] Really important are the choices you make because your experiences affect who you are.

[8] Once, when I was beginning a new school, I walked into the cafeteria of that school where I would be studying. [9] People were all over, and no one knew or cared who I was. [10] No one, except for the kid who threw his mashed potatoes at me, even saw me. [11] After I retaliated by slipping a slice of pizza into his backpack, I sat down to think. [12] Who would I be in my new school — a nerd, a jock, an activist? [13] I decided to devote all my energy to student government and nominated myself for office the very next day. [14] I gave free pizza to everyone who promised voting for me. [15] Society gave me a chance to prove myself by giving me a new school, even though I had burned down the old one. [16] My choices have led me to my true self. [17] Today I can proudly say that I am a successful politician and the owner of 2,592 pizzerias.

187. Which of the following, if any, is the best revision of Sentences 1 and 2?

(A) No change.

(B) Omit "that" from Sentence 1.

(C) Place Sentence 2 before Sentence 1.

(D) Delete Sentence 2.

(E) Add "irregardless" to Sentence 2.

188. In the context of this essay, which sentence, if any, would be a good addition to the first paragraph?

(A) No change.

(B) Self-definition is a lifelong task.

(C) No one really understands his or her own identity.

(D) Identity is a private matter.

(E) Your identity is set at birth.

189. What is the best revision, if any, of Sentence 6?

(A) No change.

(B) Your society in this current time also gives you a definition.

(C) The society, in which you live in this current time, also gives you a definition.

(D) The society in which you live also defines you.

(E) Society, in this current time, also defines you.

190. To improve Sentence 8, what should the writer do?

(A) No change.

(B) End the sentence after "cafeteria."

(C) Delete the words between the commas.

(D) Change "was beginning" to "had begun."

(E) Change "would be studying" to "will study."

191. Which is the best revision, if any, of Sentence 14?

(A) No change.

(B) I gave free pizza to everyone who promised they would vote for me.

(C) I gave free pizza to whoever promised their votes to me.

(D) I gave free pizza to everyone who promised to vote for me.

(E) Giving free pizza, everyone promised to vote for me.

192. What change, if any, would you make to this essay?

(A) No change.

(B) Mention politics and pizza in the first paragraph.

(C) Insert additional examples of choices in the first paragraph.

(D) Delete the first paragraph.

(E) Place Sentences 16 and 17 in a concluding paragraph, expanding on the ideas they contain.

Answers to Exercise One

In the following figure the errors from the original course description are boldfaced and crossed out, with a possible correction following each one, as well as an occasional addition of a missing word or mark. All corrections are boldfaced and underlined. Check the corresponding numbered explanations that follow the revised course description.

6901 World Domination (3 credits): Professor Peck, Mr. Lapham, Ms. Austin. One two-hour lecture period per week is required. Three periods of fieldwork per week ~~is~~ **are** also required.

1

This course on world domination and dictatorship ~~involve~~ **involves** both lecture and ~~that they put into practice~~ **practical application of** what students ~~will learn~~ **learn**.

2 **3** **4**

~~A student~~ **Students** will report to their faculty advisors once a month. Everyone must keep a journal of revolutions started, governments overthrown, and peasants**'** oppressed. Readings include Karl and Groucho Marx's masterful essay, "Laughing All ~~T~~**t**he Way to ~~T~~**t**he Throne**,"**, and Chairman Mayo's autobiography, *Hold the Bacon*. This **reading list** is sure to interest students ~~who's~~ **whose** career plans are to be an emperor**,** tsar**,** dictator**,** or reality-show winner. By the time the course concludes, students **will have** gathered all necessary information about what it takes to rule the world. We will be discussing topics ~~like~~ **such as** propaganda, media manipulation, and telegenic coronation clothes (including crown-jewel selection). Working in the field, ~~spy networks will be set up~~ **students will set up spy networks**~~,~~; **this** **fieldwork** will count as a quarter of the grade. The ~~students's~~ **students'** task **that is required for graduation** is to outmaneuver everyone **else** in the course by becoming the first to conquer a hostile country ~~that is required for graduation~~. Exams also ~~emphasizes~~ **emphasize** ~~real~~ **really** practical skills**,** and theoretical ideas. Students ~~only~~ write **only** two papers.

5 **6** **7** **8** **9** **10** **11** **12** **13** **14** **15** **16** **17** **18** **19** **20** **21** **22** **23** **24**

Admission to this course and ~~it's~~ **its** sequel (Universal Domination) ~~are~~ **is** by permission of the Department of ~~Politically~~ **Political** Science. ~~Irregardless~~ **Regardless** of age or class rank, applicants should be as motivated ~~than~~ **as** the average freshman and should try ~~and~~ **to** visit the departmental office for an interview.

25 **26** **27** **28** **29** **30**

1. The subject is *three periods,* a plural, so the verb *(are)* must also be plural.

2. The subject *course* is singular, so the verb *(involves)* must also be singular.

3. To keep the sentence parallel, the noun *lecture* should be coupled with another noun, not with a subject/verb combo.

4. The *practical application* is simultaneous to the learning, so future tense isn't what you want. Go for present *(learn).*

5. The paragraph refers to *students* (plural), so a shift in one spot to singular is inappropriate. Also, *a student* should never pair with *their,* because singulars and plurals don't match.

6. The original sentence includes the possessive *peasants'* for no valid reason. The possessive form should be linked to a noun, but here it precedes a verb form *(oppressed).*

7. In titles, articles (such as *the* in this title) shouldn't be capitalized.

8. When a comma follows quoted material, the comma is placed inside the closing quotation mark.

9. In the original sentence the pronoun *this* is vague. Insert the clarifying expression *reading list.*

10. The contraction *who's* means "who is," but the sentence calls for the possessive *whose.*

11. Items in a series are separated by semicolons only when one or more of the items contain a comma. In this series, no item contains a comma, so semicolons aren't necessary.

12. A future deadline *(by the time the course concludes)* calls for future perfect tense *(will have gathered).*

13. *Like* excludes the items listed and refers to items that are similar. In this sentence the listed items are examples and should be preceded by *such as.*

14. The original sentence contains a dangler, *working in the field.* An introductory element containing a verb form must refer to the subject, and *spy networks* aren't *working in the field.* Reword the sentence so that the *students* are *working in the field.*

15. Two complete sentences may not be joined by a comma. Substitute a semicolon or make two sentences.

16. The pronoun *this* is too vague all by itself. Substitute a noun *(fieldwork)* to clarify the meaning.

17. To create a possessive form for a plural ending in the letter *s,* just add an apostrophe, not an extra *s.*

18 The student is *in* the course and so must be compared to everyone *else*.

19 In the original, this misplaced description seems to say that *a country* is required for gradua-tion, not the *task*. Descriptions should be close to the word they describe.

20 The plural subject, *exams*, requires a plural verb, *emphasize*.

21 The description *practical* should be intensified by an adverb *(really)*, not by an adjective *(real)*.

22 If you unite two complete sentences with the word *and*, a comma precedes the *and*. If you unite two of anything else (in this sentence, two nouns — *skills* and *ideas*), no comma precedes the *and*.

23 The descriptive word *only* should precede the word being compared — in this case, *only two* as compared to *three* or *four* or whatever the professor assigns.

24 Possessive pronouns have no apostrophes.

25 *Admission* is singular and takes a singular verb, *is*.

26 The adjective *Political* describes the noun *Science*. *Politically* is an adverb and may describe only verbs *(speaking politically)* or other descriptions *(politically inexperienced)*.

27 A statement should end with a period, which is missing in the original.

28 *Irregardless* isn't Standard English. Substitute *regardless*.

29 *As* and *than* don't belong in the same comparison. An *as* comparison is for equal items and a *than* comparison for unequal items.

30 *Try and* implies two actions, but the sentence refers to one that should be attempted. The proper expression is *try to*.

Answers to Exercise Two

In the following figure the errors from the original letter are boldfaced and crossed out, with a possible correction following each one, as well as an occasional addition of a missing word or mark. All corrections are boldfaced and underlined. Check the corresponding numbered explanations that follow the revised letter.

Higgen Publishing Company

459 ~~elm~~ **Elm** Avenue — *31*

Bronxton, VT 05599

October 31, 2010

Mr. Chester Slonton

33 Warwickville Road

Alaistair, CA 90990

Dear Mr. Slonton:

Thank you for sending us your novel, ~~"The Lily Droops at Dawn."~~ *The Lily Droops at Dawn.* To read — *32*

~~over~~ **more than** 1,000 pages about a love affair between plants is a ~~very~~ unique experience. In your — *33* *34*

talented hands, both of the plants ~~becomes~~ **become** characters that are well-rounded and ~~of great~~ — *35*

~~interest~~ **interesting** to the reader. Before Mr. Higgen, ~~whom~~ **who** you know is our founder, commits to — *36* *37*

publishing this masterpiece, I must ask for some ~~real~~ **really** minor changes. — *38*

Most of the editors, including Mr. Higgen, ~~was~~ **were** confused about the names. You are absolutely right — *39*

in stating that each of the lovers ~~are~~ **is** in the lily family~~,~~ ; scientifically they have similar characteristics. — *40* *41*

Calling the lovers Lila and Lyle would not ~~of~~ **have** been a problem if the characters were distinguished — *42*

from one another in personality or habits or appearance. Unfortunately, your main characters ~~resembles~~

resemble each other in petal color and height. True, one of the lilies is said to be ~~smartest~~ **smarter**, but the — *43* *44*

reader doesn't know which. — *45*

A second problem ~~are~~ **is** the love scenes. You mention in your cover letter that you can make them ~~more~~ — *46* *47*

lengthier. Mr. Higgen feels, and I agree, that you write ~~vivid~~ **vividly**; nevertheless, we think you could cut — *48*

them ~~alot~~ **a lot** without losing the reader's attention. After all, once a person has read one flower proposal, — *49*

he or she has essentially read them all.

Finally, the ending needs work. When the lily droops, the book ~~ended~~ **ends**. Are you comfortable with a — *50*

tiny change~~,~~ **?** Market research shows that books with happy endings appeal to the readers, whoever — *51*

~~he or she~~ **they** may be. These volumes sell ~~good~~ **well**. Instead of drooping, perhaps the lily could spread — *52* *53*

it's petals and welcome the ~~dawn. Or~~ **dawn or** become a rose. — *54* *55*

Higgen Publishing would like this novel for ~~their~~ **its** fall list. I hope that you are open to the changes I — *56*

~~had~~ outlined in this letter. I cannot help ~~but mention~~ **mentioning** that Higgen Publishing is probably the — *57* *58*

only publisher with experience in plant romance volumes. I look forward to ~~having talked~~ **talking** with you — *59* *60*

about the editing process.

Sincerely,

Cynthia Higgen

31 Proper names are capitalized.

32 The title of a full-length work (in this case, a novel) is italicized or underlined, not enclosed in quotation marks.

33 *Over* precedes a singular word, and *more than* precedes a plural.

34 *Unique* is an absolute, so no degrees of uniqueness (*very unique, a little unique,* and so on) exist.

35 *Both* is plural and should be matched with the plural verb *become*.

36 The original sentence isn't parallel because it pairs the simple description *well rounded* with the phrase *of great interest*. The correction changes the phrase to a simple description, *interesting*.

37 The pronoun *who* is needed to act as a subject for the verb *is*.

38 *Real* is an adjective and appropriate for descriptions of people, places, things, or ideas. The adverb *really* intensifies the description *minor*.

39 *Most of the editors* is a plural subject and requires a plural verb, *were*.

40 *Each of the lovers* is a singular subject and requires a singular verb, *is*.

41 A comma may not join two complete sentences. Use a semicolon instead.

42 *Would of* doesn't exist in Standard English. The proper expression is *would have,* here changed to the negative *would not have*.

43 The plural subject *characters* needs the plural verb *resemble*.

44 *Smartest* is for the extreme in groups of three or more. Because only two lilies are compared, *smarter* is correct.

45 The contraction *doesn't* contains an apostrophe.

46 The singular subject *problem* takes the singular verb *is*.

47   Double comparisons aren't correct. Use *lengthier* or *more lengthy*.

48   The verb *write* may be described by the adverb *vividly* but not by the adjective *vivid*.

49   The expression *a lot* is always written as two words.

50   The present-tense verb *ends* works best with the rest of the sentence, which contains the present-tense verb *droops*.

51   This sentence, a question, calls for a question mark instead of a period.

52   The plural pronoun *they* refers to *readers*.

53   *Good* is an adjective, but the sentence calls for the adverb *well* to describe the verb *sell*.

54   A possessive pronoun, such as *its,* never includes an apostrophe.

55   The expression *or become a rose* is a fragment and may not stand as a separate sentence.

56   A company is singular, so the matching pronoun is *its.*

57   The helping verb *had* is used only to place one action in the past before another past action.

58   *Cannot help but mention* is a double negative.

59   Every sentence needs an endmark. This statement calls for a period.

60   *Having talked* implies a deadline, and the sentence doesn't support such a meaning.

Answers to Exercise Three

In the following figure the errors from the original article are boldfaced and crossed out, with a possible correction following each one, as well as an occasional addition of a missing word or mark. All corrections are boldfaced and underlined. Check the corresponding numbered explanations that follow the revised article.

61 Hold the Tights: ~~a~~ **A** Former Television Star Plays Shakespeare

Silver, the actor that played a talking horse on the Emmy-winning series *Mr. Said***,** is now starring in the **62**

63 Royal Theater production of ~~"Hamlet."~~ *Hamlet***.** The handsome blond recently agreed to discuss his

64 approach to acting. It ~~were~~ **was** never about talking, in ~~Silvers'~~ **Silver's** view. As he ~~had~~ munched oats **65**

and sipped delicately from a water pail, the colt explained that he learned to talk at the age of one. ~~Him~~ **66**

67 **His** talking was not fulfilling enough~~,~~**;** only acting met his need for recognition. **68**

69 "I started by reciting monologues for ~~whomever~~ **whoever** would listen," he said. **†**Then one day I got a **70**

call from a Hollywood agent offering me the part of Mr. Said." Tossing his mane in the air, Silver continued,

"I ~~plays~~ **played** that role for nine seasons. You get typecast. Nobody ~~want~~ **wants** to take a chance on your **72**

71 dramatic ability if ~~they~~ **he or she** can find someone else for the role." He added, "Sitting by the phone one

73 day, ~~it rang~~ **I heard the phone ring,** and my agent told me that I had ~~a~~ **an** audition." That audition resulted **75**

74 in ~~him~~ **his** getting the part. Silver is the only horse that ~~have~~ **has** ever played Hamlet, as far as he knows. **77**

76

The actor has ~~all ready~~ **already** ~~began~~ **begun** rehearsals. His costume includes a ~~traditionally~~ **traditional** **80**

78 velvet coat but no tights. "Between you and ~~I~~ **me**," he whispered, "the tights snag on my fur." Director Ed **81**

79 Walketers asked Silver to consider shaving, and ~~he~~ **Silver** also tried several types of material for the

82 tights. Even Silver's wife got involved in this key costuming decision. "No one tried harder than ~~her~~ **she** to **83**

find tights I could wear," Silver said. Nothing was suitable for this ~~extremely~~ **unique** situation. **84**

Silver is equally ~~as~~ involved with the role itself. "I relate to Hamlet's problems," he explained. "~~Us~~ **We** **86**

85 horses often find it hard to take action and ~~being~~ **to be** decisive." The role is also exhausting; Silver

87 ~~lays~~ **lies** down for a ~~quickly~~ **quick** nap every day before ~~having gone~~ **going** onstage as Hamlet. **90**

88

89

61   The first word of a title and a subtitle should always be capitalized.

62   *Silver* identifies the horse being discussed. The original sentence has a comma at the beginning of the long, descriptive expression (*the actor who played a talking horse on the Emmy-winning series* Mr. Said) but none at the end. The second comma is necessary because the information supplied is extra, not essential to the meaning of the sentence. It should be set off from the rest of the sentence by a pair of commas.

63   The title of a full-length work (in this sentence, a play) should be in italics or underlined.

64   The singular *it* pairs with the singular verb *was*.

65   A singular possessive is formed by the addition of an apostrophe and the letter *s*.

66   The helping verb *had* places one past action before another past action, but in this sentence the actions take place at the same time. Drop the *had*.

67   The possessive pronoun *his* should precede an *-ing* form of a verb that is being used as a noun (in this sentence, *talking*).

68   Two complete sentences shouldn't be joined by a comma. Use a semicolon instead.

69   The subject pronoun *whoever* is needed as the subject of the verb *would listen*. The preposition *for* may have confused you because normally an object follows a preposition. However, in this sentence the entire expression *(whoever would listen)* is the object of the preposition, not just the pronoun.

70   A quotation mark belongs at the beginning and the end of the quotation.

71   The past tense verb matches the meaning of the sentence.

72   The pronoun *nobody* is singular and requires a singular verb, *wants*.

73   Only singular pronouns (in this sentence, *he or she*) can refer to the singular pronoun *nobody*.

74   In the original sentence, *it* (the phone) is sitting by the phone — illogical! Reword in some way so that the speaker is sitting by the phone. Another possible correction: Add a subject/verb combo to the beginning of the sentence so that it begins "When I was sitting by the phone."

75   The article *an* precedes vowel sounds, such as the *au* in *audition*.

76 The possessive pronoun *his* should precede the *-ing* form of a verb that is being used as a noun (in this sentence, *getting*).

77 Because *only one horse* is the meaning of the pronoun *that,* the verb paired with *that* is singular. *Has* is singular, and *have* is plural.

78 The single word *already* means "before this time," the meaning required by the sentence.

79 *Begun* is the form of the verb *to begin* that is used with a helping verb. Here it's paired with *has.*

80 The adjective *traditional* describes the noun *coat.*

81 *Between* is a preposition and thus takes an object. The pronoun *me* is an object.

82 Two males appear in the sentence *(Silver* and *Ed),* so the pronoun *he* is unclear. Substitute a noun.

83 The missing word in the original is *did,* as in *than she did. Her* is inappropriate as the subject of the implied verb *did.*

84 *Unique* is an absolute and can't be compared, so the *extremely* must be deleted.

85 The comparison *equally* should not be followed by *as.*

86 *We* is the subject pronoun needed here. *Us* is for objects.

87 To keep the sentence parallel, *to be* should be paired with *to take action.*

88 *To lay* is "to place something else somewhere." *To lie* is "to rest or to recline," the meaning here.

89 The noun *nap* must be described by an adjective *(quick),* not an adverb *(quickly).*

90 The sentence is in present tense, and two actions are mentioned — *lies* and *having gone.* See the mismatch? Change *having gone* to *going* and you stay in the present, the best tense for habitual actions.

Answers to Exercise Four

In the following figure the errors from the original manual are boldfaced and crossed out, with a possible correction following each one, as well as an occasional addition of a missing word or mark. All corrections are boldfaced and underlined. Check the corresponding numbered explanations that follow the revised manual.

---

91 — Installing ~~You're~~ **Your** New Widget Wheel

92 — To install the widget wheel, ~~a computer should first be turned off~~ **first turn the computer off**, **and** then **93**
follow these simple steps.

94 — *Important:* If you have an A4019 or a ~~newest~~ **newer** model, please discard this manual. You must ~~have sent~~
95 — **send** for manual number 218B, or, in the case of a computer that previously ~~has~~ **had** a widget, for manual **96**
97 — number 330B. ~~Being that~~ **Because** your computer is not covered in this manual, discard ~~it~~ **the manual**. **98**
Faulty directions have been responsible for explosions and ~~that software crashed~~ **software crashes**. **99**

100 — 1. Unpack the widget wheel**,** which looks like a shark**'**s tooth. **101**

102 — 2. Unpack the two disk poles. Grasp the disk pole that is more **nearly** circular. ~~Lining~~ **Line** up the teeth with **103**
104 — the teeth on the widget. *Note:* Teeth should be brushed ~~alot~~ **a lot** with a WidgetBrush. ~~s~~**See** the **105**
enclosed order form for more information.

106 — 3. After the teeth are ~~tight~~ **tightly** clenched, ~~a person should~~ insert the widget disk into slot C. However, if **107**
the widget disk has a blue strip, ~~in which case it should be inserted into slot D~~ **insert the widget into**
108
slot D. Don't mix up the slots as the computer will catch fire. Neither of these slots ~~are~~ **is** open when **109**
the computer is standing upright. ~~Sit~~ **Set** the computer on its side before beginning this step.

110 — 4. Turn on the computer. If the screen is blank**,** call the service specialist at 914-555-5039. If the screen
111 — blinks ~~rapid~~ **rapidly** from red to green (or from blue to yellow in model 2W4T), run ~~further~~ **farther** from
112 — the screen. ~~This~~ **Blinking** means the widget was installed ~~improper~~ **improperly**; the computer is **113**
114 — altogether unusable. **115**
116

117 — 5. You are almost ready to enjoy your new widget~~!~~**!** Place a hand **that is not wearing any rings, including**
118
wedding rings, on the mouse ~~that is not wearing any rings, including wedding rings~~. Depending upon
the model number, ~~either~~ press **either** firmly or softly. Some widgets can work ~~good~~ **well** no matter **120**
119 — what the pressure.

91 The contraction *you're* means "you are." In this sentence you want the possessive pronoun *your*.

92 An introductory verb form *(To install the widget wheel)* must refer to the subject, but the subject in the original sentence is *a computer*. Reword the sentence so that the subject is the person who is installing — the understood *you*.

93 The adverb *then* is not capable of uniting two complete sentences on its own. Delete the comma and insert *and*.

94 The *-est* comparison singles out one extreme from a group of three or more. In this sentence you're talking about a comparison between two things only — model A4019 and the group of everything *newer*. (The group counts as one thing because the items in the group aren't discussed as individuals.)

95 The verb *send* is in present tense and addresses what the installer must do now, not what the installer must have done previously. The present perfect tense *(have sent)* implies a connection with the past.

96 The word *previously* tips you off to the fact that you're talking about past tense, so *had* works better than *has*.

97 The expression *being that* is not standard; use *because* instead.

98 The pronoun *it* must have a clear meaning, but the original sentence provides two possible alternatives, *computer* and *manual*. The correction clarifies the meaning of *it*.

99 Two terms linked by *and* need a similar grammatical identity in order to keep the sentence parallel. The original sentence joins a noun *(explosions)* with a clause *(that software crashed)*. The correction links two nouns, *explosions* and *crashes*.

100 A description beginning with *which* is usually set off by a comma from the word it describes.

101 The tooth belongs to the shark, so you need the possessive *shark's*.

102 *Circular* is an absolute. It may be approached but not compared. The disk pole may be *circular* or *more nearly circular*.

103 The original sentence is a fragment; it has no complete thought. The correction has a subject (the understood *you*) and a verb *(line)* and a complete thought.

104 The expression *a lot* is always written as two words.

105 A sentence always begins with a capital letter.

106 *Tightly* is an adverb, needed to describe the verb *clenched*.

107 *A person* is a new expression in this piece, which has been addressing *you* either directly or by implication. For consistency, change *a person* to the understood *you*.

108 The original is a fragment, not a complete sentence. The reworded version has a complete thought.

109 The pronoun *neither* is singular and takes the singular verb *is*.

110 *Sit* is what the subject does by bending knees and plopping onto a chair. *Set* means that you're placing something else into some position.

111 An introductory expression with a verb is usually set off by a comma from the main idea of the sentence. Insert a comma after *blank*.

112 The adverb *rapidly* is needed to describe the action *blink*.

113 *Farther* is for distance, and *further* is for time or intensity. Here you need the distance word.

114 The pronoun *this* is too vague. Go for the specific term, *blinking*.

115 The adverb *improperly* is needed to describe the action *installed*.

116 A comma isn't strong enough to link two complete sentences. Dump the comma and insert a semicolon.

117 Don't double up on endmarks. One per sentence does the job.

118 The description is in the wrong place in the original sentence. Place it after *hands,* the word being described.

119 The duo *either/or* should link words or expressions with the same grammatical identity. In the original sentence, a verb-description combo is linked to a description. Move *either* so that two descriptions are linked.

120 The adverb *well* is needed to describe the verb *can work*.

Answers to Exercise Five

In the following figure the errors from the memo are boldfaced and crossed out, with a possible correction following each one, as well as an occasional addition of a missing word or mark. All corrections are boldfaced and underlined. Check the corresponding numbered explanations that follow the revised memo.

121 ~~"~~Memorandum~~"~~

To: Eliot Simpson

From: Nina Winter

122 Date: ~~september~~ **September** 23, 2020

123 Re: Bid for ~~Hacker'~~ **Hacker's** Wallpaper Factory

124 This morning Jenna Pamek and ~~myself~~ **I** met with Oscar Hacker, President of

Hacker Wallpaper. We presented our bid to renovate his wallpaper factory, ~~that~~

125 ~~which has been~~ **is** located on the corner of 71st Street and Alexander Avenue. **126**

127 The two of us, ~~who~~ **whom** Mr. Hacker ~~will have~~ praised for our work on the **128**

129 paste factory, ~~set~~ **sat** down to try ~~and~~ **to** go over the financial aspects of the **130**

131 project. Although mathematics ~~were~~ **was** hard for me when I took it in college, I

132 explained the numbers ~~real~~ **really** well. When I ~~had~~ left, I was convinced that Mr. **133**

Hacker would give the job to this fine company of **ours**~~'~~. **134**

135 No matter what Jenna ~~will have~~ said, everyone ~~were~~ **was** satisfied with ~~their~~ **136**

137 **his or her** gift basket. ~~It is totally a lie and not true at all~~ **It is untrue** that one of **138**

139 the gift baskets ~~were~~ **was** filled with money. Mr. Hacker objects to ~~me~~ **my** bribing **140**

141 him. Jenna was just upset~~,~~ because she had to listen to Mr. Hacker explain that a

142 square ~~had~~ **has** four sides, and the "square" in our design has five. "You should

143 ~~of~~ **have** studied geometry~~"!~~**!"** Mr. Hacker exclaimed. **144**

145 Jenna, ~~whom~~ **who** everyone thinks is close friends with Mrs. Hacker, was ~~very~~ **146**

wrong when she said that I stapled ~~her~~ **Mrs. Hacker's [or Jenna's]** hair to the **147**

table. Pulling out the staple, ~~the table was damaged~~ **I damaged the table** **148**

~~and that~~ **, and** it will need repairs. Either Mr. Hacker or his assistants ~~is~~ **are** **150**

149 willing to testify that I never touched the stapler. Mr. Hacker awarded the

contract to our competitor because our bid was too high and for no other reason.

121 A centered title should not be placed in quotation marks.

122 The names of months are capitalized.

123 An apostrophe appears at the end of a word only when the word is a plural ending in the letter *s* or a singular name (such as my own, Woods).

124 The pronoun *myself* is used only for emphasis or to explain an action that doubles back on the subject.

125 After a comma, the pronoun *which* usually introduces a description containing a subject/verb combo (a clause, in other words). The pronoun *that* generally begins a description that is not set off by commas.

126 The present perfect verb, *has been,* ties an action in the past to the present time. In this sentence, no time span is indicated, so simple present tense works best.

127 *Who* is for subjects and *whom* for objects. In this sentence, *Mr. Hacker* is the subject; *whom* is an object.

128 The future-perfect verb *(will have praised)* implies a deadline, but the sentence has no deadline. Instead, the action is in the past, which the past-tense verb *praised* expresses.

129 To *set* is to place something. Here you want *sat,* which is the past-tense version of what you do when you plop into a chair.

130 *Try and* expresses two separate actions, but the meaning of the sentence is *try to* — one action.

131 The subject *(mathematics)* is singular and requires a singular verb *(was).*

132 The description *(well)* is intensified by *really,* an adverb, not by the adjective *real.*

133 Two actions — the leaving and the being convinced — are simultaneous, so *had* is inappropriate here. The helping verb *had* places one past-tense action before another.

134 No possessive pronoun (such as *ours*) ever needs an apostrophe.

135 The action is in the past, so *said,* a past-tense verb, is what you want here.

136 The pronoun *everyone* is singular, so it pairs with the singular verb *was.*

137 The pronoun *their* is plural and thus doesn't match the singular pronoun *everyone.* Opt for *his or her* — the singular choice that includes, well, everyone.

138 The original sentence is repetitive. I show one possible correction; yours may differ.

139 The subject of the sentence is *one*, not *baskets*, so the verb must be singular.

140 Mr. Hacker doesn't object to *me*. (He's actually quite fond of *me*.) He objects to the bribe. The possessive pronoun *my* places the emphasis on the bribe, not the person.

141 A semicolon joins two complete sentences, but it isn't appropriate between a complete sentence and a subordinate idea. No punctuation is needed here at all.

142 An unchangeable fact (that a square *has* four sides) is always expressed in present tense.

143 The expression *should of* doesn't exist in Standard English. Go for *should have* or the contraction *should've*.

144 Because the quotation is an exclamation, the exclamation point belongs inside the quotation marks.

145 Place your finger over *everyone thinks* and you see that *who* is needed as the subject of *is*.

146 The word *wrong* is an absolute; you're either *wrong* or you're *right*. The intensifier, *very*, isn't appropriate in an absolute situation.

147 Two females are mentioned in the sentence, so the meaning of *her* isn't clear. Add a name (either one!) to clarify.

148 An introductory verb form *(Pulling)* must refer to an action performed by the subject. The table can't pull!

149 The *that* isn't needed here. In the corrected version, the *and* is followed by a complete sentence *(it will need . . .)*, so a comma should precede the *and*.

150 With an *either/or* sentence, the subject that is closer to the verb rules. Therefore, the plural subject *assistants* takes the plural verb *are*.

Answers to Exercise Six

Presentation slides, projected on the wall, magnify every little mistake. Check out these answers and explanations so your next presentation will be letter-perfect.

Slide #1

151 Marketing ~~potential~~ **Potential** for Pierced-Elbow Rings

152 The target buyer is~~:~~

- 21–92 years old

153 - ~~has two piercings~~ already **pierced twice** in other body parts

154 - ~~Concerned~~ **concerned** about ~~their~~ **his or her** appearance 155
~~and what they look like~~
156

Slide #2

Specifications of Pierced-Elbow Rings

157 - ~~they~~ **They** ~~dont~~ **don't** pinch the elbow's skin~~.~~ 158
159
160 - Manufacturing cost ~~are~~ **is** minimal.

- Karen Oleson, the designer, specifies ~~allergy free~~ **allergy-**
161 **free** metal. 162

163 - Some of the rings ~~is~~ **are** made of plastic.

Slide #3

164 Themes ~~And~~ **and** Holiday Promotions include the following~~:~~ 165

166 - greased rings for ~~Labor day~~ **Labor Day** in honor of the "elbow
grease" a person uses when ~~you are~~ **he or she is** working 167

168 - ~~back to school~~ **back-to-school** rings that ~~looks~~ **look** like 169
rings in binders

170 - ~~Telephone~~ **telephone** rings with ~~alot~~ **a lot** of ring tones 171
172 (~~purchasing~~ **purchased** separately)

- engagement rings decorated with wedding bells ~~laying~~ **lying**
over clasped hands 173

Slide #4

Marketing challenges will ~~have been~~ **be**
174
175 - ~~Long sleeved~~ **Long-sleeved** shirts cover the rings.

176 - When **the rings catch** ~~catching~~ on cloth, **you must apply**
178 antiseptic ~~that kills germs must be applied~~. 177

179 - You ~~only~~ have **only** two elbows, and we ~~can't~~ **can** hardly sell 180
more than two rings per person.

151 Important words in a title should be capitalized, unless you're following scientific style, in which case just the first word of the title in written with a capital letter.

152 An introduction to a bulleted list doesn't take a colon (one dot atop another) or any other punctuation if the introductory expression isn't a complete thought. If you finish an introduction with "is," you haven't completed anything. No punctuation is needed here.

153 Items in a bulleted list should be parallel. Because the first and third items complete the thought begun by the introduction, the second item should also.

154 When you see a list, think *match.* All the items may be capitalized, or none. Here, lowercase makes more sense because in a sense, each item joins with the introduction to form a complete sentence.

155 The bullet points talk about *The target buyer,* a singular. Therefore, *their* (a plural) is a mismatch. Opt for *his or her,* another singular.

156 Don't repeat yourself! Once you say *appearance,* the expression *what they look like* is unnecessary. (It's also not parallel — another no-no.)

157 Each item in this bulleted list is a complete sentence, so the first word *(They)* takes a capital letter.

158 The contraction *don't* needs an apostrophe to substitute for the missing letters in the original *(do not).*

159 Add a period to the end of this sentence, because all sentences need endmarks.

160 The subject, *cost,* is singular, so the verb must also be singular. *Is* is a singular verb. (Doesn't that sentence sound strange?)

161 Once you know the name *(Karen Oleson),* the extra information *(the designer)* should be set off by commas.

162 Two words, *allergy* and *free,* combine to form one description of *metal.* The hyphen creates a single description.

163 The subject pronoun, *some,* may be either singular or plural. Because it is followed by *of the rings, some* is plural and takes a plural verb.

164 Unimportant words (*and,* for example) aren't capitalized in a title.

165 Grammarians see an introduction that ends with *the following* as a complete statement, even though a list follows. Therefore, a colon is appropriate here.

166 The holiday, *Labor Day,* needs two capital letters.

167 The expression *a person* is singular and should be matched with *he or she,* which is also singular, and *is,* a singular verb.

168 Three words *(back, to,* and *school)* are linked by hyphens to create one description of *rings.*

169 The pronoun *that* refers to *rings.* Because *that* represents a plural word, it takes a plural verb *(look).*

170 All the items in a bulleted list should match, and this one is the only one with a capital letter. Writing *telephone* in lower case is better than capitalizing the other three because the bullets aren't complete sentences.

171 *A lot* is always written as two words.

172 The ring tones may be *purchased,* not *purchasing.*

173 When something is resting or reclining, the verb you want is *to lie. To lay* is "to place something somewhere." Here, *lying,* a form of *to lie,* fits the meaning.

174 The future perfect tense *(will have been)* implies a deadline — not the meaning here. Simple future works better.

175 Place a hyphen between *long* and *sleeved* to fashion one description of *shirts.*

176 The original sentence begins with an implied subject, but an implied subject must be the same as the stated subject in the sentence. But *antiseptic* isn't *catching on cloth,* the *rings* are.

177 Whenever you have a choice between active and passive voice, choose active *(you must apply).*

178 An *antiseptic* kills germs, by definition, so *that kills germs* is repetitive.

179 Descriptive words should be as near as possible to the words they describe. In the original, *only* appears to describe *have.* The logical meaning, however, is *only two elbows* — not three or four!

180 Double negatives aren't cool, and *can't hardly* is a double. Change the *can't* to *can* and you're fine.

Answers to Exercise Seven

If this were a real standardized test, by now you'd be sleeping and a machine the size of a small country would be scanning your answers and tallying your score. Sadly, here you have to check your own work. The payoff is that the explanations reinforce some important points about writing.

181 **C.** The original sentence contains a description attached to the wrong word. The introductory verb form *(Being a teenager)* must describe the subject, but in the original it's attached to *a large part of my life.* Choice (C) fixes the problem by changing the subject. Did I catch you with (E)? Grammatically it's fine, but because the rest of the paragraph is in first person (the *I* form), the first sentence should be also.

182 **E.** The switch from active voice *(I love)* to passive *(is frowned upon)* isn't justified. Choices (D) and (E) stay active, but (D) misuses a word. *Accept* is "to receive freely." The word that rules something out is *except.* Therefore, Choice (E) is the best answer.

183 **C.** The original sentence isn't parallel because *explaining* is paired with *having relaxed.* Choice (C) corrects the parallelism error and keeps the correct tense — present — because the author is discussing an ongoing, current situation.

184 **E.** Sentence 7 is a general statement that explains why tests are a pain and socializing is fun. You may use it in the first paragraph (not an option in the answer list) or in the third paragraph, which is where Choice (E) places it, because the introduction and the conclusion discuss the same ideas.

185 **B.** The description *only* should precede the comparison. Here the writer is talking about *one scene,* not *many scenes* or the whole movie, so *only* belongs in front of *one*. The tense changes in Choices (D) and (E) aren't justified by the meaning of the sentence.

186 **A.** Surprised? The last paragraph of this essay is the conclusion, explaining the author's point of view. You don't need to label it as opinion — Choice (E), because the reader already knows. Why else would the writer make these statements? Nor do you need additional examples or a different order. The conclusion could be expanded by adding a statement reinforcing the ideas in the essay (Sentence 7, for example), but the answer choices don't include that option.

Answers to Exercise Eight

Last but not least, here are the answers that belong to this lovely essay on the virtues of being oneself. Take a look at the answers and explanations to see whether you found all the errors — grammatical errors, that is. I'll let you figure out what else this writer is doing wrong. Buying votes is just a start!

187 **B.** When you introduce a quotation with a speaker tag *(A wise man once said),* the tag is followed by a comma and the first word in the quotation is capitalized. A quotation introduced by *that* has no comma and no capital letter, unless of course the first word is a name. In this case, dropping *that* solves both the capital letter and the comma problem.

188 **A.** The first paragraph is short, but it does the job of introducing the ideas in the essay. The other four choices are off-topic.

189 **D.** If you're living in a society, the time is *current,* so you don't need *in this current time*. Repetition is boring! Go for the short version whenever possible. Choice (E) doesn't allow for society's influence at other times in history.

190 **B.** By the time you get to *cafeteria,* you already know that the writer is enrolled (and presumably *studying*) in that school. Why add extra words?

191 **D.** You can't promise *voting,* only *to vote* or *a vote*. Therefore, the original doesn't work. Nor can you pair *everyone* with *their* or *they,* because *everyone* is singular and those other pronouns are plural. Bingo, Choices (B) and (C) fall apart. Choice (E) fails because the introductory verb form *(Giving)* must describe the subject, and *everyone* isn't giving pizza. Choice (D) is the answer you seek.

192 **E.** Essays should be focused, so adding examples at random to paragraph one doesn't work. Nor does deleting the first paragraph, as it serves a purpose: to set the stage for the anecdote in the second paragraph. What's missing is a true conclusion. The closest thing this essay has to a conclusion is the last two sentences. Give them their own paragraph and expand on the ideas to create a stronger ending.

Index